EL ABETH BA R TT WNING

Women Writers

General Editors: *Eva Figes* and *Adele King*

Published

Margaret Atwood, Barbara Hill Rigney
Jane Austen, Meenakshi Mukherjee
Elizabeth Barrett Browning, Marjorie Stone
Elizabeth Bowen, Phyllis Lassner
Anne Brontë, Elizabeth Langland
Charlotte Brontë, Pauline Nestor
Emily Brontë, Lyn Pykett
Fanny Burney, Judy Simons
Willa Cather, Susie Thomas
Colette, Diana Holmes
Ivy Compton-Burnett, Kathy Justice Gentile
Emily Dickinson, Joan Kirkby
George Eliot, Kristin Brady
Elizabeth Gaskell, Jane Spencer
Sylvia Plath, Susan Bassnett
Christina Stead, Diana Brydon
Gertrude Stein, Jane Palatini Bowers
Eudora Welty, Louise Westling
Edith Wharton, Katherine Joslin
Women in Romanticism, Meena Alexander
Virginia Woolf, Clare Hanson

Forthcoming

Nadine Gordimer, Kathy Wagner
Doris Lessing, Margaret Moan Rowe
Katherine Mansfield, Diane DeBell
Toni Morrison, Nellie McKay
Jean Rhys, Carol Rumens
Christina Rossetti, Linda Marshall
Stevie Smith, Romana Huk

Women Writers

Elizabeth Barrett Browning

Marjorie Stone

MACMILLAN

First published 1995 by
THE MACMILLAN PRESS LTD
Houndmills, Basingstoke, Hampshire RG21 2XS
and London
Companies and representatives
throughout the world

ISBN 0–333–48858–X hardcover
ISBN 0–333–48859–8 paperback

A catalogue record for this book is available
from the British Library

Printed in Malaysia

For my parents
Sheila and Bill Parfitt
and
my story-telling grandmothers

Contents

Acknowledgements

I am grateful to the following libraries for permission to refer to and quote from Barrett Browning's manuscripts: the Armstrong Browning Library, Baylor University, Waco, Texas; the British Library; the English Poetry Collection, Wellesley College Library; the Henry W. and Albert A. Berg Collection, the New York Public Library, Astor, Lenox and Tilden Foundations; the James Marshall and Marie Louise Osborn Collection, Yale University Library; and the Pierpont Morgan Library. I would like to thank the librarians in these libraries for their assistance. I owe a special debt of gratitude to Betty Coley of the Armstrong Browning Library and Scott Lewis of *The Brownings' Correspondence* for sharing their expertise regarding the Brownings, as well as to the Social Sciences and Humanities Research Council of Canada for a grant supporting my research on Barrett Browning's manuscripts. A longer version of Chapter 3 appeared in *Victorian Literature and Culture*, 21 (1993). I would like to thank the editors for permission to reprint it.

My editor, Adele King, and my colleagues at Dalhousie and elsewhere gave me many helpful suggestions. I would particularly like to thank Malcolm Ross, who read all of the manuscript, for his astute comments on structure; Cory Davies and Mary Arseneau for stimulating conversations and for reading several chapters with a rigorous editorial eye; and my colleague and husband, Andy Wainwright, for helping me find a point of entry into the myths surrounding Barrett Browning (and out of them again). Mervyn Nicholson and Ronald Tetreault helped me to see some of the many weaknesses in an early version of the chapter on 'Romantic Revisionism'. Patricia Monk generously shared her computer expertise and Julia Swan meticulously proof-read the manuscript.

Most of all, I am indebted to Andy and our children for enduring life with someone possessed by 'EBB'.

Editors' Preface

The study of women's writing has been long neglected by a male critical establishment both in academic circles and beyond. As a result, many women writers have either been unfairly neglected or have been marginalised in some way, so that their true influence and importance has been ignored. Other women writers have been accepted by male critics and academics, but on terms which seem, to many women readers of this generation, to be false or simplistic. In the past the internal conflicts involved in being a woman in a male-dominated society have been largely ignored by readers of both sexes, and this has affected our reading of women's work. The time has come for a serious reassessment of women's writing in the light of what we understand today.

This series is designed to help in that reassessment.

All the books are written by women because we believe that men's understanding of feminist critique is only, at best, partial. And besides, men have held the floor quite long enough.

EVA FIGES
ADELE KING

1 Fighting on Her Stumps: The Woman, the Poet, the Myths

I

Elizabeth Barrett was a legend before she ever met Robert Browning. In his first letter to Barrett in 1845, Browning compared her to 'some world's-wonder in chapel or crypt', recalling how he had almost been introduced to her three years earlier. She ironically replied to this rather tactless comment, 'BUT . . . you know . . . if you had entered the "crypt", you might have caught cold, or been tired to death' (*RB–EBB* 1:4–5). As every schoolgirl knows, Browning did enter the 'crypt' and he was not 'tired to death'. Elizabeth Barrett, the legendary poet-recluse, was transformed into Elizabeth Barrett Browning, the legendary heroine of a romance chaste enough to be safely enjoyed even by the proverbial Victorian 'young person'. It is a romance summed up in five famous words.

Just as it is sometimes difficult to approach Shakespeare because he is an institution, it is difficult to approach Barrett Browning because she is a legend. The romantic story of her elopement and marriage has become so much a part of our culture that we are collaborators in it against our will, just as we are complicit in the ideological forces that have nurtured it for over a century now. Let us count the ways in which we have encountered 'How do I love thee?' In

Valentine cards, of course. On tea boxes, if not yet on cereal boxes. On the American children's television show, 'Sesame Street'. In movies like the 1964 Peter Sellers comedy, *The World of Henry Orient*, where two zestfully romantic pubescent girls pursue the pseudo-Byronic lover played by Sellers as he pursues his amours. In a Canadian Post Office advertisement featuring 'a dreamy-eyed teenage girl' posting a letter, with the superscription, ' "How shall I mail this? Let me count the ways" ' (Stephenson 2). In a bathetic advertisement for ladies' fashions, 'How shall I glove thee? Let me count the ways'.[1]

Louise Bernikow's witty parody captures the sentimental scenario trailing in the wake of this too famous sonnet:

> Enter the legend: sweet, invalid, dear Miss Barrett. . . . Doll's face, those ringlets round her head. Dear Miss Barrett, lying there the day long, wasting away, waiting for – at last, it comes, the life-force incarnate, virile Robert Browning! . . . Miss Barrett runs away with Mr. Browning, into the warm sun, cured. Somewhere along the way she commits to paper [the *Sonnets from the Portuguese*, expressing] the sum of what is on her mind.[2]

At least in some popular versions, Miss Barrett is granted the legs to run away with the Perseus who rescues her, like Andromeda chained to the rock, from her dragon of a father – Mr Barrett, the patriarchal tyrant of Wimpole Street. Another late nineteenth-century version makes her passivity absolute. In Francis Thompson's words, Robert 'Browning stooped and picked up a fair-coined soul that lay rusting in a pool of tears'. Daniel Karlin's *The Courtship of Robert Browning and Elizabeth Barrett*, which cites Thompson (10), reveals how insidious the romantic legend

enshrouding Barrett Browning can be. No other critic
has more subtly and incisively analysed the myths
surrounding the Brownings' courtship. Yet Karlin
reinscribes some of the most deeply rooted of these
myths by emphasizing the miraculous transformation
in Elizabeth Barrett brought about by Browning's
'strong and self-possessed identity' (11), and by
considering Barrett the poet only in a supplemental
chapter that perpetuates the traditional image of the
pining recluse.

Thompson's version of the Brownings' romance is a
striking example of the 'poetics of rescue' Adrienne
Munich explores in *Andromeda's Chains*, her wide-
ranging study of the multiple images of bound women
and chivalric male saviours in Victorian literature and
art. As its stubborn vitality in our own century attests,
however, the legend of Elizabeth Barrett Browning's
romantic rescue does not reflect a cultural paradigm
that is merely Victorian. Nor is it a paradigm as
benign as its chivalric trappings might suggest.
Barrett Browning herself acutely noted the 'contempt
of the sex' discernible in those who depicted women as
languishing lilies passively waiting to 'be "defended"
by the strong and mighty' men around them (*LMRM*
3:81).

Since ideology itself is inescapable, the only way out
of such gender-inflected ideologies is through ideology.
In the last two decades, feminist scholars engaged in
what might be termed a 'critics of rescue' have done
much to counteract the 'poetics of rescue' casting
England's first unequivocally major female poet as a
weeping coin rusting in her own tears or an Andromeda
chained to the rock of her father's house. Most
notably, the recovery of lost traditions of women's
writing initiated in the 1970s restored *Aurora Leigh* to
its central place in Barrett Browning's canon. After

Cora Kaplan's 1978 edition of *Aurora Leigh and Other Poems*, it was no longer possible to overlook the fact that the woman who penned 'How do I love thee?' was also the author of a feminist novel-epic that went through over twenty editions between 1857 and 1900. As the reception of *Aurora Leigh* suggests, Barrett Browning does not fit the common profile of the woman writer who has been excluded from literary history because she was constrained by economic or educational limitations, or because she wrote principally in marginalized or unpublished forms. On the contrary, Victorian reviews of Barrett Browning's works and her impact on other writers indicate that she was widely viewed as a major poet, in England, America and some European countries from the 1840s – well before the publication of *Aurora Leigh* – up to the 1890s.

How do we reconcile Barrett Browning's fame and critical stature as nineteenth-century author with the virtual disappearance of most of her canon in our own century? This key question gives rise to the particular mix of critical approaches I mobilize in considering how her texts entered into and altered literary and social history. Feminist and new historicist critical approaches that emphasize particular historical contingencies and acknowledge the critic's own position as a historical subject seem especially helpful in the case of Barrett Browning. 'All inherited works of literature have it in their power to force a critical engagement with any present form of thought . . . by virtue of the historical differentials which separate every present from all the past', McGann observes in *The Romantic Ideology*.[3] Reconsidering Barrett Browning's unprecedented career entails an examination of present critical ideologies not only because, in McGann's words, a 'good deal' of *Aurora Leigh* 'still seems ideologically advanced to this day' (157), but also because in this instance the 'historical differentials' – the conflicts between nineteenth-century and twentieth-century assessments of her achievement – are so stark and unresolved.

The 'new historicism' advocated by McGann and many others has much in common with the 'third phase' of feminist criticism delineated by Elaine Showalter in *The New Feminist Criticism*. Feminist criticism in this phase moves beyond the exposure of sexist stereotypes typical of the early 1970s, and the subsequent drive to rescue buried women writers, to 'a radical rethinking of the conceptual grounds of literary study'.[4] Rather than seeking to insert recovered texts into a pre-existing order of cultural 'monuments', it systematically deconstructs the embedded assumptions shaping canon formation and literary histories. 'Third phase' feminist criticism is a logical extension of the 'new women's history' of the 1970s which, as Judith Lowder Newton points out, fostered many of the postmodern assumptions of the 'new historicism', a critical movement too often artifically separated from the women's movement that helped to generate it. Newton observes that 'a number of critical practices', including feminist practices, had long been informed by the 'postmodern' assumptions of the new historicism: the assumptions, for instance, that 'human subjectivity is constructed by cultural codes', or that 'all our representations of the world, our readings of texts and of the past, are informed by our own historical position', or that ' "history" is best told as a story of power relations and struggle'.[5] Such conceptualizations rapidly became a part of feminist literary histories in part because of the 'new French feminism', with its philosophical focus on deconstructing the symbolic systems of cultural representation;

and in part because, as Sydney Janet Kaplan notes, the Anglo-American recovery of women writers led to the redefinition of 'traditional parameters' used to define historical periods.[6]

Despite the numerous cultural forces propelling feminist criticism generally into this 'third phase', the questioning of 'traditional parameters' has remained less fully developed than might have been expected in the growing body of work on Barrett Browning. Ever since Ellen Moer's *Literary Women* (1976), critics have focused primarily on *Aurora Leigh*'s place in a gynocentric tradition, not on the reframing of nineteenth-century literary history that is called for when we consider the prominence and influence of Barrett Browning's entire canon in her own time. Cora Kaplan's analysis of *Aurora Leigh* as an 'overlapping sequence of dialogues with other texts' ('Introduction' 16) treats it more as a text rupturing the nineteenth-century literary tradition than as a work revealing the need to deconstruct the tradition itself. Angela Leighton's *Elizabeth Barrett Browning* (1986) offers a ground-breaking rereading of the complex sexual and textual politics involved in Barrett Browning's courting of the muse throughout her career; Helen Cooper's *Elizabeth Barrett Browning: Woman and Artist* (1988) perceptively traces the evolution of Barrett Browning's woman-centred poetics; and Glennis Stephenson's *Elizabeth Barrett Browning and the Poetry of Love* (1989) provides close readings of a wide range of love poems. Yet all of these studies focus principally on Barrett Browning's contributions to a tradition of women writers, to genres particularly associated with women writers, or to her development as a woman-poet. In a more direct challenging of canonical formations, Leighton's *Victorian Women Poets* (1992) argues for the inclusion of Barrett Browning and seven other 'major' women poets in anthologies and literary studies of nineteenth-century poetry (2).[7] Nevertheless, her principal focus remains Barrett Browning's place in a separate tradition of women poets writing 'against the heart'.

Dorothy Mermin's *Elizabeth Barrett Browning: The Origins of a New Poetry* (1989) is the only recent reinterpretation that contextualizes Barrett Browning's achievement in 'the male Victorian line' of 'major' poets, to use her words (2). Drawing at times on the earlier scholarship of Alethea Hayter, Mermin links Barrett Browning to Tennyson, Browning, Clough, Meredith, Swinburne and the Rossettis in comparisons threaded throughout her comprehensive study. In making such comparisons, however, Mermin acknowledges the difficulty she initially experienced in matching Barrett Browning's works 'up with the grids through which [she] was accustomed to read Victorian poetry'. This difficulty was resolved only when she found an 'entrance' to the 'obscure but richly attractive world' of Barrett Browning's *oeuvre* in the struggle of 'the first of English women poets' to find 'woman's place in the central tradition of poetry' (8). This struggle is Mermin's focus, not the ways in which Barrett Browning's writings, which were far from 'obscure' in her own time, reveal the limitations of the 'grids' themselves, or the transformations in these grids between the mid-Victorian period and the present. Cooper similarly alludes to the difficulty of reconciling Barrett Browning's works with the grids of literary history in concluding that her writings were dismissed because they 'did not fit with the periodization and concerns of male literature' (4).

Much in this study moves towards a contrary conclusion. I argue that many of Barrett Browning's works 'fit' very well in the generic, thematic and stylistic grids constructed by literary historians, from the late nineteenth to the late twentieth century. In many cases, only the sex of their writer disqualifies them. Significantly, many of these grids were not established or consolidated until the early twentieth century, during the period in which literary studies was established as a discipline, when a growing body of professional male academics were reacting against the inroads of the nineteenth-century 'women's rights' movement and the wave of women writers accompanying it. In this climate of backlash, the 'schools' referred to by earlier critics (the 'Lake School' of Wordsworth and Coleridge, the 'Satanic School' of Shelley and Byron, the 'Tennysonian School') were replaced by the discursive fields of Romantic and Victorian poetry, structured by gender exclusions still operative today.

While such gender exclusions in themselves help to explain the disappearance of much in Barrett Browning's canon, including *Aurora Leigh*, they often interact in complex ways with exclusionary genre and period paradigms. The chapters that follow indicate how intersecting ideologies of gender and genre, sometimes compounded by the artificial barriers of historical periodization, have acted to obscure or conceal Barrett Browning's poetical achievement in a range of poetical or literary modes. Throughout I draw on nineteenth-century assessments of her texts because they often reveal strikingly different pre-suppositions concerning generic categories, period boundaries and traditions of writers than those that prevailed in our own century.

As 'third-phase' feminist criticism and new historicist approaches alike emphasize, such a project remains incomplete if it focuses only on the past. It should also illumine the 'ideological involvements of the criticism, critical theory, and reading we practice, study, and promote' (McGann 160). Barrett Browning's canon and her poetical influence in her time remain important in our own because they expose the underpinnings of metanarratives which remain very influential despite the critiques they have in some cases provoked: among them, Harold Bloom's history of Romantic revisionism and histories of the nineteenth-century ballad that completely exclude not only Barrett Browning but women poets collectively. As Margaret Homans observed in 1980 (7), and the author-editors of *Engendering the Word* have more recently confirmed, the fields of poetry and poetics have proven to be particularly resistant to feminist critiques.[8] The extent to which Barrett Browning's canon remains excluded from literary histories and anthologies is a telling example of such resistance.

One would not expect, of course, to find Barrett Browning included along with Browning in the male line of Romantic revisionists Harold Bloom constructs, given his relentlessly male-centred poetics. But her works have also been passed over by those feminists who have radically critiqued androcentric construc-tions of Romanticism or the Romantic tradition, including Homans herself. Joanne Feit Diehl largely disregards Barrett Browning's role in the transmission of Romanticism, even though she is deeply concerned as Homans is with Emily Dickinson's response to the Romantic poets and Barrett Browning was the primary female medium of Romanticism for Dickinson.[9] In Anne Mellor's *Romanticism and Gender* (1993) Barrett Browning is not mentioned, although Mellor moves 'beyond the historical confines of the Romantic period (1780–1830) into the mid-nineteenth century' in considering Emily Brontë (186), and generally calls for more investigation of 'the *continuity* in British literary culture from 1750 to 1900' (211). In studies focusing on Victorian poets or on Barrett Browning alone, her connections with the Romantics have been similarly neglected. Critics typically approach the transition between Romantic and Victorian poetry through the earlier works of Tennyson and Browning, not through hers – despite the fact that she had a profile almost as high as Tennyson's and higher than Browning's by 1844.

By resituating Barrett Browning's works in their historical context and by considering previously neglected manuscripts, this study reconstructs her poetical development not only in light of the particular conflicts she experienced as a woman-poet, but also in light of the traditions we associate with Romanticism – both Romanticism as it has been defined in the past and as it is now being redefined. Chapter 2 argues that, like the Romantic poets, Elizabeth Barrett was fascinated by the mysteries of consciousness and the power of the mind in meditation, and that many of her texts are more remarkable for their Romantic audacity of authorship than for any peculiarly female anxiety of authorship. Since many of Barrett Browning's earlier works foreground the continuities rather than the discontinuities between Romantic and Victorian poetry, they point to the spots of blindness created by period paradigms. As much as the young Robert Browning and more than Tennyson, Elizabeth Barrett was drawn to major Romantic poetical forms such as the lyrical drama and the visionary poem incorporating an internalized quest romance. And more than either of the two poets she clearly regarded as her greatest rivals, her writings reflect the continuing attraction of Romantic Prometheanism, the Romantic cult of transcendent artistic genius, Romantic tropes of the sublime and the revisionary struggle with Milton and

Dante. Barrett Browning clearly subscribed to many Romantic ideologies, as McGann and others have defined them. But she was also led to question many of these, given the critical distance fostered by her gender.

The continuities between Romantic and Victorian poetry are also manifested in Barrett Browning's ballads, which were enormously popular and critically praised in her own time. Many of her ballads have female protagonists and some of them were first published in annuals. But, as Chapter 3 indicates, there is little evidence in Barrett Browning's own comments about the Romantic ballad tradition, in the intricate intertextuality of her ballads, or in the response of her contemporary readers to support the customary categorization of them in a separate female genre – a categorization ironically perpetuated in recent feminist criticism. Ideologies of gender, combined with ideologies of genre privileging certain forms of the ballad over others, have obscured the influence Barrett Browning's widely disseminated ballads had in the period between the Romantic ballad revival and the later ballads of the Pre-Raphaelite poets.

Barrett Browning produced a significant body of dramatic monologues as well – poems that help to uncover the gender and genre ideologies underlying the many histories of the form focusing principally on the innovations of Browning and Tennyson. Like some of Tennyson's works, Barrett Browning's dramatic monologues draw attention to prototypes of the form in Romantic and pre-Romantic forms that tend to have female speakers, such as the ballad, the monodrama and the complaint. Because her many published and unpublished experiments with the dramatic monologue demand more detailed treatment than I can give them here, they are not included in this study. For different reasons, I do not consider the *Sonnets from the Portuguese*, in part because they already have a very high profile in histories of the Victorian sonnet sequence, in part because they have been ably analysed by Leighton, Stephenson, Mermin and Agajanian, among others. Unlike the famous *Sonnets*, Barrett Browning's volumes of polemical political poetry, *Casa Guidi Windows* and *Poems before Congress*, remain unjustly neglected – despite the important work of Julia Markus and Helen Cooper in rescuing the former text and in interpreting it in light of its historical context. But since I have already addressed the political poems in another context (see 'Cursing'), Chapter 4 of this study is completely given over to Barrett Browning's greatest work, *Aurora Leigh*, while Chapter 5 analyses the critical tradition that erased it from literary history along with most of her other writings.

Aurora Leigh has typically been approached as a *Kunstlerroman* reflecting Barrett Browning's own poetical development. While there is much to support this approach, it is also a generic classification that has tended to perpetuate the traditional focus on Barrett Browning's life rather than her art, meanwhile obscuring two important dimensions of her greatest work: first, the narrative sophistication apparent in Barrett Browning's dramatic representation of Aurora's consciousness and formation; and second, the extent to which *Aurora Leigh* was written and read as a work of polemical 'sage discourse' in the tradition of Carlyle and Ruskin's prophetic writings on the tribulations of their times. As a work with a dramatic speaker whose reliablity is in doubt more often than critics have assumed, *Aurora Leigh* grows out of Barrett Browning's experimentation with dramatic speakers in her published and unpublished work of the 1840s. As a work of prophetic sage discourse, it subverts the phallocentric tradition it energetically enters both by destabilizing the infallible authority typically assumed by the Victorian sage, and by comprehensively deploying the gynocentric emancipatory strategies developed in Barrett Browning's earlier works.

'Emancipatory strategies' is Patricia Yaeger's term in *Honey-Mad Women*, and it is my contention in much of this book, but especially in the chapter on *Aurora Leigh*, that Barrett Browning is very much a 'honey-mad' woman in Yaeger's sense of the term.[10] Indeed, in the graphically sensuous 1844 poem 'Wine of Cyprus', with its striking similarities to Emily Dickinson's 'I taste a liquor never brewed', Barrett presents herself as literally honey-mad, as she transforms a gift of Cyprian honey wine from her classical mentor Hugh Stuart Boyd into a symbol of the classical heritage she has lustily downed in her studies with him. More importantly, Barrett Browning employs almost all of the emancipatory strategies Yaeger identifies. Thus, to name just a few, she de-centres masculine metaphors and myths; she transforms silent or marginalized women into speaking subjects, as in the 1838 dramatic monologue, 'The Virgin Mary to the Child Jesus'; and, anticipating the insights of feminists like Teresa de Lauretis and Lynda Boose, she represents women short-circuiting a male economy in which they function as objects of exchange.[11]

Barrett Browning's use of these emancipatory strategies has been passed over by some prominent contemporary feminist theorists – Rachael Blau DuPlessis and Alicia Ostriker, for instance – in part because of the tendency, even among postmodern feminist critics, to construct historical metanarratives contrasting nineteenth-century women writers with their twentieth-century counterparts, usually to the disadvantage of the earlier writers. Rita Felski comments on the way in which 'the feminist application of poststructuralist thought is frequently underpinned by a vague periodization of culture' which represents 'a notion of the "modern" or "postmodern" understood as a radical rupture with the conceptual frameworks of the past', including the 'tired fictions of patriarchal bourgeois humanism'.[12] These presuppositions have contributed to a sometimes dismissive view of Barrett Browning as an essentially conservative writer, despite the undeniably progressive and feminist dimensions of *Aurora Leigh*. Most notably, ever since Mary Jane Lupton's popularizing study of *Elizabeth Barrett Browning* was issued by New York's Feminist Press in 1972, critics have reiterated the view that Barrett Browning 'remained basically detached from the struggle for women's liberation' (Lupton 56), and they have emphasized as Cora Kaplan does the limitations of her liberal bourgeois subject position.

In fact, however, both the composition and the reception of *Aurora Leigh* point to Barrett Browning's close ideological affiliations with Victorian feminist activists. Moreover, the apparently conservative and class-bound elements of her writing need to be viewed in the context of surrounding textual ironies (like the man she married, she is often an intricately ironic writer), and in the larger historical context mediating the production and reception of her works. Felski's comment on contemporary feminist debates and their relation to social praxis applies very well to the example of Barrett Browning. 'If it is the case that a supposedly conservative subject-based politics has been a powerful and effective force in mobilizing large numbers of women to assess critically and change aspects of their own lives, then it is important for feminism to develop an analysis of the subject which is not theoretically inadequate, yet which is able to account for the emancipatory potential of the women's movement as a politics that has been strongly grounded in the dynamics of everyday life' (54).

Since we cannot appreciate how Barrett Browning became the most influential woman-poet of her age without some understanding of the dynamics of her own 'everyday life', the remainder of this chapter takes a closer look at the woman behind the myths. In place of the usual biographical survey, however, I provide a reconstruction of Elizabeth Barrett the poet as she lived, thought and wrote in the years leading up to the publication of her 1844 *Poems*. This approach is a tactical one, designed to counteract both the persistent myths obscuring Barrett Browning's achievement and the relative neglect of the works that first established her fame. The 1844 *Poems*, together with the letters and the poetical manuscripts from the same period, dramatically reveal the misrepresentations perpetuated by the romantic story I began with: the legend casting Elizabeth Barrett as a pining recluse rescued by Robert Browning. The story behind the 1844 *Poems* is very different from the legend. It is the story of a woman writer fighting for life and fame in the face of personal tragedy and broken health. It is the story of a woman writer empowered by a matrix of other women writers. It is the success story of Elizabeth Barrett Barrett – to use the double-barrelled name that appeared on the title page of her 1844 *Poems* (in contrast to the less forceful 'Elizabeth B. Barrett' that had graced the title page of her 1838 volume). The 1844 *Poems* established Elizabeth Barrett Barrett as Tennyson's rival in the eyes of many of her contemporaries. These two volumes are to her career what Tennyson's 2-volume 1842 *Poems* are to his, and should be recognized as such. Yet, despite the recovery of *Aurora Leigh*, many of the widely influential works in Barrett Browning's 1844 *Poems* remain unread or unappreciated.

Such neglect is a lingering legacy of the process of textual transmission traced in my final chapter, but it cries out to be repudiated as vigorously as Aurora repudiates her cousin Romney's patriarchal legacy in *Aurora Leigh*. In anthologies and literary histories after 1900, where the poetical achievement of 'Elizabeth' or 'Mrs Browning' was relegated to footnotes or to supplementary sections of chapters on Browning, the originality, the range and the critical success of Barrett Browning's 1844 *Poems* were completely eliminated, along with *Aurora Leigh*. In effect, Elizabeth Barrett Barrett the poet was erased, and replaced by the woman chiefly known as one man's daughter and another man's wife. Who was the woman who published two famous volumes under this name, and who signed her manuscripts with the initials 'EBB' before she became Elizabeth Barrett Browning? How did she live? How did she think? What were some of the most important influences on her formation as a poet increasingly in possession of her own powers? 'I shd like to know what poets have been your sponsors, . . . – and whether you have held true to early tastes, or leapt violently from them – & what books you read, & what hours you write in. How curious I could prove myself!', Barrett wrote early in her correspondence to Browning (*RB–EBB* 1:15). The same questions have too seldom been asked of her.

II

We can begin reconstructing Elizabeth Barrett Barrett,

woman and poet, by emphasizing what she was not. Unfortunately, the myths surrounding her life are perpetuated even in revisionary feminist criticism. In Christine Battersby's *Gender and Genius*, an illuminating study of the gendering of genius as male in Romantic and post-Romantic culture, the debilitating effects of nineteenth-century constructions of femininity are illustrated by 'Elizabeth Barrett lying on her sick-bed, awaiting Robert Browning's invigorating presence'. Barrett had so 'internalised the models of her age "condemn[ing]" her to freakishness, to (fatal) sickness, and to maleness for her pretensions of genius' she was psychically maimed, Battersby implies. 'The doctors made Elizabeth Barrett Browning into a morphine addict' who employed 'the euphoric side-effects of her medicine to counter the discouragement . . . doled out to female authors' (88–90).

Battersby's vision of Elizabeth Barrett is another rendition of the legend of the 'crypt', only in this case Victorian doctors lurk as villains in the antechamber and the 'world's wonder' is a helpless addict. However much of an invalid Barrett may have been, we can be sure of several things about the woman and the poet who produced the 1844 *Poems*. Barrett was not a woman who turned to opium because she was demoralized by the response to her genius. She was not a woman whose genius was denied. She was not a neurotic female expending her creativity in tearful poems, although she was well aware that, in Cheryl Walker's words, woman's sorrow is 'literary capital';[13] and she furthermore believed with Keats and Emily Dickinson that real poetic power necessarily involves the experience of human suffering. She did not consider herself a freak, although her lively sense of humour made her quick to see and sometimes mock eccentricities in others. She was not awaiting the 'invigorating presence' of Robert Browning or any other man. She was far too busy reading and writing – 'in a horizontal posture' when necessary (*BC* 4:222), which she had long found 'very useful in enabling an invalid to get thro' a good deal of writing without fatigue' (*BC* 4:81).

The letters of the early 1840s make it plain that Barrett suffered between 1838 and 1841 from a debilitating tubercular illness that left her bedridden and spitting blood for a period of over two years (*BC* 6:144, 187). She did not, as some versions of the legend suggest, exploit a lingering psychosomatic complaint, although there is no doubt that her illness was intensified by psychological trauma and that she converted the deprivations of her bedridden state into opportunities for her creativity. The greatest psychological blow was the death of her beloved brother Edward by drowning in July 1840, at Torquay, where he had gone to accompany Elizabeth in her illness. 'That was a very near escape from madness, absolute hopeless madness', Barrett wrote a year later to the older, established woman writer Mary Russell Mitford, who became her closest correspondent in the early 1840s. 'The mind seemed to myself broken up into fragments. And even after the long black spectral trains . . . had gone back from my bed, – *to understand*, to hold on to one thought for more than a moment, remained impossible' (*BC* 5:83).

Barrett, already gravely ill, came very close to death in the summer and fall of 1840. But out of the despair of that period came some of her finest early sonnets, including 'Grief'. Her use of the combination of morphine and ether she called her 'elixir' (*BC* 5:222) may have contributed to the 'spectral trains' she experienced after Edward's death, but it was not an addiction she turned to because of discouragement as a poet. Morphine was a standard prescription for a variety of ailments, given to Barrett, it seems, because of the insomnia that was no doubt aggravated by the series of medical regimens that did not permit her to get out of bed, and that afflicted her with leeches, blisters and a variety of medications (*BC* 4:52, 236). Clearly the morphine led to a form of addiction, but what one very rarely sees mentioned in studies of Barrett Browning, aside from Alethea Hayter's, is how, like Samuel Coleridge or Thomas De Quincey, she converted opium-enhanced reverie into an additional source of poetical creativity.

Similarly, she nourished her creativity by using her long hours in bed to engage in omnivorous reading of Greek and Latin texts, poetry, contemporary periodicals and novels. Far from being deterred by the medical advice that warned her against aggravating her illness by unfeminine reading and exertion, Barrett continued to read her volume of Plato, which fortunately looked like 'a novel on the outside'; and she continued to write poetry expressly against the warnings of one of her physicians, Dr Barry (*BC* 4:131, 94). The long Gothic ballad, 'The Legend of the Brown Rosarie', was written covertly against Dr Barry's orders in the summer of 1839. 'The Brown Rosarie' is hardly the kind of poem likely to seem safe to Dr Barry. Barrett called it her 'wild and wicked ballad', and amusingly described the scene in which Dr Barry discovered her with 'a pen guilty of ink' by her side: ' "In the very act, Miss Barrett! In the very act!' " (*BC* 4:169, 174).

While Barrett's physicians warned her that writing poetry might endanger her life, she literally wrote herself back to life, spurred on not by romance but by that last infirmity of noble minds, the love of fame. She thought seriously of Napoleon and Joan of Arc as possible subjects for a major poem in the early 1840s (*BC* 5:171–3, 228), and she displays something of the ambition and heroic ardour of both. For instance, in an 1843 letter to Mitford, she expresses her intense desire for fame by echoing the old ballad of Chevy Chase in which the hero fights upon his stumps after his legs are cut off. Likewise, Barrett tells Mitford, she will ' "fyghte" (write) upon [her] stumps' to win fame. 'Oh I confess it!' she declares. '. . . so little has aspiration been crushed by sorrow & ill health – To fighte upon my stumps, remains to me in a certain sense, *& I do it*' (*BC* 6:299). This fighter 'on her stumps' wrote to the painter Benjamin Haydon in April of 1843 saying that she lived only for poetry – 'in other respects the game is up' – but the poetry in her 'is like a *will to be written*' (*BC* 7:84).

The fighting spirit finds another outlet in the spirited epistolary debates that Barrett carried on with her various regular correspondents in the early 1840s. Sharpening the rhetorical skills later apparent in Aurora's debate with Romney in Book 2 of *Aurora Leigh*, Barrett debated with the Greek scholar Hugh Stuart Boyd concerning points of classical scholarship, politics, and the abilities of women; with Mitford concerning the merits of a multitude of authors, the value of fame, the character of 'pen and ink' people versus non-authors, and a range of other subjects; with the poet, dramatist and critic Richard Hengist Horne concerning her theories of rhyming, and what and what not to include in the survey of contemporary writers she collaborated on with him in 1843–4, *A New Spirit of the Age*; and with the painter Benjamin Robert Haydon concerning the nature of genius, his friendship with Keats and the greatness of Wellington versus Napoleon.

Barrett's comments in her letters to Haydon and

others reveal that, like many of her contemporaries, she attributed genius to women as well as men – despite the anxieties about the nature of female genius reflected in her famous 1844 sonnets to George Sand. Her letters thus imply that genius was not so consistently gendered as male in this period as Battersby claims. Discussing her 'hero-worship' of genius with Mitford, Barrett says, 'I cd. kiss the footsteps of a great man – or woman either – & feel higher for the stooping' (*BC* 4:185). And in a letter to Henry Chorley, she ranked George Sand as 'the first female genius of any country or age' (*LEBB* 1:233). Haydon, who in his own case took the Romantic cult of genius to grandiose and finally tragic extremes, clearly thought of Barrett, his 'invisible' correspondent, as a genius like himself, and found 'something so original in a couple of Geniuses corresponding . . . yet never seeing each other' (*BC* 6:291) that he had his 'immortal Urn', in which he had made tea for other geniuses like Keats, sent to her home so that she could drink from it, before having her name engraved on it along with the other 'immortals' (*BC* 7:78).

Often in the letters of this period we see the boldness that led Barrett to read the French novels by Sand and Balzac no respectable woman was supposed to touch, and that made her 'insolent with a pen in [her] hand" ', in the words of her cousin and friend John Kenyon – words that she took great delight in quoting to other friends (*BC* 7:57). She initiated the older Mitford into what she called her 'lion and tiger hunting with La jeune France' (*BC* 6:191), and shared with her an admiration of the works of Beaumont and Fletcher, despite the fact that they had been condemned by the critic Christopher North as ' "fit reading for the *stews*" ', and by an eminent historian as unsuitable for any ' "woman of common respectability" '. 'So we will hold our respectability to be *un*common – like our reading', Barrett quipped to Mitford (*BC* 6:173).

Along with reading voraciously and widely, she also repeatedly expressed a Ulyssean desire for travel and for experience of other countries, especially Italy, as she fought her way back to life in 1842. In June of that year she defended against Mitford's criticisms the 'continental wandering' of their mutual friend Kenyon, and confessed her longing to do 'the exactly same sinful thing. Think of the German pinewoods! & again, those of the Appenines! – Think of the Alpine glories – thrusting into the sun's face their everlasting snows!' (*BC* 6:23). Some of the unpublished manu-script poetry from this period reveals that Barrett was fascinated by the idea of travelling to Italy well before she knew Browning or thought of escaping there with him. In a 77-line fragment beginning 'Italy! World's Italy!' in one of the Berg notebooks, she imagines hurling herself in spirit 'from one elm top to the next', 'up the rocks' and across the peaks of the Alps to sing in Italy of the English poets whose songs 'ceased upon thy shore / From their English evermore'.[14] The fragment, which may be the opening of a projected long poem, is remarkable for the energy of aspiration it expresses. Its central images subsequently appear in the passage in Book 5 of *Aurora Leigh* in which Aurora prepares to leave England for Italy: 'if we could ride with naked souls', Aurora says, 'I would have seen thee sooner, Italy, / For still I have heard thee crying through my life, / Thou piercing silence of ecstatic graves' (ll.1191–5).

Just as Barrett heard Italy 'crying through' her life before she corresponded or met with Browning, she also began translating Petrarch and writing love poetry well before their meeting, suggesting that the roots of the *Sonnets from the Portuguese* may have been as much literary as romantic. Translations from Petrarch and from the minor Italian love poet Felice Zappi appear in one of the Berg notebooks and in the 'Sonnets Notebook' now in the Armstrong Browning library.[15] This particular Berg notebook was given to Barrett in 1840, and includes many poems published in the 1844 *Poems*. The 'Sonnets Notebook' similarly dates from the 1842–4 period. A third notebook at Yale, the 'Poems and Sonnets' notebook, also includes several published and unpublished love poems, some of them dated 1844 in Barrett's hand. Two intriguing fragments in this notebook – 'We are not equal' and 'I dared to love' – may reflect an initial response to Browning's ardent profession of love. But the earlier love poems in the Yale notebook and her Petrarch translations pre-date Browning's first letter, indicating that Barrett was interested in love as a poetic subject before he entered her life.

The love poetry of the early 1840s is one of a number of signs suggesting that Barrett experienced a physical and a poetical rebirth two years before she first met Browning on 20 May 1845. In October of 1842, she expressed her hope of being 'really & essentially better' (*BC* 6:118). She later looked back on the spring of 1843 as the time when this hope began to be fulfilled: in May of 1845 she wrote to the American writer Mrs Sigourney that 'for the last two years' she had been 'gradually & essentially better' (*BC* 10:191). Barrett's sense of new life is vividly recorded in a May 1843 letter to Mitford in which she vividly describes her intense love of the colour green, her girlhood penchant for dressing in green, and her desire to furnish a room entirely in 'leaf-green' – like the room she was later to give to Aurora Leigh (*BC* 7:113). Although she goes on to say, 'My green leaf has fallen away', she records in the same letter how she has risen from her sickbed to walk from her room across the threshold of the adjoining room (her father's). By July of that year, she was leaving her own room, her father's room, and the Wimpole Street house for afternoon outings in a carriage, and writing to the American poet Cornelius Mathews, 'The bright sunshine is reviving me, & I seem to be putting out leaves' (*BC* 7:218).

Earlier letters from Mitford to Barrett indicate how important a role the older woman played in helping the younger woman she called 'almost a daughter' turn again to life and to high poetic aspirations (*BC* 6:217). Regularly sending Barrett flowers for her sickroom in 1841 and 1842, Mitford also sought, in vibrantly descriptive letters, to woo the younger woman towards the gardens and fields she gathered them in: 'My dear Love', she cried out in one such letter of June 1842, 'how I wish we could transport you into the garden where they grow!' (*BC* 6:8). Mitford also played a vital role in fostering Barrett's ambition – in effect, 'mothering' the poet's mind in Ruth Perry's sense of the term, as the Brownings later did for each other (Mermin, *Mothering*). In one extraordinary letter of March, 1842, Mitford writes:

> My love and my ambition for you often seems [sic] to be more like that of a mother for a son, or a father for a daughter (the two fondest natural emotions), than the common bonds of even a close friendship between two women of different ages and similar pursuits. I sit and think of you, and of the poems that you will write, and of that strange, brief rainbow crown called Fame, until the vision is before me as vividly as ever a mother's heart hailed the eloquence of a patriot son. (*BC* 5:275)

Barrett Browning's turn towards human and contemporary subjects, away from the self-confessedly mystical and abstract subject matter of her 1838 volume *The Seraphim, and Other Poems*, has often been attributed to Browning's influence. But the letters and the poems themselves show that much in her own nature and experience led to that change, and that Mitford significantly contributed to it well before Barrett ever met Browning. For instance, in praising Barrett's ballad, 'The Romaunt of the Page', Mitford entreated her 'to write more ballads' and poems of that order: 'that is to say, poems of human feelings and human actions' (*BC* 5:135).

The poems Mitford pictured Barrett writing in her vision of the younger woman's future fame began to appear with amazing plenitude by the spring of 1843. In February 1843, Barrett wrote the lyrical Wordsworthian quest romance, 'The Lost Bower' (*BC* 6: 334), turning back to happy memories of her girlhood. These were days of 'tree-climbing & wall-climbing' that she had described as being 'too hard to look back at now' in an 1841 letter to Mitford (*BC* 5:67). But near the beginning of 1843, she was looking back and finding in the child the mother of the reborn woman and poet she was to become. Leighton's insightful analysis of 'The Lost Bower' (1986, 70–5) shows how the 'little water Naiad' (l.180) in the elusive fountain of music at the bower's centre is an incarnation of Barrett's muse, reflecting the growth in her of a female poetic identity no longer fostered principally by the male-centred tradition that had dominated her earlier works. Signs of the same new growth appear in the embodiment of wild and spontaneous girlhood Barrett created in her hauntingly resonant semi-autobiographical essay about the ten-year-old Beth, also written in the early 1840s (*BC* 1:360–2).

Like the majority of nineteenth-century women writers discussed by Valerie Sanders in *The Private Lives of Victorian Women*, Barrett Browning's self-writing is fragmentary, unpublished, mediated by fiction and marked by self-censorship. But the 'Beth' essay, which Sanders does not consider, is the most revealing of her several surviving autobiographical fragments, perhaps because it is the most indirect. It seems to have been written in the same period as Barrett's autobiographical sketch for Horne (*BC* 7:352–5), perhaps in part to amuse Barrett's young cousin Elizabeth or 'Ibbit' Hedley, a beautiful and spirited child born in Florence who may have suggested some features of Aurora Leigh. Like 'My Own Character', which Barrett wrote when she was twelve, and 'Glimpses Into My Own Life and Literary Character', written during her fourteenth and fifteenth years (*BC* 1:347–56), the description of Beth's character reveals Barrett's girlhood ambition and force of personality. But more overtly than either of the two earlier essays, it also conveys the fiery feminist spirit of the girl who desired to be 'the feminine of Homer' and Byron, while at the same time despising 'the word "feminine" ': 'Beth thanked her gods that she was not & never wd. be feminine. Beth could run rapidly & leap high' (*BC* 1:361).

Taken together with 'The Lost Bower' and the manifestations of poetical activity that soon followed it, the 'Beth' essay indicates that the awakening Barrett experienced in 1843 follows the classic pattern defined by Susan Rosowski in her well known essay on Kate Chopin's *The Awakening* and parallel texts.[16] That is, it was clearly an awakening growing out of a resurgence of her repressed girlhood ambitions and desires, and an experience of rebirth with psychological, sensual, spiritual and creative dimensions.

Significantly, soon after writing 'The Lost Bower' Barrett went on to write 'The Dead Pan', in which she symbolically bids goodbye to the classical literary heritage her Greek studies with Boyd had immersed her in. The end of 'The Dead Pan' calls for a poetry of the present and 'the Real' (1.249) which she fails to achieve in that poem itself, where the classical past is evoked with graphic sensuality compared to the wooden and abstract evocation of the Christian present. But her turn to a poetry of the present is strikingly manifested in her famous poem of social protest, 'The Cry of the Children', written in the summer of 1843 and published in *Blackwood's* in August.

Barrett's 'poetical fit', as she termed it, continued through the summer and fall of 1843. In mid-July she wrote to Mitford, 'I am writing such poems . . . allegorical-philosophical – poetical-ethical' (*BC* 7:242). These poems included the main part of 'A Vision of Poets', a major and still neglected work revealing her affinities with the Romantic 'visionary company' of poets, and expressing her intense aspirations for poetic fame. The manuscript of 'A Vision of Poets' – in three sections in three notebooks now in the Berg Collection – indicates that Barrett probably began writing it in 1838 before her serious illness. The fact that she was able to take it up again and complete it in 1843 is one more sign of her poetical rebirth.

The fame Mitford had prophesied in 1842 began to come to Barrett even before the publication of her 1844 *Poems. The Seraphim, and Other Poems* (1838) had revealed her originality and the impressive learning already glimpsed in her 1833 translation of Aeschylus's *Prometheus Bound*. Wordsworth was only one of the many who thought highly of the 'Genius and attainments' revealed by her 1838 volume (*BC* 4:347,338).

Between 1838 and 1844, poems published in annuals and periodicals in England and America fuelled the growing interest in this new 'genius'. Two of her romantic ballads published in the 1839 and 1840 issues of *Findens' Tableaux*, the annual edited by Mitford, attracted particular attention: 'The Romaunt of the Page' and 'The Legend of the Brown Rosarie' (entitled 'The Lay of the Brown Rosary' in its heavily revised form in the 1844 *Poems*). Because *Findens' Tableaux*, resembling expensive modern coffeetable books in its format, was difficult to obtain, 'The Legend of the Brown Rosarie' circulated in manuscript copies among the circle of Barrett's American admirers that included James Russell Lowell and his poet-wife Maria, Sophia Peabody (later Nathaniel Hawthorne's wife), and the American feminist transcendentalist Margaret Fuller. During this period Lowell, Cornelius Mathews and other American writers solicited contributions from Barrett for American periodicals such as the shortlived *The Pioneer*. Her letters to American admirers such as Mathews and Lowell, eager to promote their own literary reputations in England through her assistance, reveal her acumen in cultivating her growing fame in America. She was adept in 'doing literary business', like the American women writers considered by Susan Coultrapp-McQuinn; and, as Robert Gladish observes, she 'seemed to keep amazingly well abreast of all that was published on both sides of the Atlantic'.[17]

Two substantial critical essays appearing in 1842 in the *Athenaeum* – 'Some Account of the Greek Christian Poets' and 'The Book of the Poets', the latter a remarkably wide-ranging survey of English poetry from the Middle Ages to the Romantics – further contributed to Barrett's stature among her contemporaries. Anna Jameson, the art historian and women's rights advocate who was to become such a close friend of Barrett after her marriage, read the 'Greek Christian Poets' with ' "great pleasure" '; while Browning sent a copy of it with his comments to Barrett through their mutual friend John Kenyon, expressing his desire to meet her (*BC* 5:303; 290).

Although Browning did not gain the introduction to Barrett he desired in 1842, his admiration for her powers continued to grow. Karlin rightly emphasizes that Browning 'recognized Elizabeth Barrett's "genius" long before he had any personal motive for doing so' (44). Like Harriet Martineau, Browning saw 'The Dead Pan' in manuscript in 1843 when Kenyon was circulating the poem among numerous writers and scholars, and described it as '*most* noble!' – praising in particular the irregular experimental rhymes subsequently censured by reviewers (*BC* 7:137, 269). Kenyon also sent part of 'The Dead Pan' to Wordsworth, who sent Barrett part of an unpublished poem of his own (*BC* 7:55, 23).

Another index of Barrett's increasing fame in 1843 appears in her dealings with Edward Moxon, the publisher of Tennyson's 1842 *Poems* and her 1844 *Poems*. In December of 1842, when Barrett first broached the publication of a volume of miscellaneous poems with Moxon, he refused because of the losses he had suffered from poetry (*BC* 6:254). But by the spring of 1843, Barrett heard through Kenyon of Tennyson saying to Moxon, ' "There is only one female poet whom I wish to see . . . & that is Miss Barrett" '; meanwhile Moxon himself was sending repeated messages through Kenyon that he would be happy to consider publishing any new volume of Miss Barrett's poems (*BC* 7:4, 2, 37).

When the 1844 *Poems* appeared, many works in them won high praise not only from the reviewers, but also from political organizations like the Anti-Corn Law League, and from writers like Thomas Carlyle and Margaret Fuller. The response in America was particularly enthusiastic. In its obituary on Elizabeth Barrett Browning, *Harper's Magazine* recalled that her 1844 volumes 'had a more general and hearty welcome in the United States than any English poet since the time of Byron and company'. In her review for *The Tribune*, Fuller ranked the writer of the 1844 *Poems* 'in vigour and nobleness of conception, depth of spiritual experience, and command of classic allusion, above any female writer the world has yet known'.[18] With characteristic flamboyance, Edgar Allen Poe dedicated his 1845 volume *The Raven and Other Poems* to Barrett, whom he proclaimed the 'noblest of her sex' despite his mixed review of her 1844 volumes. This led Barrett to quip to Kenyon, 'What is to be said, I wonder, when a man calls you the "noblest of your sex"? "Sir, you are the most discerning of yours" ' (*LEBB* 1: 249).

Browning too first wrote to Barrett in January of 1845 to declare not his love for 'dear Miss Barrett', but his love for her 'great living poetry' with its many excellencies: 'the fresh strange music, the affluent language, the exquisite pathos and true new brave thought' (*RB–EBB* 1:3). The 'I love you too' Miss Barrett was an enthusiastic addition, evidently prompted by a renewed desire to 'see' this legendary poet, as he put it, in a phrase modern feminist theorists of the male gaze might find ominous. Browning first addressed Barrett as a peer and a rival. It was critics and biographers, chiefly after the turn of the century, who transformed her into the muse who inspired his poems, the wife who confessed her chaste love in the *Sonnets from the Portuguese*, the 'of Robert' subsumed in the tale of his genius, to use the patronymic form familiar to readers of Margaret Atwood's *The Handmaid's Tale*.

The strength of will and energy manifested in the 1844 *Poems* are also apparent in Barrett's famous flight with Browning to Italy in September of 1846. One popular biography of the Brownings, Frances Winwar's *The Immortal Lovers* (1850), entitles the chapter on their secret marriage and flight 'Fugitive Angel', after the cloyingly sentimental portrait of the infant Elizabeth complete with wings that was her father's favourite. This image infantilizes Barrett Browning in a passivity characterized by dependency on her father, only to be replaced by dependency on her husband, when in fact her action was more akin to the flight of the fugitive black woman she dramatically depicted with such fierce intensity in 'The Runaway Slave at Pilgrim's Point', one of the first poems completed after her marriage.

Between 1844 and 1850, Barrett Browning published a number of poems – most notably, her 'Runaway Slave' poem in the 1848 Boston abolitionist annual *The Liberty Bell*, and a group of seven poems in *Blackwood's* in 1846. But it was largely on the basis of the 1844 *Poems* that her name was proposed in the *Athenaeum* for the Poet Laureateship on Wordsworth's death in 1850. Moreover, she clearly was regarded by many as a suitable candidate, contrary to Margaret Forster's suggestion that the *Athenaeum* proposal was not made 'entirely seriously' (245). The publication of a new and expanded collection of *Poems* in 1850 further consolidated her reputation. The extent of Barrett Browning's fame before *Aurora Leigh* appeared in 1857 is apparent in the quotations from reviews used as advertisements in the first American edition of that work – quotations concerning her previous publications. 'Mrs. Browning is entitled to dispute with

Tennyson the honor of being the greatest living poet of England', the *Illustrated News* declared. *Casa Guidi Windows* (1851), Barrett Browning's lyrical epic on Italian liberation, added to her fame in some quarters (chiefly in America). But her position as Tennyson's rival at mid-century remained principally based upon the 1844 and 1850 editions of her collected poems.

Aurora Leigh seemed to ensure Barrett Browning a permanent place in literary history. Swinburne wrote in his 1898 preface to the work that had passed into more than twenty editions by then: 'The advent of *Aurora Leigh* can never be forgotten by any lover of poetry who was old enough at the time to read it. Of one thing they may all be sure – they were right in the impression that they never had read, and never would read, anything in any way comparable with that unique work of audaciously feminine and ambitiously impulsive genius. It is one of the longest poems in the world, and there is not a dead line in it.' In his 1857 *The Elements of Drawing*, Ruskin praised *Aurora Leigh* as 'the greatest poem which the century has produced in any language'. George Eliot paid tribute to it in the *Westminster Review*, and in her letters revealed that she had read it three times because no other book gave her 'a deeper sense of communion with a large as well as beautiful mind'. Gaskell took her epigraph for *The Life of Charlotte Brontë* from *Aurora Leigh*, just as she had taken many of her chapter epigraphs in the earlier *North and South* from Barrett Browning's 1844 and 1850 poems. And Susan B. Anthony carried *Aurora Leigh* with her in her trunk as she crisscrossed America lecturing on women's rights, inscribing in her copy of it her wish that women might grow 'more and more like Aurora Leigh'.[19]

Women did grow more and more like Aurora Leigh over the next century, but at the same time *Aurora*

Leigh disappeared from literary history, along with the poet viewed in her own time as Tennyson's rival. Irene Cooper Willis' 1928 book on Barrett Browning in the 'Representative Women' series dismissed the work that had inspired Anthony as a book once approved by the 'Mammas of England' and 'nowadays . . . starred as suitable reading in the syllabuses of "Literature" classes in young ladies' finishing schools'.[20] In our own time, women readers are far more likely to share Anthony's response to *Aurora Leigh* than Willis'. Gilbert and Gubar's description of it as 'an epic of feminist self-affirmation' is representative (575). Although *Aurora Leigh* was followed by two additional volumes of poetry, the polemical political sequence *Poems before Congress* (1860) and the posthumously published *Last Poems* (1862), it is now typically read as the culminating expression of Barrett Browning's unprecedented gynocentric poetics.

Understandably, then, the question of how this poetics was formed has attracted much interest – particularly since it seems to be singularly absent in Barrett's first published writings, *The Battle of Marathon* (1820) and *An Essay on Mind, with Other Poems* (1826). Far from embodying an incipient gynocentric poetics, these works of juvenilia acutely manifest the 'metaphorical transvestism or male impersonation' that Gilbert and Gubar read as a reflection of the nineteenth-century woman writer's 'anxiety of authorship' (66). Moreover, elements of male impersonation persist even in some of the works Barrett Browning included in her 1844 *Poems*, reflecting the formidable difficulties she experienced in her attempts to enter a male poetic tradition. Consequently, as Deborah Byrd notes (24), critics have focused on the ways in which Barrett Browning 'draws upon or swerves from male writers', particularly the poetical 'grandfathers' she professed her reverence for in the famous 1845 letter to Henry Chorley in which she cried, 'I look everywhere for grandmothers and see none' (*LEBB* 1:232).

There is far from unanimous agreement, however, on the nature of Barrett Browning's relationship to these poetical 'grandfathers', or on the extent to which she in fact developed a fully gynocentric poetics. Whereas some stress the extent to which she remained in the shadow of her male precursors, others stress the revisionary 'swerves' that transformed her into a grandmother herself for subsequent women poets. Leighton's Lacanian conflation of Barrett Browning's poetical grandfathers with Edward Barrett, the poet's father, is one important instance of the former approach. Even in her later works, Leighton argues, Barrett Browning's 'poetics depends on an intimate and highly biographical relation to the figure of power that represents her muse' – the father whose inspiration she never ceased to court (1986, 14).

My own examination of the poetry Barrett Browning published in the 1840s bears out the opposing emphasis of critics like Mermin, Cooper and Byrd, who discern a distinct movement away from male perspectives and influences in Barrett Browning's writing during this period. In the published works, one of the first striking manifestations of this shift is the focus on Eve's experience in *A Drama of Exile*. It is even more visible, however, in the manuscripts of the 1840s: most notably, in a fragment associated with *A Drama of Exile*, in the love poems of the early 1840s, and in the preliminary version of 'The Runaway Slave at Pilgrim's Point'. All of these not only reveal Barrett Browning shifting from male to female perspectives, but also give some indication of when and why this important shift occurred.

As Chapters 2 and 3 suggest, one of the principal catalysts contributing to Barrett Browning's 'swerve' away from her poetical grandfathers was the revisionary poetical practice she inherited from the Romantics. But her biographical formation and other aspects of her cultural milieu also played vital roles in her increasingly woman-centred consciousness. The influence of her mother and other family members has been underestimated, along with the influence of her many female friends and correspondents. Given the importance of many of these women in mid-Victorian culture, personal and cultural influences often overlap for Barrett Browning. But there also existed an entire matrix of women writers whom she did not personally know who shaped her consciousness and textual practice.

Her mother's influence came first, as Barrett Browning later indirectly acknowledged in *Aurora Leigh*: 'But still I catch my mother at her post / Beside the nursery door' (1:15–16). Leighton's Lacanian readings of many of Barrett Browning's poems indicate that Mr Barrett, *pater familias*, still looms large over reconstructions of the poet's career, even when the focus shifts from her life to her art. While Edward Moulton-Barrett undoubtedly did strongly influence his daughter's poetical development, however, Forster has persuasively shown that Mary Moulton-Barrett was also actively concerned in educating her eldest daughter and in encouraging her childhood literary endeavours. Forster's reconstruction of their relationship is supported by manuscripts from the period of Elizabeth's childhood, now in the Armstrong Browning Library. Elizabeth's mother even developed a game in which she played the part of her daughter's 'publisher' (*BC* 1:286).

The influence of Barrett Browning's mother has

been easily overlooked not only because of her early death when her eldest daughter was only twenty-two, but also because, for a long period of her artistic formation, Elizabeth seems to have overlooked her first 'publisher' herself. As she became increasingly successful in her juvenile literary endeavours, her father took a strong interest in them, arranging the publication of *The Battle of Marathon* when she was only fourteen. The idealization of a powerful father figure was a natural consequence for the young Elizabeth, but she also developed an equally important psychological alliance with her brother Edward, born a year after her in 1807.

In fact, it might easily be argued that Elizabeth's mother was displaced less by the poet's father than by the poet's closest brother Edward, following the pattern of intense 'fraternal alliance' that Marianne Hirsch discerns in a number of nineteenth-century women novelists in *The Mother–Daughter Plot*.[21] Inheritor of his father's name, Edward was the first-born male in a family of twelve in which, as Charlotte Porter and Helen Clarke note, the four daughters did not count in the line of eight sons Mr Barrett ended by naming Septimus and Octavius (*CW* 1:xii). Long before the premature death of Elizabeth's mother in 1828, Edward had become his older sister's closest confidant in the Herefordshire home, Hope End, where they passed their childhood. He was affectionately known as 'Bro' to the elder sister who herself was called 'Ba' by family members, and it is little wonder that his death by drowning in 1840 left her prostrate with inexpressible grief.

In a reversal of the intense brother–sister relationships characteristic among the Romantics – William and Dorothy Wordsworth, Byron and his half-sister Augusta, Shelley's Laon and Cythna in *The Revolt of*

Islam – Bro came to function as muse and second self for the young Elizabeth Barrett, while her mother, immersed in child-bearing, receded in importance. The autobiographical fragments, 'Glimpses Into My Own Life and Literary Character' and 'My Character and Bro's Compared' (*BC* 1:348–58), reveal the trauma Elizabeth endured at fourteen when the brother she identified with so strongly left home for the formal schooling and opportunities denied to her. After Bro's death in 1840, she turned to another brother, George, as her chief poetical confidant, and not simply to her father as the often reprinted dedication to the 1844 *Poems*, 'To My Father', implies. Indeed, she was bitterly observing by 1843 that 'Papa . . . does not believe in poetry, & wd. drive me sometimes "distract" with melancholy, if I believed him' (*BC* 7:206). In the same period, her letters to George are filled with details of her poetical activity and aspirations.

Despite the pattern of fraternal alliance noticeable in Barrett Browning's case, the mother did not remain displaced in either her life or her works. The 1843 awakening that brought the resurgence of Barrett's girlhood energy and ambition was accompanied by a return of the repressed mother. Critics writing in the early 1980s discerned a woman-centred poetics in *Aurora Leigh* that remained pervaded by 'mother-want' (Steinmetz), or by the attempt to reclaim the 'iconic' visionary maternal face that haunts Romantic and Victorian poetry (Rosenblum, 'Face to Face', 322). Such approaches reflect the general focus on the daughter's perspective and the elision of the mother's experience typical of feminist criticism produced in these years – when many critics were primarily daughters themselves (Hirsch 19). But, as Sandra Donaldson demonstrates, it is a focus Barrett Browning developed beyond, both in *Aurora Leigh* where she presents Marian as both mother and daughter, and in powerful late works like 'Mother and Poet'. *Casa Guidi Windows* as well is, in Mermin's words, 'a hymn to progress and human possibility that is also, and not coincidentally, a song of motherhood' (173). Nevertheless, Barrett Browning's representations of maternal subjectivity are by no means unambivalent: significantly, some of her most dramatic mother figures are indirectly or directly asssociated with murder or cursing (Phelps 232). What fascinate her, as 'The Runaway Slave at Pilgrim's Point' indicates, are the convolutions of the maternal passions.

The shift in focus to the mother's experience in Barrett Browning's life and writing is accompanied by intensifying alliances with her own sisters, Henrietta and Arabella, and with other women – alliances that may have grown stronger in part because of tensions in her marriage. As her letters to Mrs David Ogilvie, Anna Jameson and Isa Blagden suggest, relationships with other women remained very important to Barrett Browning after her marriage. One particularly intense relationship she formed with the American medium Sophia Eckley in the late 1850s ended in disillusion-ment when she began to suspect Sophia as a charlatan. In *Through a Glass Darkly*, Katherine Porter attributes Barrett Browning's relationship with Sophia to the fascination with spiritualism that she shared with many of her contemporaries in the 1850s. But evidence also points to possible intervals of relative alienation from her husband leading Barrett Browning to turn to intimacy with other women, and to the consolations that spiritualism seemed to offer.

'So ended on earth the most perfect example of wedded happiness in the history of literature', Frederic Kenyon wrote in 1897, describing Barrett Browning's

death in her husband's arms (*LEBB* 2:452). No doubt
the Browning marriage was 'extremely happy' much
of the time (Mermin 5). Yet perfect 'wedded happiness'
exists only in fairy tales. In the Brownings' case, there
may be traces of a more complicated human story in
Barrett Browning's late dramatic monologues of
passionately possessive women betrayed by love, such
as 'Bianca Among the Nightingales', and in the
manuscript of 'My Heart and I', another monologue
of betrayal included in *Last Poems* – not to speak of
Browning's powerful representation of a marital
breakdown in 'James Lee's Wife'.[22]

Cultural context is certainly as important as
personal experience, however, in accounting for the
intensely woman-centred perspective we encounter in
so many of Barrett Browning's works from the 1840s
on. Ellen Moers was among the first to situate the
author of *Aurora Leigh* in the matrix of a female literary
tradition that included Mary Wollstonecraft, Madame
de Staël, and George Sand, all of them powerful
precursors for the woman who could find no poetical
'grandmothers'.

Compelling evidence for the direct impact of
Wollstonecraft at a formative stage in Barrett
Browning's development appears in an 1842 letter
to Mitford in which she ironically explains her
incompetence in needlework. 'I ought to have been
well whipped at six years old', she observes, '& then –
that is, now – I shd. whip [i.e. do the whip stitch]
better'. But, as she points out, she never learned 'the
duties belonging to [her] femineity' [sic] because
needlework was never put to her as a duty. 'And then',
she adds:

I was always insane about books & poems – poems
of my own, I mean, – & books of everybody's else –

> and I read Mary Wolstonecraft [sic] when I was thirteen: no, twelve! . . and, through the whole course of my childhood, I had a steady indignation against Nature who made me a woman, & a determinate resolution to dress up in men's clothes as soon as ever I was free of the nursery, & go into the world 'to seek my fortune'. '*How*', was not decided; but I rather leant towards being poor Lord Byron's PAGE. (*BC* 6:42)

The 'whip' pun suggests how much Barrett Browning's light wit conceals here, coming from someone aware as she was of the abolitionist controversy concerning whipping on the West Indian slave plantations that had created her own family's wealth. There were, she later wrote to Browning, 'infinite traditions' in her family of how her great-grandfather Edward Barrett had 'flogged his slaves like a divinity' (*RB–EBB* 2:759). The parallel between women and slaves was one that Wollstonecraft and Barrett Browning's female contemporaries often drew.

The woman–slave parallel is made more explicit in what may be the most dramatic manifestation of Barrett Browning's youthful adherence to what her mother called 'yours & Mrs. Wolstonecrafts system' [sic] (*BC* 1:132): the 'Fragment of an "Essay on Woman" '. Although the attribution of this fragment has been questioned by Margaret Reynolds (*AL* 61), it appears to have been written around 1822 when Barrett was sixteen, but not published until 1984 (Hoag). Modelled on Pope's 'Essay on Man', the fragment scornfully criticizes men for singing of their own powers, while praising women only for their weakness:

> Imperious Man! is this alone thy pride
> T'enslave the heart that lingers at thy side?

Smother each flash of intellectual fire,
And bid Ambition's noblest throb expire?
Pinion the wing, that yearns for glory's light,
Then boast the strength of thy superior flight?

Kay Moser has shown how imbued the 'Fragment of
an "Essay on Woman" ' is with Wollstonecraft's
diction and arguments. But with the exception of some
unpublished remarks by Tricia Lootens (29), the
connections between Wollstonecraft's writings and
Barrett Browning's mature works remain unexplored.

The importance of Madame de Staël in Barrett
Browning's poetical development likewise remains
relatively unexplored, despite Kaplan's analysis of the
many echoes of *Corinne* in *Aurora Leigh* ('Introduction',
16–21). The Romantic woman of letters is among the
women of genius saluted in the 'Essay on Woman',
but Mermin suggests that de Staël never could have
aroused 'a very passionate enthusiasm' in the young
Barrett (27). This assumption is not supported by
Barrett's later description of de Staël, along with
Sand, as one of the two great women writers produced
by France; or by her defence of the same writer to
Mitford as a woman of genius, compared to a woman
of talent such as Fanny Burney (*BC* 6:252, 196–7). In
the 'Beth' essay, de Staël is the only woman the
militant young heroine does not despise (*BC* 1:361).
Elsewhere, Barrett metaphorically associates her hero-
worship of the poets she staunchly defended and
Mitford decried with hiding in 'Madme. de Staël's
petticoats' (*BC* 4:249). And she declared *Corinne*, the
work about a doomed female genius that also influenced Byron and Sir Walter Scott, an 'immortal
book', deserving to be read 'three score & ten times'
(*BC* 3:25).

George Sand's impact on Barrett Browning's thinking about women and writing was even greater than de Staël's. Patricia Thomson and Sandra Donaldson have explored her liberating 'love affair' with her great French contemporary; while Cooper has pointed out the subversive significance of Barrett's use of the sonnet form to address Sand (63). Relatively early in her correspondence with Browning, Barrett vigorously defended Sand's novel *Consuelo* against his criticisms. Where he saw only a lack of dramatic power, she saw a 'female Odyssey', written by an author who was 'man and woman together' (*RB–EBB* 1:160, 159). After seeking an introduction to Sand in Paris in 1852, Barrett Browning noted how she 'seemed . . . to be *the man*' in the circle of respectful younger men that surrounded her (*LEBB* 2:56). Aurora Leigh is named in part after Sand, whose maiden name was Aurore Dupin; and like Sand, who appeared one evening in Paris wearing ivy around her brows (*LEBB* 2:230), Aurora Leigh crowns herself with a wreath of 'headlong ivy' (Book 2:46). Sand's contribution to the bold feminism of *Aurora Leigh* is furthermore indicated by Barrett Browning's interest in her 'views upon the *sexes*' in 1855, when she was at work on her own 'female Odyssey' (*LEBB* 2:222).

Barrett Browning found no woman writer to match Sand's genius among her English precursors and contemporaries. But her letters make it clear that she read very widely among the hundreds of women writers who, as Mellor points out (1), 'produced at least half of the literature published in England between 1780 and 1830'. Maria Edgeworth, Anna Seward, Amelia Opie, Ann Radcliffe, Lady Morgan (Sydney Owenson), Mary Shelley, Joanna Baillie, Felicia Hemans, Letitia Landon and many others, indeed almost all of the most influential Romantic women writers explicitly named by Mellor (2), are discussed in Barrett Browning's correspondence – particularly her correspondence with Mitford, who was personally acquainted with many of these authors. For example, in one extended exchange, she disagreed with Mitford's high estimate of Jane Austen, whom she saw as at best a graceful 'Dutch painter' of English 'middle life', whose 'ladyhood' was 'stronger than her humanity' (*BC* 7:214). Reflecting the Romantic sensibility that led her to prefer de Staël to Burney, her response to Austen strikingly resembles Charlotte Brontë's famous description of Austen's novels as a 'carefully fenced' garden with 'neat borders', but with 'no open country, no fresh air' (cited Moers 48). Other references to Romantic women writers reveal her interest in the buried lives of women such as Seward. After reading a life of William Hayley, she remarked to Mitford, 'how little is said of Miss Seward "the Muse"! It disappointed me. Is there a life of *her*?' (*BC* 5:244).

Barrett Browning's references to women writers are also characterized by a spirit of internationalism and a marked interest in French and American authors. When Mitford mentioned an anthology of women writers she had been asked to contribute to in 1842, Barrett asked 'why not *include* all the female writers of Europe' in 'this *blue* book as people are sure to call it'. 'Germany Spain & Italy wd. fill as many pages as our England – & it wd. give a completeness & interest to the work' (*BC* 5:228). She also read 'a long dynasty of French memoirs' by women (*LEBB* 1:235). These French memoirs and her curiosity 'beyond the patience of [her] Eve-ship' were in fact what led her to begin reading Sand (*BC* 6:162). Proleptically, she was greatly moved by one Frenchwoman's memoirs, recounting the intense anguish, joy, and internal conflicts of a late-life marriage, deferred because of the man's imprisonment (*BC* 7:240).

She developed particularly close connections with the American antebellum feminist abolitionists considered in Jean Fagan Yellin's *Women and Sisters*, as 'The Runaway Slave at Pilgrim's Point' indicates. 'The Runaway Slave' was published in the Boston abolitionist annual, *The Liberty Bell*, like the later abolitionist poem 'A Curse for a Nation'. Yellin's discussion of the sonnet 'Hiram Powers' "Greek Slave" ' reveals how this poem too incorporates the tropes and the concerns of the American feminist abolitionists (123–4). Among individual American writers, Barrett Browning came to know Margaret Fuller well in Italy before the latter's death by shipwreck in 1850, and admired the force of genius that she did not find fully reflected in Fuller's writings (*LEBB* 1:459–60). And she praised Harriet Beecher Stowe, the author of *Uncle Tom's Cabin*, as a writer who had changed the world with a book before she came to know and admire her as a woman whose religious speculations revealed not a 'deep thinker' but one 'singularly large and unshackled' (*LEBB* 2:424).

Barrett Browning's turn to socially controversial issues in the 1840s may have been influenced in part by the American feminist abolitionists, in part by the long tradition of English women writers who were pioneering figures in the nineteenth-century discourse of social protest. Harriet Martineau, one of the most important women in this tradition, is the English woman writer whom Barrett most admired in the 1840s along with Anna Jameson. She termed Martineau 'the noblest female Intelligence between the seas', and noted that both Martineau and Jameson had a 'European reputation' (*BC* 7:302; 8:86). Barrett read other important writers contributing to social protest literature as well: Charlotte Elizabeth Tonna, for instance (*BC* 6:62). 'The Cry of the Children' has invariably been attributed to the influence of Barrett's correspondent Horne and his parliamentary 'Report on the Employment of Children and Young Persons in Mines and Manufactories' (*CW* 3:362). But the impact of works by women writers like Martineau and Tonna in the 'hungry' 1840s may be an equally important influence on its genesis.

One of the highly topical social issues in the 1840s was the education and rights of women. In an 1845 letter, Barrett described herself as '*not* . . . a very strong partizan on the Rights-of-Woman side of the argument', and stated, 'I believe that, considering men & women in the mass, there IS an *inequality* of intellect, and that it is proved by the very state of things of which gifted women complain' (*LMRM* 3:81). The few passages reflecting views of this sort in Barrett Browning's letters have often been cited as proof of Barrett Browning's antipathy to the feminist activists among her contemporaries, usually without acknowledging the contexts that complicate their import.

The case for Barrett Browning's ideological opposition to the Victorian women's rights movement has been made most fully and intelligently by Deirdre David. Foregrounding the contradictory and conservative elements in Barrett Browning's ideological practice, David has interpreted her as a 'traditional intellectual' in Antonio Gramsci's sense of the term, and argued that she was 'smugly scornful of the intellectual capabilities of women unlike herself', 'barred by illness from participation in any female or feminist community', deprived of a 'sustaining female literary tradition', 'androcentric' in the sexual politics reflected in her letters, and indifferent to 'the struggles for cultural and social equality in women'.[23] David's exclusive focus on the conservative elements in Barrett Browning's thought usefully corrects simplistic ideal- izations of her as a feminist foremother. But the appreciation of the complexities of Barrett Browning's ideological practice is not furthered by fitting her into the straitjacket of a Gramscian traditional intellectual, which itself does not allow for contradiction or change.

Barrett Browning's comments on the capabilities and rights of women, both in her letters and in *Aurora Leigh*, typically appear in dialogical or ironic contexts. In the letter in which she comments on the 'Rights-of- Woman', for instance, she expresses great anger at men who exaggerate the weakness of women 'in order to parade their protection', and who use both the chivalric theory of woman's glory and the 'pudding- making and stocking darning theory' to discourage women from expressing themselves as writers and social critics. Barrett Browning's thinking about the rights of women also changed quite substantially between the 1840s and the 1850s. Certainly by the 1850s she had closer ties with British feminist activists than is generally recognized, in part through her friendship with Anna Jameson. In 1855, Barrett Browning signed the petition for reform of the marriage laws circulated by Barbara Leigh Smith (later Barbara Bodichon) and her committee; while in 1858 she encouraged her friend Mrs Ogilvie to contribute to England's first periodical published entirely by women, the newly established *English Woman's Journal* edited by Bessie Parkes.[24] Her affilia- tions with mid-Victorian feminist activists help to explain the enthusiastic reception of *Aurora Leigh* among the Langham Place group, which included Bodichon, Parkes and Frances Power Cobbe.

Barrett Browning's connections with the major

women novelists among her contemporaries –
Charlotte Brontë, Elizabeth Gaskell, and George Eliot
– form a complex web of interactions and affiliations
most apparent in the traces of *Ruth*, *Jane Eyre*, and
Villette in *Aurora Leigh*, and in the many traces of *Aurora
Leigh* in Eliot's works. As for women poets among her
precursors and contemporaries, Barrett Browning
read them with a keenness intensified by her search for
poetical 'grandmothers', a shrewd awareness of the
critical double standard they encountered, and an
often uneasy sense of identification and rivalry. Byrd
notes the importance of Barrett Browning's interaction
with women poets such as Felicia Hemans, Letitia
Landon, Mary Howitt, and Caroline Norton, although
her claim that Mitford's encouragement first led
Barrett to study such women is somewhat inaccurate
(30). The 1824–6 Wellesley notebook indicates that,
long before she met Mitford, the young Barrett was
reading Landon and comparing her to Hemans with
'an acute consciousness of issues of gender', as
Mermin notes (31). For instance, Barrett observes in
her notebook that the *Literary Gazette* praised Landon
relative to other female authors only; and she criticizes
Landon for casting her thoughts into the 'prettiest
attitudes' – but too much 'the *same* attitudes' –
revealing her uneasiness about the poses making some
women's poetry resemble the 'attitudes' made fashionable by Lady Hamilton in the late eighteenth century.

In her maturity, Barrett Browning remained acutely
aware of 'the ordinary impotencies & prettinesses of
female poets' (*LMRM* 3:412). But it is fallacious to
assume that she responded to women's poetry as a
'body of texts' with common tropes and rhetorical
strategies, rather than entering into dialogical relationships with a 'particular poem' or 'a specific female
precursor' (Byrd 31). She did both, but modern

readers tend to miss the individual dialogical relationships because we are no longer familiar as Barrett
Browning's contemporaries were with particular poets
and poems. For instance, she emphatically described
Joanna Baillie as 'the first female poet in all senses in
England' (*LEBB* 1:230). At the same time, however,
she did not see herself or Baillie as writing in a female
tradition distinct from the mainstream of English
poetry.

There is much to be gained from the ongoing
endeavour to reconstruct Barrett Browning's complex
connections with a female literary tradition in the
'epic age' of women writers (Moers 14). But since
Barrett Browning was not an underground writer in
her own age or a writer always marginalized by
her gender, it is also important to conceptualize her
achievement in the context of a poetic tradition
conventionally defined in terms of predominantly
male writers. As Battersby points out in her discussion
of artists such as Hannah Hoch, a woman artist
remains buried in the 'insignificance' of 'Otherness'
until we construct a narrative that binds her 'output
together into an *oeuvre*' and anchor that narrative in
the 'chains of influence and inheritance out of which
"culture" is constructed' (142–3). In her own poetical
development, Barrett Browning overcame the
debilitating sense of otherness reinforced for nineteenth-
century women writers by their exclusion from the
position of 'the speaking subject as male' and their
identification with nature (Homans 12). Criticism
needs to follow suit in exploring how her poetic output
enters into and alters the narrative of nineteenth-
century literary culture that we ourselves have
inherited.

2 The Scene of Instruction: Romantic Revisionism

'Byron, Coleridge ... how many more? ... were contemporaries of mine without my having approached them near enough to look reverently in their faces ... and young as I was, I cannot get rid of a feeling of deep regret that, so, – it shd. have been' (*BC* 7:319). Elizabeth Barrett was born in 1806, eleven years after Keats and six years before Browning. Her first published works, *The Battle of Marathon* (1820) and *An Essay on Mind, with Other Poems* (1826), pre-date the appearance of Tennyson's juvenilia in *Poems by Two Brothers* (1827). Her formative years therefore belong to the Romantic, not the Victorian period. But her affiliations with Romantic poets and traditions have been largely unexplored, with the exception of her connections with Wordsworth. Dorothy Mermin's conclusion that for the young Elizabeth Barrett 'as for the young Matthew Arnold Romanticism meant mostly nature poetry, especially Wordsworth's' (63), is shared by Angela Leighton (1986, 13) and Helen Cooper, while Kathleen Blake and Antony Harrison alternatively emphasize Wordsworthian elements in the poetics of *Aurora Leigh*. Margaret Reynolds considers Barrett Browning's general adherence to the 'tenets of Romanticism', yet again singles out only Wordsworth among the poets (*AL* 13).

Although there is little reason to question

Wordsworth's importance as one of Barrett Browning's Romantic precursors, there is good reason to question both the idea that she saw him principally as a nature poet and the neglect of other equally important Romantic influences on her cultural formation. She identified Wordsworth as the 'poet-hero of a movement esssential to the better being of poetry' (*CW* 6:304) less because of his gendered representations of nature than because of his experiments with poetic diction, the ballad form and marginalized dramatic speakers, which significantly influenced her own ballads and dramatic monologues. Her other most ambitious poetical works published from 1820 to 1844, the subject of this chapter, reveal lines of influence and resistance connecting her not only with Wordsworth, but also with Romantic writers collectively. Margaret Morlier has illuminated one of these lines in analysing Barrett Browning's complex critique of Romantic representations of the goat-god Pan: her depictions of Pan bring out the egoism and the violence associated with Pan's attempted rape of Syrinx that male Romantic poets characteristically leave in the background (137). This chapter considers some of the many other lines of transmission connecting Barrett Browning to the younger generation of male Romantic poets in particular: Keats, Shelley and above all Byron.

Like Victorianism, Romanticism is notoriously difficult to define. Jerome McGann concludes that it is better to speak of 'phases of Romanticism';[1] while in *Romanticism and Gender* Anne Mellor takes issue with McGann himself in observing that 'we can no longer continue to speak monolothically of "British Romanticism", of a "Romantic spirt of the age", of "*the* Romantic ideology" ' (209). Generally, however, the work of influential critics such as M. H. Abrams,

Harold Bloom and Geoffrey Hartman through the 1960s and 70s marked a shift away from the focus on nature as the primary subject in Romantic poetry to a focus on the preoccupation with epistemology and with 'imagination, vision and transcendence' in Wordsworth as well as other Romantic poets (Mellor 1). McGann's critique of this approach as a replication of Romantic ideology marked another general shift in critical focus, this time to the instability of perception and language in Romantic texts, and to the ideological conflicts and political and social realities repressed by the preoccupation with vision and transcendence, in Romantic poets and their critics alike. Meanwhile, new historicist and feminist critics began to question the traditional approach to Romanticism in terms of six major male poets writing in the 'higher' poetical genres − an approach evident in McGann's *The Romantic Ideology* itself. As Mellor suggests, 'what we have traditionally defined as "Romanticism" ' might be better conceptualized as ' "masculine" Romanticism', in opposition to a still largely uncharted ' "feminine Romanticism" ' with very different 'thematic concerns, formal practices, and ideological positionings . . . To mention only the most immediately obvious, the women writers of the Romantic period for the most part foreswore the concern of their male peers with the capacities of creative imagination, with the limitations of language, with the possibility of transcendence or "unity of being", with the development of an autonomous self, with political (as opposed to social) revolution, with the role of the creative writer as political leader or religious savior' (2–3).

While my previous chapter indicates that 'feminine Romanticism' was undoubtedly very important to Barrett Browning's development, I nevertheless focus here principally on her connections with 'masculine

Romanticism' because she simply does not fit the pattern Mellor attributes to Romantic women writers. It is true that her 1838 volume, *The Seraphim, and Other Poems*, contains a certain amount of domestic and memorializing poetry in the vein of Hemans and Landon – poetry leading Antony Harrison to conclude that she was primarily concerned with constructing female subjectivity and extending the domestic sphere (114–19). But Harrison arrives at this conclusion without considering the lead poem in the 1838 volume or Barrett Browning's other most substantial works up to 1844. Leighton more persuasively observes that 'Barrett Browning begins where L.E.L. left off' in locating female conventions of sensibility within 'systems of socialisation' and 'social reality'; yet she still defines her as 'a true inheritor of the tradition of female sensiblity which Hemans and L.E.L. had popularized' (1992, 80). My own view, to the contrary, is that Elizabeth Barrett wrote much of the time as a 'true inheritor' of the male Romantic poets. As Mellor acknowledges in treating both Emily Brontë's *Wuthering Heights* as 'an example of "masculine" Romanticism' and the features of 'feminine' Romanticism in Keats' works, any writer, 'male or female', can occupy either subject position (4). Like Brontë, Barrett Browning endorsed the 'masculine' Romantic values of 'revolu-tionary energy, of imagination, of that life-force in nature and the mind which Percy Shelley called "Power" ' (Mellor 204). Moreover, because her primary medium is poetry and because she was familiar with classical models, her formal practices are more closely associated with 'masculine Romanticism' than Brontë's *Wuthering Heights* is.

Both the subject and the compositional process of Barrett Browning's unfinished poem 'The Develop-ment of Genius' reveal how much she was influenced by the self-writing practices of the male Romantics. Despite its eighteenth-century form, the earlier *An Essay on Mind* similarly reflects her self-reflexive concern with epistemology and with what Wordsworth described as 'the growth of the poet's mind'. Although her attempt to construct the 'unitary, transcendental subjectivity' Mellor associates with Wordsworth's 'egotistical sublime' was thwarted by her gender (149), Barrett Browning is remarkable for her highly self-conscious and overt poetic aspirations – particularly in contrast to a self-repressed writer like Dorothy Wordsworth.

She also endorsed the male Romantic vision of poets as the 'unacknowledged legislators of the world', to use Shelley's famous words. This key component in 'the Romantic ideology' critiqued by McGann and others persists in Barrett Browning's works from her juvenilia to her maturity, although she subtly subverts certain aspects of it herself in *Aurora Leigh*. Many of her works from 1820 to 1844 also reflect the inter-mixed strains of Romantic revolutionary idealism and millenialism later apparent, in a revised and gyno-centric form, in *Aurora Leigh*. What tends to disappear is the Romantic Hellenism she initially shared with Byron, Shelley and many others, the predilection for masculinized images of the sublime, and the use of generic forms favoured by the Romantics: descriptive-meditative lyrics, the lyrical drama, and allegorical or visionary poetic modes like that employed in Keats' *The Fall of Hyperion*, which Barrett Browning's 'A Vision of Poets' (1844) uncannily resembles.

Her fascination with the Titanic figures of Prometheus and Satan and the ambitious daring of her revisionary impulse are the features of Barrett Browning's poetry up to 1844 that most obviously link her to 'masculine' Romanticism and to the 'Satanic

School' of Byron and Shelley in particular. Significantly, she referred to her 'early association with "*Fire-thieves*!" ' (*BC* 4:34). Her comment captures not only the Romantic Prometheanism reflected in her love of Aeschylus' *Prometheus Bound*, which she translated once in 1833 and again in 1845, but also her emulation of her Romantic precursors, all of them 'fire-thieves' too in their rebellious revisioning of their precursors. Her revision of Aeschylus in *The Seraphim* (1838) produced a lyrical drama akin to *Prometheus Unbound* in several respects, reflecting as Shelley's text does a later phase of Romantic Prometheanism. In the 1844 *Poems*, Aeschylus recedes in importance while Milton and Dante, the two precursor-rivals who dominate the works of the major Romantics, become the principal focus of Barrett's revisionary enterprise. Much as Wordsworth, Blake, Shelley and Byron engage in the revisionary 'wrestling' with Milton mapped out in Harold Bloom's *The Anxiety of Influence* and *A Map of Misreading*, she sets out to 'complete' Milton's *Paradise Lost* in *A Drama of Exile*, thereby engaging in one common type of 'revisionary swerve'.[2] In the process, she simultaneously echoes and revises Byron's *Cain*, itself a rewriting of Milton's angelology and metaphysics. 'A Vision of Poets', the other major work in her 1844 *Poems*, is written in Dante's shadow rather than Milton's, although it also strikingly reveals the difficulties she experienced in trying to enter an entire tradition of 'king-poets', to use her own term.

In her study of female creativity, Paula Bennett argues that Bloom's paradigm of the 'anxiety of influence' is 'at best only indirectly relevant' to the struggle of the woman poet. 'The woman writer's principal antagonists are not the strong male or female poets who may have preceded her within the tradition, but the inhibiting voices that live within herself' –

voices arising out of her fear that 'in fulfilling her destiny as a poet, she will be forced to hurt or fail those whom she loves . . . Her struggles, in short, are not literary but part of life'.[3] Much in Emily Dickinson's or Christina Rossetti's response to Barrett Browning casts doubt on Bennett's assumption that women writers' anxieties are not concerned with the forbidding example of powerful precursors. But it seems even less applicable to Barrett Browning, whose principal struggles were with an alienating tradition of poetical 'grandfathers'. These struggles were necessarily 'literary', although feminist critics since Sandra Gilbert and Susan Gubar have revised Bloom's emphasis significantly by analysing the 'anxiety of authorship', not the 'anxiety of influence', apparent in her earlier works (*Madwoman* 49, 69–70).

While I consider several manifestations of Barrett Browning's 'anxiety of authorship' below, I place greater emphasis on the remarkable audacity of authorship her works between 1820 and 1844 reveal. In the process, I make fairly direct use of Bloom's paradigm because Barrett Browning's audacity as a woman poet makes her very much like the male Romantic 'strong poets' as Bloom describes them – although we should not forget that some Romantic women writers also displayed a remarkable 'authorial self-confidence, even arrogance' (Mellor 8). Barrett Browning furthermore resembles the male Romantics, however, in being obsessed by poetic origins and a sense of belatedness; and like them, she begets herself as a poet through bold acts of creative 'misprision' or misreading. In keeping with Bloom's model, her works up to 1844 also enact a 'primal scene of instruction' among the progenitors who both fostered and inhibited her own creativity (*Map* 41–62).

Given her status as a daughter in the house of the

literary fathers, Barrett Browning's formation understandably does not follow the Freudian Oedipal
pattern of Bloom's paradigm. It is less overt and more
internally conflicted, like the struggle of daughters
with fathers, that aspect of the 'family romance' Freud
neglected. Nevertheless, her development generally
reflects the phases of poetic incarnation Bloom outlines.
Thus her earliest works like *The Battle of Marathon*
embody the initial phase of desire for 'absolute
assimilation' with poetic precursors, while subsequent
works manifest the phase in which this desire is
'uneasily allied to a competitive element' presaging
the third phase, the 'rise of individual inspiration'.
This crucial phase enables entry into the fourth, fifth
and sixth phases, in which 'poetic incarnation proper'
takes place (*Map* 51–5). Bloom's map of poetical
evolution of course reflects his reliance on Romantic
organic metaphors for the growth of the poet's mind.
But the fact that his paradigm is itself a 'repetition' of
Romantic ideology (McGann 95) makes it all the
more applicable to Barrett Browning, given her
participation in that ideology.

For somewhat different reasons, the 'patriarchal
Bloomian model' (Gilbert and Gubar 48) is also
relevant to Barrett Browning's poetical development
because Bloom's masculinist, muscular poetics repli-
cate the androcentric Romantic ideologies that her
audacity of authorship confronted and helped to undo.
It is no accident that the genealogical metaphors
underpinning the Bloomian model are precisely those
that Barrett invokes and subtly subverts in representing
the grand company of immortal 'king-poets' in 'A
Vision of Poets'. Bloom's unremitting focus on a
mighty male line of poetical fathers and sons who
'wrestle' in Oedipal rivalry over the 'whoring' mother-
muse of inspiration makes his poetics, if anything, more

exclusively phallocentric than the tradition the young
Barrett faced in the wake of the major Romantic poets.
Such extreme androcentrism has invited acts of
misprision on the part of feminist critics, who have
appropriated and applied Bloom's model in ways that
illumine its blindness as well as its insights. Indeed,
Elisa Kay Sparks observes, 'Any woman, any feminist
literary critic, who wants to discuss the creative
process and . . . to retell the myth of poetic engenderment, must confront T. S. Eliot and Harold Bloom as
her two strongest, male critical precursors'.[4]

My use of Bloom's paradigm of poetic influence is
intended as just such a retelling of 'the myth of poetic
engenderment', in keeping with Barrett Browning's
own revisionary mythopoeis culminating in the textual
practice of *Aurora Leigh*. As Cooper suggests, the
metaphor of 'fire-thief' applies particularly well to
Barrett Browning because her 'disobedient act of
writing' as a woman in a male poetic tradition
'resonated to Prometheus's theft of fire from the Gods'
(15). The works of her earliest years express a
Promethean audacity similar to that embodied in
Aurora Leigh, although an audacity without a solid
basis in experience and poetic practice. 'Ah, when I
was ten years old, I beat you all you & Napoleon &
all, in ambition', she confessed to Horne in 1841 (*BC*
5:110). In a convolution not accommodated by
Bloom's map of poetic incarnation, the bold confidence
and high poetical ambitions of Barrett Browning's
precocious youth were subsequently muted by the
anxieties of gender conspicuous in the works she wrote
in her late teens, her twenties and her early thirties.
Yet her youthful audacity never entirely disappeared –
even in the face of the domestic ideology of 'true'
womanhood that increasingly dominated the early
Victorian period. The fire thief retained her essential

audacity, although her acts of begetting herself as a poet necessarily became more oblique than Bloom's metaphors of overt rivalry suggest.

The persistence of Barrett Browning's Promethean aspirations through the 1820s and 30s helps to explain the poetical awakening that resulted in the 1844 *Poems* – the collection in which her youthful audacity of authorship resurfaced with renewed force, this time grounded in her maturing poetic powers and in her sense of an emerging tradition of women writers. Alan Richardson has noted the 'colonization of the feminine' evident in the Romantic poets' incorporation of attributes conventionally associated with women, including maternal feeling.[5] What we see in Elizabeth Barrett's 1844 *Poems* is nothing less than a counter incursion into the field of high poetic conquest dominated in her youth by the male Romantics.

'Altho' ambition is a grand angelic sin, I fell a good way from the sphere of it, soon after I left the nursery', Barrett wrote to Kenyon in 1838 (*BC* 4:16). In the nursery, the young Barrett's ambition was fired by her reading of the Classics and of Pope, as she told Horne in 1843. 'The Greeks were my demi-gods, & haunted me out of Pope's Homer . . . The love of Pope's Homer threw me into Pope on one side, & into Greek on the other & into Latin as a help to Greek.' But along with her youthful 'fits of Pope', there were also fits of 'Byron – & Coleridge' (*BC* 7:353–4). Despite her description of Wordsworth as 'the king-poet of our times', Barrett thought Coleridge had 'an intenser genius' (*BC* 6:28, 75). Her interest in Keats, Shelley and Blake came later. Her 1831–2 diary reveals her close reading of both Keats and Shelley, with particular admiration for Keats' *Hyperion* fragment (*Diary* 91, 102). Significantly, given her affiliation with 'masculine' Romantic traditions, she did not particularly like

Keats' romances – works that aroused his own unease because of their association with a 'feminine' poetic mode (Mellor 183). Many references to Keats and Shelley appear in her letters of the early 1840s, where a preference for Keats is discernible. Keats may have been a 'poet of the senses', but 'it is of the senses idealized', she observed to Browning (*RB–EBB* 1:187). There is a human side to his 'fine genius' (*BC* 6:113) that she finds wanting in Shelley, that 'high, & yet too low, elemental poet, who froze in cold glory between Heaven & earth' (*BC* 5:60). As for Blake, the Romantic poet least known in the early nineteenth century, Philip Kelley and Ronald Hudson detect echoes of his *Jerusalem* in Barrett's letters of 1837 and 1841 (*BC* 3:219–21; 5:117–18); while her reading of *Songs of Innocence* in 1842 (*BC* 5:308) contributed to the imagery and the radicalism of 'The Cry of the Children' and 'The Runaway Slave at Pilgrim's Point' (Stone, 'Cursing', 160).

During the earlier years of her girlhood, Byron was clearly the Romantic poet who loomed largest on Barrett's horizon. In 'Glimpses into My Own Life and Literary Character' she wrote that 'at four' she 'first mounted Pegasus', and that in her eleventh year, when for '8 months' she thought of nothing but 'the ambition of gaining fame', she wrote her Homeric epic in the style of Pope, *The Battle of Marathon* (*BC* 1:349–51). But if the form of this epic imitation is after Pope, its 'spirit . . . is chiefly Byronic' (Borg 61). Since Byron is the only major Romantic poet for whom Pope remained an important influence, this conjunction is less odd than it appears. Byron is the first poet Barrett mentions among her contemporaries in the 'Preface' to *The Battle of Marathon*, where she affirms that 'Poetry is the parent of liberty' (*CW* 1:9). Literary histories have often told the story of the grief-stricken fourteen-year-old Tennyson who, hearing of Byron's death in the Greek war of liberation in 1824, rushed out of doors and wrote on a piece of sandstone, 'Byron is dead'.[6] But the eighteen-year-old Barrett's publication the same year of 'Stanzas on the Death of Lord Byron' has been forgotten.

Barrett's first two poems to be published in a periodical – two poems on Greek liberation accepted by the *New Monthly Magazine* in 1821 (Barnes 91) – also reflect the impact of Byron's Romantic Hellenism. Mermin suggests that Barrett identified so strongly with Greece as a 'damsel in distress' both in *The Battle of Marathon* and in her poems on Greek liberation because she could find no individual heroic women to identify with. Hence her 'imaginative identification is political and impersonal', contributing to her 'lifelong habit of associating geography with gender and imagining England as male and Greece and Italy . . . as female' (23–7). But the gendering of Barrett Browning's geography was also significantly shaped by de Staël's *Corinne*, while her youthful Hellenism derives as much from the ardent political Republicanism she associated with Byron as from her identification with Greece as a 'damsel in distress'.

Nevertheless, as Mermin suggests, Barrett is clearly seeking heroic female figures to identify with in *The Battle of Marathon* – figures she may also have found in Byron's representations of active, assertive heroines. Thus she presents Athens as the 'one little city rising undaunted, and daring her innumerable enemies, in defence of her freedom' (*CW* 1:6). She also focuses on the goddess Minerva – 'in her hand her father's lightnings shone' (l.1027) – much as in her earliest poems she focuses on potent female goddesses generally, Aurora most conspicuous among them (*HUP* 1:81,86,91,97). Minerva inspires the hero Aristides:

his mind 'with all Minerva glows' (l.778). Indeed, the bloody, bone-crunching battle 'mid seas of gore' (l.1279) that Barrett so zestfully depicts often seems to be a struggle between two mighty goddesses, Minerva and Venus, rather than Greek and Persian heroes. Likewise, the Athenian matron whom Barrett introduces to rally on the troops conventionally weeps but nevertheless speaks up when all the Athenian men are 'by despair deprest' (l.709). 'The mother wept, but 'twas the Patriot spoke' (l.746), Barrett writes, passing over the conflict she so movingly explored near the end of her life in 'Mother and Poet'.

The Byronic Hellenism and the republican spirit of *The Battle of Marathon* are also conspicuous in *An Essay on Mind*, published when Barrett was twenty. Addressing 'Graecia' with 'feelings wild' as 'My other country – country of my soul!', she elegizes Byron as 'The pilgrim bard, who lived, and died for thee' (ll.1144–7,1191). The form of *An Essay on Mind* is modelled on Pope's verse essays, while its survey of analogies for 'the operations of the mind' (*CW* 1:57) further reflects eighteenth-century influences in the allusions to 'metaphysicians' like Locke, Descartes, Buffon, Leibnitz, Berkeley, and Condillac. But in its numerous references to Byron, 'the Mont Blanc of intellect' (l.70), in its manner of turning 'the pow'rs of thinking back on thought' (l.201), and in its high claims for Poetry rather than Philosophy as Mind's greatest creation, *An Essay on Mind* is more Romantic in spirit than *The Battle of Marathon*. Barrett Browning later dismissed both works because they exhibited the 'imitative faculty' typical of youthful poetic aspiration: as she puts it in *Aurora Leigh*, how strange it is that 'nearly all young poets should write old' (Book 1:1012). But she described her *Essay on Mind* as 'imitative in *its form*', yet 'not without traces of an individual thinking & feeling – the bird pecks through the shell in it' (*BC* 7:354).

Barrett begins by considering 'th' unequal pow'rs, the various forms of Mind'. Why did 'Homer sing', why 'do I not the muse of Homer call', why is it not true that 'Tom Paine argued in the throne's defence' or that 'Byron nonsense wrote'? she asks, with negative constructions that emphasize her anxieties about her own powers (ll.29–40). Then she surveys 'the various stages of life in which genius appears' and the diverse 'elements of Mind', before treating the 'creations of Mind' – Philosophy and Poetry (*CW* 1:246). In her 'Preface' to *The Battle of Marathon*, Barrett had happily assumed that the primacy of Poetry had not been denied 'in any age, or by any philosopher' (*CW* 1:2). But in the 'Preface' to *An Essay on Mind*, she vigorously counters the long tradition of such denials in Plato, Newton, Locke and Boileau, invoking Byron to support her claim that ' "ethical poetry" ' is ' "the highest" ' poetical form and stressing the 'inspiritings to political feeling' poetry provides. 'Poetry is the enthusiasm of the understanding; and, as Milton finely expresses it, there is a "high reason in her fancies" ', she concludes in a peroration reminiscent of Wordsworth's description of poetry in the 'Preface' to the *Lyrical Ballads* as the 'breath and finer spirit of all knowledge', the 'impassioned expression' of Science (*CW* 1:56–7).

In Barrett's consideration of the 'various forms of Mind' in *An Essay on Mind*, we can see an indirect exploration of a question she never directly addresses in this relentlessly male-centred text. How does gender influence the manifestations and development of genius? Barrett opens her poem by observing that since the Creation when 'dust' first 'weigh'd Genius down', 'The ambitious soul her essence hath defin'd, /

And Mind hath eulogiz'd the pow'rs of Mind' (ll.3–6). But when the 'ambitious soul' is weighed down by the 'dust' of a female body in a literary culture that tropes poetic identity as male, the quest for self-creation is inevitably conflicted. At the age of eleven, Barrett had confidently stated in the 'Preface' to *The Battle of Marathon*, 'Now, even the female may drive her Pegasus through the realms of Parnassus, without being saluted with the most equivocal of all appellations, a learned lady' (*CW* 1:2). By the time of *An Essay on Mind*, published when she was twenty, she was much less confident that 'the female' writer could escape an 'equivocal' reception, and more careful to conceal her own sex: nothing in this work reveals that it is written by a very learned young lady. As for the 'ambitious soul' eulogizing her own powers, her 'essence' is given a ghastly disembodiment in 'The Vision of Fame' that concluded Barrett's 1826 volume. Appearing first as a 'bright and lofty' regal woman, with a 'brow of peerless majesty', the Fame Barrett envisions sings a seductive 'chant' of 'The *worth of praise*' that is not addressed to her. Then the visionary woman fades into a paler shade of pale as 'the flesh curled up from her bones / Like to a blasted scroll' and 'dropped away'. Yet 'still the vacant sockets gleamed / With supernatural fires' (*CW* 1:119–21).

The conflicts between Barrett's gender and her 'ambitious soul' are also strikingly apparent in 'The Development of Genius', a poem she worked on for several months in 1826–7 only to have it harshly condemned by her father as 'insufferable' in its 'egotism', 'most *wretched*', and '*beyond [her] grasp*', after he had read less than half of it (*BC* 1:359). Part of this poem was published after her death as 'The Poet's Enchiridion'; part of it appeared as 'Earth' in her 1833 volume, as Mermin notes (42); while a third part appeared in the 1838 poem 'The Student'. Revealingly, in 'The Student' Barrett turns to a form akin to the dramatic monologue to conceal her intense struggles with 'Ambition, idol of the intellect': ' "Yet, must my brow be paler! I have vowed / To clip it with the crown which cannot fade / When *it* is faded" ', her student asserts (ll.11–13).

'The Development of Genius' as it is pieced together by H. Buxton Forman (*HUP* 2:99–133) is an inchoate text struggling to be born, more intensely Romantic than anything Barrett had yet written. Like Byron's protagonists and Wordsworth in *The Prelude*, her protagonist Theon 'unbare[s]' his heart (l.102) and traces the growth of his mind – in the place of the young woman poet who, unlike Aurora Leigh, could not yet write her own 'Prelude'. Like the Byronic hero, Theon is restless, alienated ('loved of none'), and cursed by a black destiny and blacker memories (ll.100–12). Like Wordsworth, Theon invokes the wind as a 'correspondent breeze', so that his voice might be 'chainless' as the wind and 'out-bear / Power, and a mountain freedom everywhere' (l.105). Like Shelley and the poet he describes in *Alastor*, Barrett's poet seeks truth and the seeds of fame in the charnel house of history until the bones of the dead stand up 'with a shout, in living crowds' (l.109) – suggestive of the dead peers that ring Browning's Childe Roland when he arrives at his dark tower. Like Blake, who in 'Auguries of Innocence' invokes a poetic sensibility so intense that a 'fibre of the brain' is torn by the outcry of a wounded hare, Barrett imagines a consciousness so sensitive that it can hear 'the grasses sprouting up' , 'the deep rush of springs / Fathoms beneath the sea', 'the blind mole creeping', 'the cracking of worn cerement / In distant grave' – each with 'a separate curious torture' 'gathered in the chambers' of the ear to 'agonize its sense' (ll.121–2). If such a mind 'could hear the thousand wheels that roll / Urging and urged within a single soul', thunder would seem 'silence to th'imagined sound' (ll.122–3), Barrett writes, in a passage anticipating the 1844 sonnet 'The Soul's Expression'.

'The Soul's Expression' was published as the lead sonnet in both the 1844 *Poems* and subsequent editions of Barrett Browning's poetry. As such, it was clearly intended to articulate a key aspect of her artistic philosophy. In this sonnet as in 'The Development of Genius' she alludes to 'the dread apocalypse of soul' that would occur, 'as the thunder-roll / Breaks its own cloud', if she ever *could* utter fully the infinite depths and reaches of her own consciousness (*CW* 2:227). Ironically, the opening lines of the sonnet – 'With stammering lips and insufficient sound / I strive and struggle . . .' – have often been cited by critics who emphasize Barrett Browning's incomplete command of her own craft. But such applications ignore the sonnet's principal subject: its articulation of the Romantic philosophy of infinite aspiration. This is a philosophy that Barrett Browning retained throughout her career and shared with Browning and John Ruskin, among others. All three believed that the highest art is necessarily imperfect because the great artist strives until the point of failure is reached. In other words, in the greatest art the sound is always 'insufficient', as Barrett Browning implied in using the sonnet 'Insufficiency' to conclude the series of sonnets published in her 1844 *Poems*. Indeed, if she ever did 'utter all [her]self into the air', Barrett writes in 'The Soul's Expression', her 'flesh would perish there' on the 'dark edges of the sensual ground'.

The 'dread apocalypse of soul' alluded to in 'The Soul's Expression' was also the subject of a projected lyrical drama Barrett planned to write with Horne in 1841, 'Psyche Apocalypté'. '[T]he awe of this soul-consciousness breaking into occasional lurid heats through the chasms of our conventionalities has struck me, in my own self-observation, as a mystery of nature very grand in itself', she wrote to Horne (*LRHH* 2:62). Although sketches and fragmentary portions of this lyrical drama were produced by Horne and Barrett, the collaboration never resulted in a finished work. Like 'The Development of Genius' and so many other Romantic poems, it remained a fragment.

The quenchless ambition and the 'apocalypse of soul' that figure so prominently in Barrett's published and unpublished works from 1826 to 1844 reveal how much she shared the male Romantic drive for transcendence most famously embodied in Wordsworth's apocalyptic revelation while crossing the Alps in Book 6 of *The Prelude*. Like the male Romantics as Marlon Ross describes them, Barrett was 'driven to a quest for self-creation, for self-comprehension, for self-positioning . . . unprecedented in literature'; and like them, she turned to masculine metaphors of quest, conquest, and power.[7] If, as Ross observes, 'Wordsworth's favorite laudatory term is "power" ', it also is one of Barrett's favourite terms. In 1845 she told the critic Henry Chorley, 'I have that admiration for *genius* which dear Mr. Kenyon calls my "immoral sympathy with power" '. Significantly, the comment was provoked by her praise of George Sand as 'the first female genius of any country or age' (*LEBB* 1:233). But in her earlier works, the example of George Sand was not yet available and she was less certain of her own power.

Moreover, the very sublime imagery that the young Barrett turned to in representing the mind's power was inflected by paradigms that excluded her female experience. Christine Battersby notes that the sublime and its associated images were 'often explicitly, and nearly always implicitly, gendered as male' in Edmund Burke's *Philosophical Enquiry into the Origin of our Ideas of the Sublime and the Beautiful* (1757). Whereas the sublime 'is exemplified by kings and commanders discharging their terrible strength . . . as well as by the grandeur of the Alps', the beautiful – 'small, smooth, delicate and graceful' – is exemplified by the female body (74). Mellor points out that Romantic women writers developed a number of complex strategies for revising or 'domesticating' the Burkean sublime, either by displacing it into the domestic sphere in Gothic romances, or by transforming its focus on solitary transcendence into an experience of communion with others (94–7).

One of Barrett's own strategies for dealing with the conflicts created by masculine tropes of the sublime is illustrated by 'A Sea-side Meditation', a poem included in her 1833 volume, *Prometheus Bound . . . and Miscellaneous Poems*. 'A Sea-side Meditation' strikingly differs from the later, similarly titled descriptive-meditative lyric, 'A Sea-Side Walk' (1838). In the later poem, Barrett chiefly employs graceful images of the beautiful to describe the human mind and nature interfused in a manner recalling the Romantic conversation poems – particularly 'Tintern Abbey' – and anticipating subsequent works in the same tradition, like Wallace Stevens' 'The Idea of Order at Key West':

> For though we never spoke
> Of the grey water and the shaded rock,
> Dark wave and stone unconsciously were fused
> Into the plaintive speaking that we used . . .
> (ll.29–32)

As its title suggests, however, the earlier 'A Sea-Side Meditation' focuses less on the interchange of the mind and nature than on the power of the mind in meditation. Here Barrett conventionally defines the '*sublime*' as all that 'doth force the mind to view the mind' in the 'awful likeness' of its own immortal power – the mountain's brow, 'the spanless plain', the 'deep's immensity' (ll.76–97). Contemplating the sea in its varying aspects, but insistently identifying it as male – 'Like a spent warrior hanging in the sun / His glittering arms' (ll.103–4), 'Swinging the grandeur of his foamy strength' (l.24) – she dares to find in the ocean's 'vast similitude' a symbol of her own soul's depths, musings, 'secrets of decay' and 'elemental strength' (ll.119–26). This identification is accomplished without the male impersonation so often found in other works from this period as she invokes the liberating example of the Athenian who 'Unchain'd the prison'd music of his lips / By shouting to the billows, sound for sound' (ll.29–30).

Barrett's 'vast similitude' for her own soul leads her to Promethean speculations on the 'power' that 'knowledge' brings, in the process revealing her fascination with the Titanic figure of Milton's Satan. If human dreams were not mortal, if 'thought's free wheels' could 'oversweep the heights of wisdom / And invade her depths', we should 'be like gods' (ll.126–36). But 'Mind struggles vainly from flesh', and its 'Babel' constructions will tumble down even as 'Hell's angel' in the apocalypse will 'confirm his rebel heart, / Shoot his strong wings, and darken pole to pole', and 'shake / The fever'd clouds, as if a thousand storms / Throbb'd into life': only to be to be hurled back by God (ll.126–50). Mermin finds in 'A Sea-Side Meditation' the 'dynamics of renunciation and submission' that pervades Barrett's earlier works (54). This dynamic does structure the dark poem preceding 'A Sea-Side Meditation' in 1833, 'The Tempest', in which the protagonist's heart is torn by a battle between 'sympathy with power, / And stooping unto power; – the energy / And passiveness, – the thunder and the death!' (ll.115–17). But in Barrett's unchaining of her 'sea-side' meditation, there is little hint of submission. Defiant power meets a greater power and is crushed in the closing epic simile of Satan's apocalyptic rebellion throbbing 'into life'. If, as a contemporary reviewer noted, 'The Tempest' is notable for its 'Byronic energy' (*BC* 4:394), 'A Sea-side Meditation' is even more Byronic in its evocation of Satan as a Promethean over-reacher.

'A Sea-Side Meditation' suggests why Barrett was drawn to *Prometheus Bound*, among the many Greek works by Aeschylus, Sophocles, Euripides and other writers that she read intensively with Boyd in the early 1830s (*Diary* 43; *HUP* 2:134–5). Like Goethe and Byron, she admired the rebellious defiance of Prometheus, so akin to that of Milton's Satan. At the same time, like Shelley, she found in Prometheus a hero free of many of Satan's defects. *Prometheus Bound* also contains a complete repertoire of the imagery of the sublime that she deploys in 'A Sea-Side Meditation' and 'The Tempest', imagery that her immersion in the Romantics led her to prefer. Lightning, thunder, tempestuous wind, the unchained sea, volcanic eruption and alpine crags: all appear in Aeschylus' great lyrical drama. Furthermore, in Aeschylus she encountered this imagery accompanied by other characteristics supporting her view that the Greeks were not classical but romantic writers.

Barrett's first translation of *Prometheus Bound*, undertaken in the first two weeks of February in 1832, is in some respects an 'astonishing feat', as Alice Falk notes

in her illuminating comparison of this and the later
translation carried out in 1845, and published in 1850.
'In a fortnight', the twenty-six-year-old with no
university training 'made a reasonably accurate,
readable, almost line-for-line verse translation of the
least easily translated Greek tragedian' (72). 'Aeschylus
presents difficulties to the manliest Greek scholar', a
reviewer observed in 1838, in paying his 'esteem' to
Barrett: 'think of these rugged obstacles to a woman's
mind!' (*BC* 4:390). But other reviewers did not esteem
Barrett's translation, and she herself soon came to
condemn it harshly as 'cold stiff & meagre, unfaithful
to the genius if servile to the letter of the great poet', 'a
Prometheus *twice* bound' (*BC* 5:297, 26). 'She was
pained not at the lack of scholarship but at the lack of
poetry', as Falk puts it (74). Thus she undertook in
her second translation a much less literal version –
in keeping with the Romantic theory of translation she
advanced in the 'Preface' to her first version, but did
not carry into practice (*CW* 6:81–2).

The final speech of Prometheus in the second, freer
translation illustrates the imagery of the sublime that
Aeschylus employs in the play, increasing its appeal
for the Romantics:

Ay! in act now, in word now no more,
　　Earth is rocking in space.
And the thunders crash up with a roar upon roar,
And the eddying lightnings flash fire in my
　　face,
And the whirlwinds are whirling the dust round
　　and round,
　　And the blasts of the winds universal leap free
And blow each upon each with a passion of sound,
　　And aether goes mingling in storm with the sea.
Such a curse on my head, in a manifest dread,

> From the hand of your Zeus has been hurtled
>   along.
> O my mother's fair glory! O Aether, enringing
>   All eyes with the sweet common light of thy
>   bringing!
>   Dost thou see how I suffer this wrong?

Although the leading Victorian critic H. Buxton Forman described these lines as a 'magnificent rendering' of a 'magnificent work', Barrett Browning's classical knowledge was faulted in the anti-Romantic movement of early Modern literature. In Percy Lubbock's words, 'She never understood that deliberate aim at attainable perfection which is at the heart of Greek literature. Hers was the romantic temper, never content with attainment.'[8]

Such assertions ignore the characteristically Romantic redefinition of the classical Barrett advanced in the 'Preface' to her 1833 translation of *Prometheus Bound*. In effect, she redefines classical poets like Aeschylus as romantic. Our 'age would not be "classical." "O, that profaned name!" . . . It does not mean what it is made to mean: it does not mean what is necessarily regular, and polished, and unimpassioned. The ancients, especially the ancient Greeks, felt, and thought, and wrote antecedently to rules: they felt passionately, and thought daringly.' In her view, Aeschylus is a representative classical writer because he is 'a fearless and impetuous, not a cautious and accomplished poet' whose chief excellences cannot be 'acquired by art': 'a vehement imaginativeness, a strong but repressed sensibility' and a powerfully metaphoric language, sometimes writhing 'beneath its impetuosity' (*CW* 6:83–4). Like her Romantic precursors, then, Barrett found something else 'at the heart of Greek literature' than the 'attainable perfection'

Lubbock privileges, a feature she attributed in 'The Greek Christian Poets' to the 'cold and lifeless' Latin poets rather than to the 'good, fervid, faulty Greeks' (*CW* 6:175).

Most of all, Barrett found in Greek literature the Titan Prometheus, 'the Romantic hero, on a super-human scale' – exhibiting the '*authadia*' or 'insolent, self-will' that some reviewers detected in her own character (Falk 73–4). As Mermin (51), Cooper (26) and Falk all point out, Prometheus held a particular attraction for Barrett because he combined heroic defiance with the conventionally female attributes of confinement, physical passivity, and self-sacrifice. Joining the 'redemptive self-denial of Christ' with 'Promethean self-will', she 'made a Christ who could be unbound and triumph without dying, a Prometheus with whom she could safely identify' (Falk 82).

Barrett's 'Preface' to her 1833 volume points the way to this fusion of Christ and Prometheus in the systematic contrast she develops between Satan and Prometheus, analogous to Shelley's differentiation of the two figures in the 'Preface' to *Prometheus Unbound*. Aeschylus' Prometheus is 'one of the most original, and grand, and attaching characters ever conceived by the mind of man', she observes. 'That conception sank deeply into the soul of Milton, and . . . rose from thence in the likeness of his Satan.' But one embodies 'the sublime of sin' and the other 'the sublime of virtue. Satan suffered from his ambition; Prometheus from his humanity: Satan for himself; Prometheus for mankind: Satan dared perils which he had not weighed; Prometheus devoted himself to sorrows which he had foreknown. "Better to rule in hell," said Satan; "Better to serve this rock," said Prometheus' (*CW* 6:85).

The contrast between Prometheus and Satan

developed by Barrett in 1833 gave rise to the lead poem in her 1838 collection, *The Seraphim, and Other Poems*, the volume that marks her entry into the second and third phases of poetic incarnation as Bloom describes them: competition with precursors and the rise of individual inspiration. In the 'Preface' to the 1838 volume, she explains how the subject of *The Seraphim* – the 'supreme spectacle' of the Crucifixion as it appears 'dilated in seraphic eyes' – 'suggested itself' to her while translating *Prometheus Bound*:

> I thought, that had Aeschylus lived after the incarnation . . . he might have turned . . . from the glorying of him who gloried that he could not die, to the sublimer meekness of the Taster of death for every man; from the taunt stung into being by the torment, to HIS more awful silence, when the agony stood dumb before the love! And I thought, how, 'from the height of this great argument,' the scenery of the Prometheus would have dwarfed itself even in the eyes of its poet . . . He would have turned . . . to the Victim, whose sustaining thought beneath an unexampled agony was not the Titanic 'I can revenge,' but the celestial 'I can forgive!' (*CW* 1:164–5).

Barrett conceals her competitive ambition by suggesting that she is only writing what Aeschylus might have written after the Christian dispensation, and by emphasizing her 'imperfect knowledge'. But she implicitly appropriates Aeschylus' achievement and invites comparison with him in saying of her 1833 and 1838 volumes, 'The subjects of my two books lie side by side'. As she acknowledged in the same letter in which she refers to ambition as a 'grand angelic sin', the subject of *The Seraphim* was a 'very daring' one (*BC* 4:15).

Although Cooper suggests that 'Barrett did not attempt a Shelleyean revision of the Prometheus myth' (15), *The Seraphim* presents striking parallels with Shelley's much more successful transformation of Aeschylus' great drama in *Prometheus Unbound*. Mermin aptly describes *The Seraphim* as a '*Prometheus Bound* without Prometheus: a lyrical dramatization not of suffering and acting, but of watching others suffer and act. The chorus ... becomes the protagonist' in Barrett's depiction of two seraphim, Ador the Strong and Zerah the Bright One, as they observe the crucifixion (62). In *Prometheus Unbound*, 'watching others suffer and act' is similarly dramatized, as Prometheus himself triumphs through love, while Asia and various mythological beings – Earth, Ocean, the Spirits of the Hours, for instance – enact the role of the chorus in classical drama, an important prototype for Shelley as well as for Barrett. Just as Shelley departs from Aeschylus in emphasizing the curse that afflicts Earth along with Prometheus, Barrett focuses on the common curse afflicting Adam and Earth. Both writers also depict Earth's transformation by the renovating power of love felt in its darkest depths (ll.970–84 in *The Seraphim* and Act III, scene iii in *Prometheus Unbound*). Even the imagery and rhymes of *The Seraphim* seem very much like Shelley's on occasion, perhaps reflecting the common influence of Dante: Ador's 'burning eyes ... wild and mournful as a star' (ll.324–5) are suggestive of Panthea's 'eyes which burn ... Like stars half quenched in mists' in *Prometheus Unbound*, for instance. Little wonder that contemporary reviewers of *The Seraphim* often compared Barrett to Shelley (*BC* 4:383, 400, 409); or that Browning selected an epigraph from Shelley to precede the discussion of her works in Richard Hengist Horne's *A New Spirit of the Age* (*BC* 8:204). In a subtle reading of the pervasive references to *Prometheus Bound* in the correspondence between Barrett and Browning, Yopie Prins has shown how the two poets 'alternate in playing the part of Prometheus' and carry out their 'mutual seduction' through 'Aeschylus' text' (435, 437). But Shelley also entered into this complex intertextual exchange.

The resemblances between Shelley's *Prometheus Unbound* and *The Seraphim* are all the more interesting given that Barrett may not have been familiar with Shelley's greatest work when she wrote *The Seraphim* and when she differentiated Prometheus from Satan in the 'Preface' to her 1833 translation of Aeschylus. Barrett mentions reading *Queen Mab* and 'Adonais' in 1831 (*Diary* 138), but there is no reference to *Prometheus Unbound* in her correspondence before 1845, when Browning urged her to '[r]estore' the lost drama of Prometheus the Fire-Bearer 'as Shelley did' the Prometheus Unbound (*RB–EBB* 1:37). As Shelley emphasized in his 'Preface', however, he was not interested in restoring the lost drama of Aeschylus, but in using the character of Prometheus to develop his own aesthetic and moral ends. Barrett's substitution of Christ's 'I can forgive' for the rebellious 'I can revenge' of Prometheus reflects a similar revisionary impulse.

The prominence Barrett gives to Christian cosmology marks one important difference between the Promethean revisionism of *Prometheus Unbound* and *The Seraphim*. As Linda Lewis has noted, Shelley's Prometheus incorporates 'the sublimeness of the perfect self-knowledge of the crucified Christ', but 'the salvation of mankind is not envisioned in Christian terms' in *Prometheus Unbound*.[9] When Barrett was given a copy of Shelley's *Essays, Letters from Abroad, Translations and Fragments* in 1840, she deleted the hostile remarks concerning Christianity, inserting her own views instead (Thorpe). Elsewhere, she criticized Shelley for failing to aspire to 'communion with . . . the heart of the God-Man' Christ, and for 'failing to keep near enough to Humanity' (*BC* 5:60; 6:243). The 'God-Man's' human agony is at the heart of *The Seraphim*:

> The pathos hath the day undone
> The death-look of His eyes
> Hath overcome the sun
> And made it sicken in its narrow skies. (ll.863–6)

Fusing the conventions of the Christian mystery play with those of Greek tragedy, Barrett concludes by focusing on Heaven, not Earth. *Prometheus Unbound*, on the contrary, blends Greek tragedy with the secular forms of opera and dance in its final vision of millenial cosmic renovation, as Ronald Tetreault has shown.[10]

Nevertheless, both *The Seraphim* and *Prometheus Unbound* reflect the stage of Romantic Prometheanism described by Lewis in which the defiant Satanic fire-thief is replaced by 'the Prometheus who bestows divine light' (192). Lewis alternatively speculates that Barrett Browning's works, like those of other nineteenth-century women writers, may reflect a still later stage of Romantic Prometheanism in which the tradition died out because 'Prometheanism/Titanism was stolen and modified by' female authors who effectively emasculated the myth (194). The phenomenon Lewis describes as emasculation might have been conceptualized very differently by the women writers involved, the Brontës among them. That aside, however, Barrett Browning's works up to 1844 play a larger and more complicated role in the unfolding of Romantic Prometheanism than literary histories suggest. The response to her 1833 and 1838 volumes alone supports this possibility, since reviewers repeatedly cited and praised the comments on Prometheus in her two 'Prefaces' (*BC* 4:373, 376; 6:375).

A Drama of Exile, the most ambitious of Barrett's 1844 works, reflects her increasingly overt engagement with two powerful precursors more immediate than Aeschylus: Milton and Byron. Her revisionary struggle with *Paradise Lost* in *A Drama of Exile* is most apparent in her representation of Eve and of Lucifer. In both cases, her rewriting of Milton is filtered through her equally complex response to Byron's subversive metaphysical drama *Cain*, a work that she alternately imitates and revises.

Much as Byron de-centres Milton's focus on Adam's and God's perspective in *Paradise Lost* by focusing on Cain's experience after the fall, Barrett de-centres Milton by explicitly focusing on Eve after the expulsion from Eden. In an 1843 letter to Horne, she explained that the 'object' of *A Drama of Exile* was 'the development of the peculiar anguish of Eve – the fate of woman at its root'. Reiterating this point, she added, 'The principal interest is set on Eve – the "first in the transgression." *First in the transgression* has been said over & over again, because of the tradition, – but *first & deepest in the sorrow*, nobody seems to have said, or, at least, written of' (*BC* 8:117). In the 'Preface' itself, Barrett is more circumspect: 'My subject was the new and strange experience of the fallen humanity, as it went forth from Paradise into the wilderness; with a peculiar reference to Eve's alloted grief' (*CW* 2:143). The private letter more frankly reveals not only her explicitly revisionary concern with Eve, but also the weight of the 'tradition' she saw herself writing against.

The force of the tradition is evident in the fact that Barrett herself apparently began treating the Miltonic matter of *A Drama of Exile* from Adam's perspective, not Eve's. This is suggested by 'Adam's farewell to Eden – *in his age*', a manuscript now in the Armstrong Browning Library. It is not clear how this manuscript relates to the germ of *A Drama of Exile*, which Barrett first referred to in 1841 under the manuscript title 'A day from Eden' (*BC* 5:146). But it is clear that the 168-line fragment 'Adam's farewell' is focused on Adam's experience after the expulsion from Eden. In lamenting the loss of Eden in his old age, Adam repeatedly speaks of 'I' and 'we', but Eve is not otherwise alluded to. In revising the poem, Barrett made the opening more like a dramatic monologue – one of the many Victorian dramatic monologues, including her own, that portray dying, solitary speakers. But these revisions simply intensifed the focus on Adam.

In the much more ambitious and gynocentic work that Barrett finally produced, she invited comparison with Milton's epic aspirations even as she powerfully expressed the sense of trespass that Bloom finds in all poets after the 1740s who emulate *Paradise Lost*, Blake, Wordsworth and Byron among them. Ingeniously justifying this trespass in her 'Preface', she first suggests that Eve's experience of the Fall has been 'imperfectly apprehended hitherto' and that it is 'more expressible by a woman than a man', then recoils into 'anxiety of authorship':

I had promised my own prudence to shut close the gates of Eden between Milton and myself, so that none might say I dared to walk in his footsteps. He should be within, I thought, with his Adam and Eve unfallen or falling, – and I, without, with my

> EXILES, – *I* also an exile! It would not do. The
> subject, and his glory covering it, swept through the
> gates, and I stood full in it, against my will, and
> contrary to my vow, – till I shrank back fearing,
> almost desponding . . . (*CW* 2:144)

In keeping with her construction of Barrett Browning
as a conservative writer serving patriarchal traditions,
Deirdre David suggests that the poet 'is made twice
passive' in this passage, 'by Milton and by God'
(*Intellectual Women* 108). But as Barrett acknowledged
in the 'Preface' to her 1838 volume, 'The disparaging
speeches of prefaces are not proverbial for their real
humility' (*CW* 1:170). Certainly her apparently humble
genuflection to Milton's greatness bears out the truth
of her comment. She 'stood full' in Milton's glory (as
opposed to 'trembled beneath' or some such phrase) is
a nicely ambiguous statement. Barrett also boldly
justifies her endeavour by an appeal to precedent – 'I
have only attempted, in respect to Milton, what the
Greek dramatists achieved lawfully in respect to
Homer' – and further implies that it is no trespass at
all on Milton's ground, since Milton's subject 'was his
by illustration only': 'Andreini's mystery suggested
Milton's epic' (145–6). Most revealingly, as Cooper
astutely observes, Barrett manifests her 'usurpation'
of masculine poetic power in the description of her
'pleasure in driving in, like a pile, stroke upon stroke,
the Idea of EXILE' that dominates her drama (60).

Feminist critics have tended to assume that Barrett's
Eve was created to counter Milton's and that Barrett
was oppressed like Virginia Woolf by 'Milton's bogie'.
Yet her relationship with Milton may well be more
complex than such a formulation suggests. Joseph
Wittreich's *Feminist Milton* indicates that many women
readers in the eighteenth and early nineteenth century

perceived Milton not as an arch-misogynist, but as their ally in the defence of women's rights and powers. Reading *Paradise Lost* as 'a text that deconstructs the traditions it summons', these eighteenth-century and Romantic interpreters found in Eve evidence for woman's dignity, reasoning powers, and equality with man before the fall.[11]

Whether Barrett found in Milton a progenitor or an oppressor, or more probably a combination of both, in *A Drama of Exile* she intensified some of the more subversive characteristics of his Eve. Thus, the vision of the redemption to come through Eve and the 'Promised Seed' that Milton's Eve only dreams about in Book 12 of *Paradise Lost* (ll.606–23) is presented to both Eve and Adam by Christ 'in a vision' in Barrett's work. 'Henceforth in my name / Take courage, O thou woman, – man, take hope', Christ says, addressing the woman first: 'a new Eden-gate / Shall open on a hinge of harmony / And let you through to mercy' (ll.1986–92). Whereas Adam gently rebukes Eve after her lament for the loss of Eden in Book 11 of *Paradise Lost* (ll.287–92), Barrett's Eve more often gently corrects her Adam, speaking as a peacemaker between humanity and the Earth Spirits (ll.1176–81), and appealing to God's pity in an implicit correction of Adam's appeal to God's power (ll.1745–7). Barrett's Adam stands 'upright' after the fall *because* he has Eve (l.490). Finally, while Milton depicts Adam and Eve departing from Paradise together, Barrett depicts Eve first prostrate in guilt and sorrow, then renewed in strength by Adam's love so that she asserts, 'I will be first to tread from this sword-glare / Into the outer darkness . . . And thus I do it' (ll.547–9).

These features in *A Drama of Exile* call in question Cooper's suggestion that Eve is 'depicted as an acquiescent woman' (124) and Harrison's conclusion that Barrett's revision of Milton is relatively limited because 'the male characters – Adam, Christ, and Lucifer himself – are the centers of rhetorical power and dominance in this poem', which ultimately serves 'to confirm and reinforce the Victorian domestic ideology' (129). Granted, Adam defines Eve's womanly function in conventional Victorian terms, but Eve's words and actions do not always conform to his assumptions about domestic relations. Moreover, neither the length of the speeches given to Eve nor the response of contemporary reviewers bears out Harrison's claim that the male characters dominate *A Drama of Exile*. Lucifer is given the longest single speech in the drama (90 lines), but Eve comes in second with a speech of 76 lines; Adam and Christ come in third and fourth with speeches of 59 and 54 lines respectively. Eve also speaks repeatedly about speaking: 'shall I speak . . . Shall I speak humbly now who once was proud?' she rhetorically asks before launching into her longest speech. Before Adam can say 'Speak as thou wilt', she argues that she has the right to speak because she is 'schooled by sin to more humility' than Adam (ll.1179–83). After the more explicit feminism of *Aurora Leigh* had alerted critics to the subversiveness of *A Drama of Exile*, a reviewer denounced its Eve for 'talking at an amazing rate. Adam can scarcely slip in a word edgewise'.[12] Actually Barrett gives Eve and Adam relatively equal air-time, but some Victorian men could not conceive of Eve having anything of value to say. The *Blackwood's* reviewer objected to Barrett's focus on 'Eve's grief as distinguished from Adam's', because it is too trivial a subject 'to sustain the weight of a dramatic poem. At the most, it might have furnished materials for a sonnet. . . . She has tried to make bricks not only without straw, but almost without clay', the reviewer asserts, implying that the mother of mankind in herself is almost a non-entity (*BC* 9:357).

Barrett in 1844 clearly had another vision of Eve in mind, one revealing the legacy of Byron and the younger Romantics, and anticipating Charlotte Brontë's famous evocation in *Shirley* of an Eve who was a 'woman-Titan', the mother of Prometheus.[13] Like Thea in Keats' *Hyperion* or Asia in Shelley's *Prometheus Unbound*, the Titanic primeval female figures Byron created in his metaphysical dramas *Cain* and *Heaven and Earth* are anything but non-entities. Truman Steffan rightly points out that Byron's Eve in *Cain* reflects a misogynist element in his thinking, evident both in the reproaches cast upon her by Adam, Adah, Lucifer, and Cain, and in the ugly curses she herself heaps on her son. But more recent criticism has also noted the liberating elements in Byron's dynamic and autonomous female characters.[14] Like the daughters of Cain in *Heaven and Earth* who call down the seraphs to be their mates, Cain's sister-bride Adah counters Byron's apparently misogynist representation of Eve in *Cain*, even though she remains secondary in importance.

Cain was praised by Barrett in her 1824–6 notebook when the controversy over this 'blasphemous' text was still intense. But in portraying Eve and Lucifer many years later she registers her resistance to Byron as well as her emulation of his revisionism. Most notably, she echoes *Cain* in *A Drama of Exile* when Adam threatens to curse Lucifer and he responds, 'Curse freely!', insinuating that Eve 'could curse too – as a woman may – / Smooth in the vowels' (ll.652–65). In place of Byron's bitterly cursing Eve, however, Barrett presents an Eve who grieves rather than curses, and who is Adam's superior in her demonstration of loving forgiveness. As I have shown elsewhere, Eve is never a curser in this drama that might well have been entitled 'A Drama of Curses', since curses and cursing are mentioned 36 times ('Cursing', 158). Eve is not an angry domineering mother, but a sympathetic loving mate as Adah is to Cain. Whereas Byron swerves from Milton in focusing on the love of Cain and Adah, Barrett reverts to the focus on Adam and Eve, but she intensifies the conjugal relationship portrayed in *Paradise Lost* and makes Eve, not Adam or Cain, her primary subject. Thus she draws on Byron to revise Milton, at the same time significantly altering his representation of Eve in *Cain*.

A similarly complex pattern of revision is apparent in the representation of Lucifer in *A Drama of Exile*. Critics have noted how Byron departed from Milton in emphasizing Lucifer's fallen beauty and in associating him with the light-bearing Morning Star. But, although at least one contemporary reviewer rightly observed that Byron's Lucifer in *Cain* rather than Milton's Satan was Barrett's primary 'model' (*BC* 9:325), the intertextual connections between Byron's revisionism and Barrett's have never been considered. Barrett's Eve echoes Byron's Adah in emphasizing Lucifer's 'glorious darkness' (l.752), but Barrett goes further than Byron in creating sympathy for Lucifer by representing the Morning Star as his bereft consort in her 'Song of the Morning Star to Lucifer' (ll.810–95). More importantly, Barrett revises Byron by portraying 'Lucifer as an extreme Adam', as she explained in her 'Preface' (*CW* 2:144), whereas Byron in effect portrays Cain as 'an extreme Adam' in whom the effects of the fall are fully manifested. Barrett's aim in making Lucifer himself the most exiled of her exiles is to bring out the power of 'Heavenly love'. In the process she humanizes him in an unorthodox and innovative manner, resisting Byron's emphasis on

Lucifer's incapacity to conceive of human or divine love.

None of Barrett Browning's contemporaries judged *A Drama of Exile* an unqualified success. But it is absolutely inaccurate to say as Alethea Hayter does that 'nobody liked *A Drama of Exile*' (78), or as Gardner Taplin does that, 'even to Elizabeth's staunchest supporters' it appeared a 'complete failure' (*Life* 126). It was praised by John Kenyon and John Ruskin, while the *Athenaeum* was representative of many reviewers in commenting that, while the work fell 'short of its own ideal', it contained 'enough of fine thought and imagination to furnish a hundred inferior but still beautiful conceptions'.[15] *A Drama of Exile* 'exhibits *power* such as we do not remember in any lady's poetry', another reviewer observed; while a third commended its Aeschylean 'mental energy and daring imagination' – 'the author of the "Prometheus" would have recognized the work of a kindred spirit in the "Drama of Exile" ' (*BC* 9:369,379).

On the whole, however, Victorian reviewers found more to praise in 'A Vision of Poets', the most substantial work in the 1844 *Poems* next to *A Drama of Exile*. 'A Vision of Poets' was greeted as 'the most remarkable poem' in the two volumes, 'a striking piece' more often 'beautiful and masterly' than not, and 'a very impressive performance' (*BC* 9:329, 346, 359). This is 'no elegant amusement of the boudoir penned on satin paper', one reviewer commented; it is 'the soul's experience, wrung from the very depths of a noble nature' (*BC* 10:339). 'A Vision of Poets' remained a frequently cited poem until the end of the century, then lapsed into the obscurity that still afflicts it. Although Hayter describes it as 'the fullest expression of Mrs. Browning's idea of the poetical character' next to *Aurora Leigh*

(154), she mentions it only in passing, like Mermin and Cooper.

Barrett strategically positioned 'A Vision of Poets' as the lead work in Volume 2 of her 1844 *Poems*, singling it out in her 'Preface' as a poem in which she 'endeavoured to indicate the necessary relations of genius to suffering' (*CW* 2:147). 'Genius' in the context of the poem is synonymous with poetic power. What Barrett explores is the nexus of power, knowledge, and pain. She presents an anonymous 'pilgrim-poet' who experiences a vision initiating him into the knowledge of suffering that grounds poetical power and revealing the immortal fame such power may bring. The fame the aspiring poet longs for is embodied in his vision, when he sees the gathered company of great 'king-poets' of the past.

If *The Seraphim* reveals striking affinities with Shelley in its revision of Aeschylus, and *A Drama of Exile* manifests Barrett's revisionary engagement with Byron as well as Milton, 'A Vision of Poets' is her most Keatsian poem. But the work it most strikingly resembles is not Keats' *Hyperion* fragment, which Barrett read in 1831, or *Endymion* which she echoes in 'A Vision of Poets' itself, but *The Fall of Hyperion*, a work that Barrett probably did not know since it was not yet published in 1844. Some of the parallels may result from the influence of *The Divine Comedy* on both poets. For, if Barrett is walking in Milton's footsteps in *A Drama of Exile*, she is clearly walking in Dante's in 'A Vision of Poets'. The poem is written in 'a simplified form of the *terza rima*', as Oscar Kuhns notes, and it contains even more 'touches' of Dante than he points out.[16] Nevertheless, the presence of many poets in addition to Dante is felt in this densely allusive work. While one reviewer rightly noted the 'altogether Dantean' nature of some of her expressions, another commented, 'you feel, as you proceed, that you are in the company of one to whom all the masters of the Greek, Latin, and Italian schools are familiar in the originals' (*BC* 10:340, 370).

Its invocation of powerful precursors and its central quest for poetic power make 'A Vision of Poets' the fullest and clearest embodiment of 'the scene of instruction' in Barrett Browning's canon. As much as *Paracelsus*, which it sometimes echoes, it presents 'incidents in the development of the soul', to use Browning's famous words from the 'Preface' to *Sordello*. But rather than dramatizing historical figures and events as Browning does in *Paracelsus* and *Sordello*, Barrett follows Dante and the Romantics in internalizing the quest of traditional romance, making it a symbolic allegory of the poet's spiritual and imaginative growth.

'A Vision of Poets' opens with the description of a sleepless poet, arising to wander in 'the darkest glades / Where the moon had drawn long colonnades' (ll.7–8), and encountering there a mysterious queenly lady like Spenser's Una who identifies herself with the moon:

'She is in heaven, and I on earth;
This is my kingdom: I come forth
To crown all poets to their worth.' (ll.52–7)

When the poet sceptically questions the lady's claim that all poets are crowned 'to their worth', pointing to the example of Keats, the lady leads him out of the dark forest to a 'wild brown moorland' where, beneath the 'broader glory' of the moon, he sees 'four pools breaking up the heath / With white low gleamings, blank as death' (ll.114–26). The lady asks him to drink from each of these progressively more repulsive pools, the second, third and fourth representing 'World's use', 'World's love', and 'World's cruelty'

respectively, the first unnamed. The symbolism
associated with each of these pools is too complex to
explore here. But the fourth, depicted with images as
grotesquely animated as those in 'Childe Roland',
suggests that 'A Vision of Poets' may have been one of
the many texts influencing Browning's later depiction
of a young knight's progression through an intensely
symbolic and increasingly cruel landscape towards the
'dark tower' bringing a vision of his lost peers.

As Barrett's pilgrim-poet drinks from the last pool,
'His brain beat heart-like, rose and sank' (1.189) –
implying that the painful knowledge of the world's
cruelty has been felt on his pulses, head-knowing and
heart-feeling fused. He then falls backward into the
swoon that brings the vision at the heart of the poem.
As the lady's kiss awakens him within his trance, he
becomes aware of her standing beside him, 'holy, pale
and high / As one who saw an ecstasy / Beyond a
foretold agony' (ll.208–10) – like Keats' Moneta or
Dante's Beatrice. Rising up at the lady's command,
the initiate finds himself before an altar in a great
church with Piranesi-like columns glimmering through
an eddying mist of incense. Before the altar stands an
angel whose eyes reflect the glory of God as Beatrice's
do in *The Divine Comedy*; beside him stands a 'phantasm
of an organ'. Ranged around both is a 'strange
company . . . pale and bound / With bay above the
eyes profound'. With 'deathful' faces, they nevertheless
radiate '[t]he power of life' (ll.271–5):

> All, still as stone and yet intense;
> As if by spirit's vehemence
> That stone were carved and not by sense. (ll.424–7)

As the moon-muse lady gradually reveals, this is the
gathered company of 'God's prophets of the Beautiful'

(l.293), whose suffering and dedication have brought them immortal fame.

In justifying the ways of her 'Poet-God' to man, Barrett presents a theodicy that provides for no transcendence of pain. The suffering of the king-poets continues after death. Eternal passion and eternal pain accompany eternal glory. All who aspire to join the ranks of the king-poets must offer up their hearts completely and accept a baptism in the salt and bitter tears of Christ, much as in Keats' *The Fall of Hyperion* Moneta states, 'None can usurp this height . . . But those to whom the miseries of the world / Are misery, and will not let them rest' (ll.147–9). 'Anguish has instructed me in joy', Barrett said in one of her early letters to Browning (*RB–EBB* 1:35). The statement, which looks forward to Emily Dickinson and Wallace Stevens, and back to Keats, reflects the conjunction at the heart of 'A Vision of Poets', where the poet-hero learns that 'not to suffer, is to want / The conscience of the jubilant' (ll.515–16).

One of the most powerful passages in 'A Vision of Poets' is the poetic catalogue in which Barrett summons up and sums up, in a few memorable lines for each, the most famous figures in the great company of dead poets – from Homer with his 'thunderous brows' to Keats and Shelley and Byron. This royal roll-call, including Greek, Latin, Italian, Portuguese, Spanish, French and English poets, was highly praised by Browning and often cited in contemporary reviews. 'How perfect, absolutely perfect', Browning exclaimed, 'are those three or four pages in the "Vision" which present the Poets – a line, a few words, and the man there, – one twang of the bow and the arrowhead in the white – Shelley's "white ideal all statue-blind" is – perfect, – how can I coin words? . . . all, all are perfect, perfect!' (*RB–EBB* 1:142).

Barrett Browning's style 'tends to be expansive rather than lapidary', as Mermin suggests (9). But in 'A Vision of Poets' she often achieves the concentrated effect she praised in Dante when she said of his poetry 'count me the drops congealed in one hailstone' (*RB–EBB* 1:52). Thus she describes Sappho, the only woman in the company of 'king-poets', with her 'gloriole'

> Of ebon hair on calmed brows –
> O poet-woman! none forgoes
> The leap, attaining the repose. (ll.319–21)

Barrett's evocation of Sappho frames her passionate leap into the sea within the calm repose of her fame, thereby reversing the long tradition of focusing on Sappho's life rather than her art. Other memorable lines include the sketch of stern Lucretius, 'nobler than his mood, / Who dropped his plummet down the broad / Deep universe and said / "No God – " ' (ll.334–7), and 'grave Corneille / The orator of rhymes, whose wail / Scarce shook his purple' (ll.363–6). Or there is the unexpected evocation of 'poor, proud Bryon', 'sad as grave / And salt as life' (ll.412–13). Or, most fondly of all in this poem that expresses Keats' belief that 'Beauty is Truth, Truth Beauty', there is 'Keats the real Adonis' kissed 'In his Rome-grave, by Venus-queen' (ll.407–11) – a description that echoes Keats' own vision of the beautiful Adonis in Book 2 of *Endymion*.

Like Keats in *The Fall of Hyperion*, Barrett is concerned to distinguish genuine poets from idle dreamers. She dramatizes this distinction through a sudden blast of satire disrupting the sublime fabric of her poet-hero's vision – provoked by the appearance before the altar of a crowd of noisy suitors for poetic fame like the rowdy applicants for fame in Chaucer's

The House of Fame. Some of these suitors, 'composing sudden sighs ... Rehearsed impromptu agonies'. 'One dulled his eyeballs, as they ached / With Homer's forehead'; another 'his smooth / Pink cheeks did rumple passionate / Like Aeschylus', prating 'On trolling tongue of fate and fate'; while yet another 'set her eyes like Sappho's – or / Any light woman' (ll.604–29). When the spokesman for this troop of dilettantes declares 'we are not pilgrims, nor yet martyrs', they are swept away by a silent 'spirit-blast' emanating from the king-poets, who make their 'presence known by power' (ll.676–7). As the references to Homer, Aeschylus and Sappho reveal, Barrett's satiric catalogue of false poets in part reflects her 'anxiety of influence' and her repudiation of her juvenile attempts to imitate the great classical poets.

A more complex 'anxiety of authorship' arising from her gender is reflected in the structure and narrative perspective of 'A Vision of Poets'. The 'Vision' is narrated in the third person by a narrator who remains shadowy and indefinite – whose presence, in fact, is discernible only towards the close of the pilgrim-poet's vision as s/he describes the pilgrim-poet approaching the altar and wonders if 'a listening life did run / Through the king-poets ... Rejoicing in a worthy son'. Then, abruptly switching into the first person, the narrator observes, 'My soul, which might have seen, grew blind' (ll.727–32). This unnamed narrator assumes greater prominence in the 'Conclusion' that forms a frame to the narrative, where s/he traces the poet-pilgrim's footsteps through a forest and encounters the poet's son, who tells the story of his father's death and subsequent fame, and who seems destined to inherit his father's genius.

The split between the poet-hero and the poet-woman who narrates his vision becomes particularly

thought-provoking if we consider the implications of
the poem's title, with its deliberately ambiguous
genitive construction. As the poem makes clear, 'a
vision of poets' refers both to what is seen and to those
who see it: both to the company of 'king-poets'
Barrett's pilgrim-poet sees, and to the dedicated
aspirants experiencing such a vision. Barrett herself is
such an aspirant, yet she seems almost completely
absent from the poem. Moreover, by translating the
metaphoric father–son relation between her pilgrim-
poet and the company of 'king-poets' into a literal
father–son relationship in her 'Conclusion', Barrett
reveals her keen sense of how much, as a daughter, she
is outside the lines of descent through which poetic
power is transmitted. Reflected in the form of the
poem, with its split between narrator and poet in
the main narrative, and between narrator and poet's
son in the framing narrative, we find the woman-poet
who has created both the vision and its frame – but, to
echo the well known words of Muriel Rukeyser, we
find her 'split open, unable to speak, in exile from
herself'.[17]

Unable to speak directly and openly, we might add –
but it is a crucial qualification. 'I do not *say everything I
think* . . . but I *take every means to say what I think*', Barrett
said to Browning (*RB–EBB* 1:9). And indeed she finds
many means to imply what she thinks in 'A Vision of
Poets'. We sense one of her thoughts in the apostrophe
to Sappho – 'O poet-woman!' – the only poet directly
addressed in her catalogue, and the one with whom
Barrett audaciously identified herself in a January
1844 letter to Haydon: 'I am "little & black" like
Sappho, en attendant the immortality' (*BC* 8:128).
Her epigraph for 'A Vision of Poets' also calls
attention to her quest for poetic fame. More importantly, like the king-poets she sees in what is, in effect,

her vision, she makes her 'presence known by power'. Indeed, everywhere in the poem we find manifestations of the power she indirectly asserts: in the assimilation of the entire European poetic tradition embodied in her catalogue of king-poets; in the subtle echoing of her precursors from Dante, Chaucer and Spenser to Keats and Browning; in the chiselled, compressed verse commended by many reviewers; in the powerful symphonic lines describing the consummation of the pilgrim-poet's sublime vision – lines that appear, ironically, just after the narrator declares the limitations in her own vision (ll.739–74).

Even more overtly, Barrett makes her absent presence disconcertingly felt in the concluding narrative frame she evidently added to the poem some weeks after writing the central portion in the summer of 1843 (*LMRM* 2:316). The 'Conclusion' of 'A Vision of Poets' has been criticized as a structural overelaboration (*CW* 2:xxiv). But it is precisely the presence of the shadowy narrator in the 'Conclusion', more of a by-stander than Coleridge's wedding guest in 'The Rime of the Ancient Mariner', yet more of a participant in the poet-hero's suffering and glorious vision than his son, that draws our attention to the absent woman-poet who has created both father and son. If 'A Vision of Poets' dramatically illustrates how a woman poet can be marginalized by a male canonical tradition, it also reveals that meaning can 'be something that happens on the margins', as theorists of narrative framing point out.[18]

From the margins of 'A Vision of Poets', Barrett takes 'every means' to express her own audacious ambition and to imply what she thinks about the lines of descent connecting 'king-poets' to their 'worthy sons'. A poet needs to have 'the historical sense' which 'compels a man to write not merely with his own generation in his bones, but with a feeling that the whole literature of Europe from Homer . . . composes a simultaneous order', T. S. Eliot emphasized in 'Tradition and the Individual Talent'.[19] In 'A Vision of Poets', Barrett writes with 'the whole literature of Europe from Homer' in her bones. Yet because hers are the bones of a woman, she is sufficiently outside the 'order' of texts Eliot invokes to critique the male-centred genealogical metaphors that uphold it: the metaphors that are consistently invoked, despite the achievement of Barrett Browning and women poets after her, in Eliot's poetics as in Bloom's.

If one accepts Bloom's paradigm of the poet's progress through a six-phase 'scene of instruction' towards poetic incarnation (*Map* 51–5), 'A Vision of Poets' indicates that Barrett in 1844 was well beyond the early phase of 'Election-love' or imitation evident in her attempt to become a female of Homer and Byron in *The Battle of Marathon*. She was well beyond too the second phase of 'Covenant-love', with its uneasy fusion of imitation and competition. The 'rise of an individual inspiration or a Muse-principle' that she depicts in her pilgrim-poet's quest for poetic power had already taken place. Together with *A Drama of Exile* and the important body of ballads in which she had also expressed her Romantic revisionary impulse by 1844, 'A Vision of Poets' charts Barrett's entry into the later phases of 'poetic incarnation' in which she establishes her own 'veritable presence' and differentiates herself into strength. After 1844, the audacity of the Promethean 'fire-thief' who dared to refashion precursors as powerful as Aeschylus, Milton and Byron would not be significantly checked again.

3 A Cinderella Among the Muses: Barrett Browning and the Ballad Tradition

In their 1867 edition of Bishop Percy's folio of ballads, John H. Hales and Frederick J. Furnivall picture the ballad before the Romantic revival as a 'Cinderella' among the Muses:

> She had never dared to think herself beautiful. No admiring eyes ever came near her in which she might mirror herself. She had never dared to think her voice sweet. . . . She met with many enemies, who clamoured that the kitchen was her proper place, and vehemently opposed her admission into any higher room. The Prince was long in finding her out. The sisters put many an obstacle between him and her. . . . But at last the Prince found her, and took her in all her simple sweetness to himself.[1]

Some readers might pause over the class- and gender-inflected assumptions in this ingenuous fairy story of a gallantly patronizing 'Prince' taking a low-born maiden 'to himself'. But few would dispute the importance of the union Hales and Furnivall fancifully describe. Every student of Romantic poetry recognizes the profound significance of the ballad revival, reflected in

Bishop Percy's *Reliques of Ancient English Poetry* (1765), in Sir Walter Scott's 'minstrelsy', and above all in the *Lyrical Ballads* published by Wordsworth and Coleridge in 1798.

Yet the ballad is seldom recognized as an important Victorian genre, even though it attracted major and minor poets throughout the nineteenth century. G. Malcolm Laws' catalogue of literary ballads in the Victorian period (1832–90) is longer than his catalogue for the Romantic period. As Laws' survey suggests, the ballad was held in particular esteem by the Pre-Raphaelite poets.[2] Tennyson, like Hardy after him, also employed innovative variants of the form throughout his long career, in works such as 'The Sisters', with its refrain 'O the Earl was fair to see!', 'The Lady of Shalott', the immensely popular 'Lady Clare Vere De Vere', 'Edward Gray', 'Lady Clare', 'Locksley Hall', 'The Revenge: A Ballad of the Fleet', and 'Rizpah'. Ballads are particularly numerous in his 1842 *Poems*, reflecting their prominence in a period marked by the success of Macaulay's *Lays of Ancient Rome* (1842) and the continuing popularity of Sir Walter Scott's ballads and narrative poems.

Although Elizabeth Barrett was no 'Prince', she too took that 'Cinderella' among the Muses, the ballad, to herself – not so much because the form was simple and sweet, but because its energy, its strong heroines, its elemental passions of love and revenge, its frank physicality and its sinewy narrative conflicts allowed her to circumvent the ideologies of passionless purity and self-sacrifice confining middle-class Victorian women. Ballads have an even higher profile in her 1844 *Poems* than in Tennyson's 1842 *Poems*. Moreover, her 'peculiar skill' in 'this species of poetry' was frequently praised (*BC* 9:341, 365).

In our own century, however, popular Victorian

ballads and Barrett Browning's ballads in particular
have been underappreciated for a number of reasons,
among them the intersecting ideologies of gender and
genre. In short, the marriage celebrated by Hales
and Furnivall seems to have ended in divorce, with
Cinderella dismissed to her proper place in the
kitchen. Ironically, despite Wordsworth's subversion
of genre and his democratizing aims in the *Lyrical
Ballads*, most reconstructions of the nineteenth-century
ballad tradition have been informed by prescriptive
categorical distinctions separating the ballad from the
romance, 'serious' poetry from popular verse, literary
from authentic folk ballads, Romantic from Victorian
poets, and female from male traditions. These critical
ideologies have had especially unfortunate con-
sequences in the case of Barrett Browning. Even
recent feminist critics disparage her ballads, ironically
by placing them in the context of a separate 'feminine
genre' of popular ballad-writing which is, in Dorothy
Mermin's words, 'sentimental' and 'retrogressive'
(91).

By considering the intertextuality of a number of
Barrett Browning's ballads and by reconstructing the
horizon of expectation against which they were
written and read, I hope to show that her innovations
can be better appreciated when we approach poems
like 'The Poet's Vow', 'The Romaunt of Margret', 'A
Romance of the Ganges' and 'The Romaunt of the
Page' in the context of the Romantic ballad revival
and the tradition it produced. In many cases, Barrett
Browning refashioned motifs and conventions from
folk ballads and Romantic narrative verse in ways that
anticipate the ballads of the Pre-Raphaelite poets. At
the same time, however, her handling of the form
differs from that of many other poets working in the
tradition because of the distinctively gynocentric focus

of her Romantic revisionary impulse. In her appropriations of the 'Cinderella' among the muses, the
ballad is used to subvert the conventional inscriptions
of sexual difference the genre appears to confirm.

The originality of Barrett Browning's ballads is
particularly apparent in her modification of what
Nancy K. Miller terms 'female plots' – that is, the
plots that 'culture has always already inscribed' for
women, plots reinscribed in 'the linear time of
fiction'.[3] Like Charlotte Brontë, Barrett Browning has
often been faulted for her handling of plot. Even
Mermin generally observes that it was fortunate
Barrett Browning did not write novels because she
'had no gift for inventing plots' (186) and the stories in
her ballads are 'invariably silly', if 'entertaining' (90).
But in many instances the 'silly' stories that Mermin
objects to in Barrett's 1838 and 1844 ballads are no
more absurd than the plots they play against in the
traditional ballads collected by Percy, such as 'Child
Waters', and in the ballads and narratives written in
the Romantic revival by the German poet Gottfried
Bürger, by Scott, and by Wordsworth and Coleridge.

The substantial revisions Barrett Browning made in
her ballads, both at the manuscript stage and after
they had appeared in periodicals and annuals, further
illumine her complex adaptation of plots and motifs
in precursor texts. These modifications also call in
question the common view that she wrote her ballads
quickly and did not take them very seriously. In 'The
Poet's Vow', Barrett Browning appropriates elements
in the anonymous ballads of the Percy collection to
carry out a critique of Wordsworth and Coleridge – a
critique she extends in the many revisions she made in
the poem after its initial publication. In 'The Romaunt
of the Page', she subverts the gender-inflected plots in
certain of the Percy ballads themselves. Significantly,

the most substantial revisions in 'The Romaunt of the Page' expand the role and motivation of the poem's male protagonist, revealing how Barrett Browning progressively complicated her 'female plots' by portraying their intersections with the social systems that create and encompass them. The changes in 'The Romaunt of the Page' thus look forward to *Aurora Leigh*, where Barrett Browning shows how the 'female plots' shaping Aurora's existence are inseparable from the gender plots of Romney and his society.

'The Poet's Vow' and 'The Romaunt of Margret', both published in 1836 in the *New Monthly Magazine*, were the first ballads by Barrett to attract the interest of readers. These were followed by 'A Romance of the Ganges', 'The Romaunt of the Page' and 'The Legend of the Brown Rosarie', published in the 1838, 1839 and 1840 editions of the annual edited by Mary Mitford, *Findens' Tableaux*. The 1844 *Poems* brought substantially revised versions of 'The Romaunt of the Page' and 'The Legend of the Brown Rosarie' before a wider public, along with several new poems identified as 'ballads' by contemporary reviewers: most notably 'Rhyme of the Duchess May', 'Bertha in the Lane', 'The Romance of the Swan's Nest', and 'Lady Geraldine's Courtship'. Barrett Browning's ballads were acclaimed by general readers as well as critics, and remained among her most popular works until the end of the century. They were often reprinted in selected editions of her poems, while particular favourites, such as 'Rhyme of the Duchess May' and 'Lady Geraldine's Courtship' were republished separately in illustrated editions until well past the turn of the century.

The vogue for ballads in the mid-Victorian period inevitably led to parodies like those in the frequently reprinted 'Bon Gaultier' *Ballads* (1845), which included in one of its later editions a parody of 'Rhyme of the Duchess May' entitled 'The Rhyme of Lancelot Bogle'. Such parodies no doubt contributed to the relatively low profile of the ballad in modern constructions of the Victorian poetical canon – and, in Barrett Browning's case, to the disappearance of her ballads from literary history altogether. The assumption that a popular *literary* work is of little artistic value has lingered longer in the case of Victorian poets than in the case of novelists such as Dickens or Wilkie Collins.

Paradoxically, in the case of popular literary ballads, the effects of this assumption have been exacerbated by narrow definitions of the genre that privilege the anonymous or 'authentically' popular folk ballad over equally popular literary 'imitations'. J. S. Bratton shrewdly notes some of the limitations of such constraining definitions in the case of Francis J. Child's enormously influential collection, *The English and Scottish Ballads*, and detects the 'same assumption of the innate superiority of the traditional ballad' in studies of the literary ballad by Albert B. Friedman and Anne Ehenpreis.[4] Barrett Browning's ballads have particularly suffered from definitions of the genre privileging the 'authentic' folk form because they move farther away from this model than literary ballads like Keats' 'La Belle Dame Sans Merci' and D. G. Rossetti's 'Sister Helen'.

These general assumptions about the popular literary ballad underlie Alethea Hayter's dismissal of Barrett Browning's ballads in 1962 as 'synthetic' confections with a 'certain narrative sweep and excitement' appealing to 'people who did not normally read poetry at all' (81). Hayter adds in extenuation that Barrett Browning 'never really took them seriously', supporting this conclusion with the well-known lines in *Aurora Leigh*:

My ballads prospered; but the ballad's race
Is rapid for a poet who bears weights
Of thought and golden image. (Book 5:84–6)

Traces of Hayter's disparaging tone persist in recent
feminist reinterpretations. Kathleen Hickok dismisses
'The Lay of the Brown Rosary' as 'an uninspired
jumble', 'The Romaunt of Margret' as completely
conventional, and 'Rhyme of the Duchess May' as a
'Spasmodic' poem (173–5). Leighton approaches 'A
Romance of the Ganges' and 'The Lay of the Brown
Rosary' as 'confused and precipitate' ballads 'which
Elizabeth Barrett wrote in response to a demand . . .
for morally educative poems' directed towards 'a
primarily female readership' (1986, 32). Although
Leighton has more recently acknowledged the 'modern
sexual politics' in 'The Romaunt of the Page', she still
describes it as 'an awkward, pseudo-Spenserian ballad'
written in 'quirky archaic registers' (1992, 82–3).

   In a series of articles subsequently incorporated
into *Elizabeth Barrett Browning: The Origins of a New
Poetry*, Mermin was the first to reinterpret Barrett
Browning's ballads as poems providing 'a covert but
thorough-going reassessment, often a total repudiation, of the Victorian ideas about womanliness to
which they ostensibly appeal' (71). 'Beneath their
apparent conventionality,' Mermin argues, the
ballads sceptically examine 'the myths and fantasies of
nineteenth-century womanhood', including 'the virtues
of self-repression and self-sacrifice' they seem to affirm
(90–1). At the same time, Mermin doubts that the
poet herself was very aware of the subversiveness of
her own poems (90). 'Almost all of her ballads cry out
to be read as feminist revisions of old tales', but
'Elizabeth Barrett told the old stories in a style and
tone that gave no hint of revisionary intention, and she

discarded the ballad form without discovering how to use it effectively against itself' (95). Detecting a more consistently subversive dimension in Barrett Browning's medieval ballads, Helen Cooper reads them as an examination of 'the sexual economy of courtship and marriage' (70), and Glennis Stephenson analyses their critique of 'chivalric conventions' and gender roles (29). Like Mermin, however, they emphasize the limits of Barrett Browning's revisionism, and approach it within the context of a 'female genre' (Cooper 70) of ballad writing which is 'squarely in the tradition of' Letitia Landon (Mermin 107). In keeping with this compartmentalization, Mermin and Cooper separate 'The Poet's Vow' with its male protagonist from the 'romantic ballads' with female protagonists – even though 'The Poet's Vow' more clearly employs the ballad form than a poem like 'The Lay of the Brown Rosary'.

Resituating Barrett Browning's ballads within the context of the Romantic ballad revival requires an approach wary of retrospectively imposed compartmentalizations by gender, genre, period and popularity. Early Victorian conceptions of the ballad seem to have been remarkably broad and inclusive, both in terms of gender and in terms of genre. While some of Barrett Browning's ballads particularly appealed to women, neither the poet herself nor the majority of her readers approached them in the context of a separate feminine tradition. A relatively inclusive generic definition is also in order because assumptions about the ballad form were more amorphous in the early Victorian period than they became after Child's collection of 'authentic' folk ballads appeared.

Like 'The Lay of the Brown Rosary', many of the works described by Barrett's reviewers as ballads might more probably be classified as romances or romantic tales today. In fact, 'Lady Geraldine's Courtship' bore the subtitle 'A Romance of the Age', yet was still referred to as a ballad by early Victorian reviewers. Albert Friedman and Hermann Fischer acknowledge the difficulty of distinguishing between ballad and romance forms in nineteenth-century narrative verse, and trace the developments that contributed to the mixing of the two modes. Fischer notes that when Scott attempted to describe the new genre of ' "romantic poetry" ' or romantic verse narrative in 1813, he did 'not distinguish between [sic] ballads, lays and romances'; moreover, Scott's own poetical works reflect an 'eclectic mixture' of conventions from 'the ballad and romance traditions'. Friedman's more condemnatory approach to the 'intrusion of romance' into nineteenth-century 'ballad poetry' reflects the genre ideologies that contributed to the neglect of Barrett Browning's ballad-romances, along with Scott's.[5]

Barrett Browning's titles for her 'ballads' ('romaunt', 'lay', 'rhyme', 'romance') and her references to these works in her letters suggest that for her, as for many of her contemporaries, all of these terms were loosely synonymous. Harriet Martineau's reference to Barrett's ballads as her 'Rhyme, Romaunt, lay-style of poem' is indicative (*BC* 9:141). I therefore use the term 'ballad' here as Barrett Browning and other Victorians used it, to refer to all of her narrative poems with clear affinities either with the characteristic features of the ballad form (the ballad stanza, the use of dialogue and the refrain, tragic and/or topical subject matter, narrative compression and intensity) or with the larger tradition of 'minstrelsy' and Romantic narrative verse. The principal exception to this rule is the group of narrative poems with dramatized speakers, including 'Catarina to Camoens', 'Bertha in the Lane',

'Lady Geraldine's Courtship', 'The Runaway Slave at Pilgrim's Point', 'Void in Law', and 'Mother and Poet'. These works were often described as 'ballads' and they share many characteristics with both folk ballads and the ballads of the Romantic revival: there are clear echoes of the old Scottish ballad 'Lady Bothwell's Lament' in 'Void in Law', for example. But since this group of poems displays even stronger affinities with the developing form of the dramatic monologue, I have chosen to treat them as such elsewhere and to make only passing reference to their ballad traits below.

Barrett Browning often expressed her love for 'the old burning ballads, with a wild heart beating in each!' (*BC* 6:268). She also probably thought of ballad writing as a natural preparation for the writing of an epic, a mode of thinking subsequently borne out by her own career as she moved from writing simpler to more elaborate ballads and narratives between 1836 and 1844, culminating in 'Lady Geraldine's Courtship', which she clearly saw as the germ of her novel-epic *Aurora Leigh* (*LMRM* 3:42). As Barrett observed in her 1842 essay, 'The Book of the Poets', the ballad is 'a form epitomical of the epic and dramatic' (6:296). Thus it seems unlikely that she saw her ballads as mere diversionary exercises in a 'feminine' genre or that she devalued her *Findens'* ballads, as Stephenson suggests (24). On the contrary, her plans for her 1844 volumes reflect the prominence she wished her ballads to have (*BC* 6:260).

Unfortunately, space did not permit Barrett to include a survey of the 'anonymous & onymous ballads' in 'The Book of the Poets', as she explained to Mitford (*BC* 6:7). Nevertheless, she revealed her enthusiastic appreciation of the Romantic ballad revival and the innovations it fostered. 'We must not be thrown back upon the "Ballads," lest we wish to live with them for ever', she fondly observes as she passes them by (*CW* 6:296). She does find room to allude to 'the *réveillé* of Dr. Percy's "Reliques of English Poetry" ', which sowed 'great hearts' like Wordsworth's with 'impulses of greatness' (298), and to the ' "Scottish Minstrelsy" ' inspired by the *Reliques* (299–300).

Scott's epic narrative *Marmion* (1808) is one product of the Romantic ballad revival that enters into the intertextuality of Barrett's 1844 ballads, contributing to the resonance of her depiction of a woman disguised as a page and a nun buried alive in 'The Romaunt of the Page' and 'The Lay of the Brown Rosary'. The pronounced Gothic strain in the 'The Lay of the Brown Rosary' also owes something to Scott, although it reflects more closely the lingering influence of 'Lenora', the immensely popular German ballad by Gottfried Bürger that was so important a prototype for Wordsworth, Coleridge, Scott and Southey in the 1790s, as Mary Jacobus and Stephen Parrish have shown.[6]

Barrett's readers and reviewers up to 1844 were quick to link her ballads to such precursors in the larger ballad tradition. Responding to 'The Poet's Vow' in 1836, Mitford wrote to Barrett, 'I have just read your delightful ballad. My earliest book was "Percy's Reliques," the delight of my childhood; and after them came Scott's "Minstrelsy of the Borders," the favorite of my youth; so I am prepared to love ballads' (*BC* 3:195). Reviewers similarly viewed 'The Romaunt of the Page' and 'The Lay of the Brown Rosary' as 'revivals of the old English ballad, to which Miss BARRETT appears to be extremely partial' (*BC* 9:370, 326). John Forster compared 'Rhyme of the Duchess May' to the Scottish border ballad 'Edom

o'Gordon' in Percy's *Reliques*, while Sarah Flower
Adams observed of the same poem, 'it has all the
rapidity of action of "Lenore", [and] the descriptive
power of Scott and Campbell, united with the deep
pathos of the earlier Scottish ballads' (*BC* 9:347,
376).

Nevertheless, Scott and company were not the most
important precursors for Barrett the balladist;
Wordsworth and Coleridge were. Her focus on
abandoned or betrayed women in early ballads such
as 'The Romance of the Ganges' has reinforced the
assumption that she was writing primarily in a
sentimental female tradition. But such figures were a
staple in traditional ballads such as 'Lady Bothwell's
Lament', in German ballads by Bürger like 'The Lass
of Fair Wone', and in lyrical ballads by Wordsworth,
such as 'The Mad Mother' and 'The Thorn'. 'The
Runaway Slave at Pilgrim's Point', which Barrett
Browning referred to as a 'long ballad' (*LMRM*
3:310), adapts motifs from 'The Lass of Fair Wone'
and the 'The Thorn' (the mother's act of infanticide
and burial of her child beneath the roots of a tree), as
well as from 'The Mad Mother'.

Barrett was also drawn to Coleridge's 'Christabel',
with its sinister symbolic mother–daughter relationship
and its innovative irregular metre. Jacobus observes
that many of the *Lyrical Ballads* are like 'Christabel' in
releasing 'subconscious impulses' in 'dramatic confrontation' (225). Much the same can be said of two of
Barrett Browning's ballads that echo 'Christabel',
'The Lay of the Brown Rosary', and 'Isobel's Child'.
The latter, published in 1838, resembles Coleridge's
poem in its loose ballad form, in its Gothic imagery
and setting, and in its symbolically indirect treatment
of the dark undercurrents in a mother's possessive love
for her dying infant. Sara Coleridge was one Victorian

reader who noticed that 'Isobel's Child' was 'like "Christabel" in manner' (*BC* 8:333).

The poems with female protagonists in the *Lyrical Ballads* seem to be those which most directly influenced Barrett Browning's choice of subject matter and perspective in many of her ballads. In representing female subjects, however, Wordsworth remained a 'man speaking to men', to cite his famous 'Preface', whereas she increasingly wrote as a woman speaking to women. William Herridge observed in 1887 that her ballads 'appeal with an especial force to the author's own sex, and strike almost every note in the scale of woman's thought and emotion' (612–13). 'The Poet's Vow' and 'Lady Geraldine's Courtship' with their male protagonists skilfully combine an appeal to both male and female readers. But in each of these works, the female characters who seem to be secondary become the centre of interest by the end of the poem.

The impact of the *Lyrical Ballads* is also apparent in Barrett Browning's use of the ballad form throughout her career to extend the social consciousness of a community of readers. Noting the conflation of the traditional ballad and the topical broadside ballad in Wordsworth's use of the form, Tilottama Rajan describes his interest in the genre as 'social not anti-quarian'.[7] Barrett Browning was similarly interested in the power of the ballad to appeal to common human sympathies: 'all the passion of the heart will go into a ballad, & feel at home', she observed (cited Mermin 90). As 'The Runaway Slave at Pilgrim's Point' indicates, she turned to a variant on the ballad form to cut across class barriers and, in this case, sexual and racial divisions as well.

In her later career, however, Barrett Browning was inclined to be more radically polemical than Wordsworth in appropriating the ballad for political purposes, following Shelley's example more than Wordsworth's. In the 1854 political poem, 'A Song for the Ragged Schools of London', she writes in the tradition of the topical broadside ballad, using the form as Shelley had used it in 'Song to the Men of England' and 'The Mask of Anarchy', and as it was widely used by the Chartists in England during the 1840s. As I have argued elsewhere, 'A Song for the Ragged Schools' adapts and strategically revises Shelley's rhetorical tactics in 'A Mask of Anarchy' to reach an audience more female than male ('Cursing', 161–2). This highly political 'Song' was written to help raise money not for the Ragged Schools in general, but for a refuge for young destitute girls that Barrett Browning's sister Arabella helped to establish, one of the first of its kind. Moreover, in a female appropriation of the broadside ballad tradition, it was first published in a pamphlet sold at a charity bazaar.

If Barrett Browning departs from Wordsworth's example in making directly political use of the ballad, she also differs from both Scott and Wordsworth in her handling of narrative. Like the traditional ballads in the Percy collection, her ballads typically exhibit a strong narrative propulsion, despite the fact that she herself did not value narrative as the highest element in poetry (*BC* 4:109). 'It is the *story* that has power with people', she recognized (*LEBB* 1:247). She was strongly influenced by Wordsworth's focus on the psychological complexities of dramatized speakers, but she was equally drawn to the narratives of human conflict in the old anonymous ballads – conflict that Wordsworth tended to avoid in lyricizing the form. Rajan rightly detects an 'elision' of political and social concerns in Wordsworth's reduction of 'narrative to a lyric tableau that constructs the world in terms of feeling rather than events or situations' (145). The result is an apolitical 'hermeneutics of sentimentalism' that privileges archetypal and universal feeling over political, social, and gender differences.

Barrett Browning's focus, on the contrary, is on configurations of plot and character that foreground ideologically grounded gender differences in their intricate intersections with other hierarchies of power: man over Nature, God over man, knight over page, parent over child, priest over nun, and, in 'The Runaway Slave', master over slave. In many cases, these configurations create ironies intensified by her revisionary echoes of earlier texts and her appropriations of common ballad motifs. Rajan points out that, because the ballad is a 'cultural palimpsest inhabited by traces of more than one ideology', it 'functions as a psychic screen on which desires having to do with ideological authority and hermeneutic community are projected and analysed' (141–2). Barrett Browning's ballads function in precisely this way. When we appreciate their allusive intertextuality, we can read them not only as inscriptions of resistance to Victorian ideologies of womanhood, but also as subversive transformations of texts and conventions familiar to early Victorian readers.

In many cases, the convolutions and excesses that disrupt the narrative propulsion of Barrett Browning's ballads embody her critique of the 'plausible' plots encoding woman's lives in earlier ballads, both 'anomymous & onymous'. As Nancy Miller points out, such plots seem 'plausible' because they embody the assumptions of the dominant ideologies promoting their constant reiteration.[8] Like Hardy in the 'The Ruined Maid', Barrett Browning undermines such plausibility and the ideologies that sustain it. Most notably, in her ballads of the 1830s and 40s, she employs the starker power structures of medieval society to foreground the status of women as objects in a male economy of social exchange, and to unmask the subtler preservation of gender inequities in contemporary Victorian ideology. Thus, like some of the 'honey-mad' women writers Patricia Yaeger discusses, she engages in 'a form of textual violation that . . . overgoes social norms by doubling them, by making them visible'.[9]

'The Poet's Vow', the 1836 ballad in which Barrett Browning most noticeably echoes the *Lyrical Ballads*, illustrates the striking differences between her handling of the ballad form and Wordsworth's. It also reveals her artful use of folk ballad conventions to carry out a revision of both Wordsworth and Coleridge. As Cooper suggests, 'The Poet's Vow' is a critique of the Romantic ideology positing Nature as female, 'the silent other' (37). Possessed by the conviction that mankind has afflicted Earth with the curse of the fall, the nameless and representative poet referred to in the poem's title vows to forswear contact with humanity, consecrating himself to communion with Nature instead. Publicly declaring his vow, he bestows his 'plighted bride' Rosalind upon his 'oldest friend' Sir Roland, offering his own lands as Rosalind's dower (ll.136–40).

Declining to be the object in this male exchange, the betrayed Rosalind, still 'half a child', rejects the 'cruel homily' the poet has found in 'the teachings of heaven and earth' (ll.165–72). Years later, after the poet alone in his hall has withered within from 'rejection of his humanness' (l.266), Rosalind dies and instructs that her bier be placed before his 'bolted door': ' "For I have vowed, though I am proud, / To go there as a guest in shroud / And not be turned away" ' (ll.371–5). On her breast, like a Lady of Shalott who refuses to be judged merely by her 'lovely face', she bears a scroll:

'I left thee last, a child at heart,
    A woman scarce in years.
I come to thee, a solemn corpse
    Which neither feels nor fears.
                    . . .
    Look on me with thine own calm look:
        I meet it calm as thou.
No look of thine can change *this* smile,
    Or break thy sinful vow:
I tell thee that my poor scorned heart
Is of thine earth – thine earth, a part:
    It cannot vex thee now.' (ll.416–29)

As Mermin notes (65–6), the 'unmistakable' echoes in these lines of Wordsworth's famous Lucy poem, 'A Slumber Did My Spirit Seal', reflect Barrett's recognition of the 'unprivileged position of woman' in the Romantic myth of a female Nature. To speak with the voice of Nature is to speak with the voice of the dead – or, as in Wordsworth's poem, with the voice of the male poet who chooses to commingle with Nature and the dead. In either case, the individual woman is buried.

The crucial difference, of course, in Barrett Browning's rewriting of the Romantic man–Nature love relationship is that in 'The Poet's Vow' we *do* hear the voice of the still unburied Rosalind speaking from the scroll as an individual woman, not as a mythic female force articulated by the male poet. Rosalind speaks, moreover, with all of the passion and bitterness of the betrayed women in the old anonymous ballads published by Percy. She bears a particularly striking resemblance to the dead Margaret in 'Margaret's Ghost', who appears at her lover's bedside to indict him for betraying his plighted troth.[10] By superimposing a traditional ballad plot of human love and betrayal on Wordsworth's lyrical ballad of fusion

with Nature, Barrett Browning foregrounds the conflicts he elides in identifying Lucy with the earth,
thereby disrupting his focus on apparently universal
feeling.

In substantially revising 'The Poet's Vow', first for
her 1838 volume *The Seraphim, and Other Poems*, and
then for her 1850 *Poems*, Barrett Browning intensified
both the narrative conflicts between the poet and
Rosalind, and the passion and forcefulness of her
ballad heroine. In the process, she extended her
critique of Wordsworth. For instance, in both the *New
Monthly Magazine* and the 1838 versions of poem, the
section entitled 'The Words of Rosalind's Scroll'
begins with, ' "I left thee last, a feeble child / In those
remembered years" '. In revising, Barrett Browning
removed the emphasis on her heroine's feebleness, and
made it clear that, though Rosalind was ' "a woman
scarce in years" ' (l.417) like Wordsworth's Lucy
when her lover consigned her to her fate, she speaks
now with a woman's desires and a woman's strength.
The revisions also intensify Rosalind's bitter scorn for
the poet's ' "sinful vow" ' (l.426). In the two earliest
versions, the second stanza of Rosalind's scroll ends
with the lines, ' "My silent heart, of thine earth, is
part – / It cannot love thee now" ' – not with the
forceful declaration cited above, ' "I tell thee that my
poor scorned heart / Is of thine earth – thine earth, a
part: / It cannot vex thee now." ' The syntactic
doubling in 'of thine earth – thine earth' undoes
Wordsworthian ideology by simultaneously exaggerating and contradicting the identification of woman and
Nature he assumes in the Lucy poems. Moreover, by
intensifying Rosalind's bitterness, Barrett Browning
forces the reader to distinguish between the betrayed
feelings of an individual woman and Nature as mythic
female presence.

'The Poet's Vow' provides a further critique of Wordsworth in demonstrating the limited redemptive influence of recollections of early childhood and in ironically subverting Wordsworth's own teaching. Additional revisions in the poem emphasize the redeeming memories the poet *should* have shared with Rosalind – memories he has apparently forgotten.[11] Meanwhile, the epigraph from 'Lines Left upon a Seat in a Yew Tree' added in 1838 implies that Wordsworth himself should have followed his own instruction. 'O be wiser thou, / Instructed that true knowledge leads to love', the epigraph reads. In Wordsworth's poem, this advice from the moralizing poet is prompted by the example of a hermit who withdrew from the world and died in the pride of his solitude. But in 'The Poet's Vow', it is the Wordsworthian poet himself who withdraws into the pride of solitary communion with Nature and who therefore needs instruction. Barrett Browning thus turns Wordsworth's teaching back on his own example.

Still other revisions in 'The Poet's Vow' emphasize the ironic contradictions between the poet's 'vow' to mate himself with the 'touching, patient Earth' (1.68) and his broken vow to Rosalind. Moreover, in the 1850 version Barrett Browning added explicit reference to *her* vow (' "For I have vowed . . ." '). This revision foregrounds both the ambiguities of the title and the narrative doublings the ballad's convoluted plot enacts. Not only is the poet's vow itself doubled, given that the poet breaks his vow to Rosalind in making his vow to Earth. The figure of the poet is also doubled, as Rosalind uses her scroll to publish her vow. In implying that the representative poet of the title may be female, Barrett Browning subverts the universalizing assumption that the poet is male. More tellingly, of the two poets in 'The Poet's Vow',

Rosalind speaking from her scroll seems to be the stronger. In the poem's words, she is 'Triumphant Rosalind!', as the words of her text and the text of her body combine to 'wring' a cry from the 'long-subjected humanness' (ll.458–66) of the poet who has 'vowed his blood of brotherhood / To a stagnant place apart' (ll.53–4).

Such passages in 'The Poet's Vow' point to its parallels with Tennyson's 'The Palace of Art', where the proud and sinful soul of the speaker who withdraws from human contact becomes 'a spot of dull stagnation'. The Victorian critic Peter Bayne aptly described Barrett Browning's poem as 'the ethical complement of Tennyson's' in its treatment of 'the cardinal sin of isolation from human interests' (38). But of the two, 'The Poet's Vow' is the more pertinent and telling critique, since Barrett Browning makes her representative male poet a lover of Nature, whereas Tennyson makes his sterile aesthete a lover of art, a type that less often appears in Romantic poetry.

Barrett Browning's representation of the poet's love of Nature in 'The Poet's Vow' incorporates a critique of Coleridge along with Wordsworth. This critique is accomplished principally through an echo of 'The Rime of the Ancient Mariner' that ironically questions Coleridge's vision of the mariner's redemption. In a passage of 'The Poet's Vow' anticipating the ending of Tennyson's 'The Two Voices', Barrett Browning describes her solitary poet looking down from his lattice to see 'Three Christians' going by to prayer, then a bridal party, and finally a little child watching the 'lizards green and rare' playing near the wall. But the poet remains unmoved, even by the child, who remains 'Unblessed the while for his childish smile / Which cometh unaware' (ll.301–2). Thus the spontaneous release that comes to the Ancient Mariner

when, 'unaware', he blesses the watersnakes does not
come to Barrett Browning's poet. The child's
spontaneous response to Nature's beauty cannot undo
the effects of a crime against the poet's own humanity
originally motivated by a misplaced love of Nature.

This ironic echo of 'The Rime of the Ancient
Mariner' emphasizes the revisionary intent of Barrett
Browning's poem and points to her reasons for making
her alienated figure a poet who sins against his
'humanness', rather than a man who sins against the
natural order, as in Coleridge's poem. Despite its use
of supernatural rather than natural incidents, 'The
Ancient Mariner' powerfully reinforces the idea
expressed elsewhere in the *Lyrical Ballads* by
Wordsworth: that Nature and natural feeling,
defamiliarized by the poet, offer sinful man redemption. But the poet's feeling of fusion with Nature that
brings redemption in the *Lyrical Ballads* of Wordsworth
and Coleridge becomes the very source of alienation in
Barrett Browning's poem.

This alienation is only overcome in 'The Poet's
Vow' when the 'wail' of the poet's 'living mind' fuses
with Rosalind's 'senseless corpse' (ll.462–3). While
'earth and sky' look on 'indifferently', God smites the
poet with his own 'rejected nature' (ll.478–83) and he
joins his fellow poet Rosalind in death, much as
William finally joins the ghost of Margaret in her
grave in the Percy ballad: 'They dug beneath the
kirkyard grass / For both one dwelling deep' (ll.491–2).
Despite the tone of reconciliation in these lines, the
note of revenge more obviously pervades the conclusion to 'The Poet's Vow'. This feature again links the
poem to the old folk tradition, in which revenge is as
common a motif as betrayal. In Barrett Browning's
rewriting of the male Romantic communion with
Nature, the Supernatural assists 'Triumphant

Rosalind' in achieving her revenge, as she recalls the arrogant male poet to a recognition of her humanness as well as his.

The focus on female subjectivity in the second half of 'The Poet's Vow' intensifies in Barrett Browning's other ballads of the 1830s: 'A Romance of the Ganges', 'The Romaunt of Margret' and 'The Romaunt of the Page'. The first of these has much in common with the exotic poems of 'psuedo-Oriental sentimentalism' popular in the early nineteenth century: poems such as Landon's 'The Hindoo Girl's Song' (Hickok 172). But 'A Romance of the Ganges' has even closer affinities with the traditional ballad. Although the poem was written to accompany an illustration in the 1838 *Findens' Tableaux: A Series of Picturesque Scenes of National Character, Beauty, and Costume*, Barrett Browning downplays the exotic elements of costume, setting and nationality. Instead, as in 'The Poet's Vow', she focuses on the burning passions of love and revenge so pervasive in the Percy ballads.

In 'A Romance of the Ganges', however, these passions are exclusively female, as the male lover becomes no more than an absent catalyst for the narrative conflict between the betrayed Luti and her unwitting rival Nuleeni. With a further twist, Barrett Browning transforms the two women of 'A Romance of the Ganges' from rivals in love into accomplices in revenge, much as Tennyson does in 'The Sisters', a ballad which she later praised (*BC* 6:212). Thus Luti leads the child-like Nuleeni to vow to ' "whisper" ' to her bridegroom on her wedding day, ' "*There is one betrays / While Luti suffers woe*" ' (ll.161–2). And to her ' "little bright-faced son" ' when he asks ' "What deeds his sire hath done" ', Nuleeni vows to whisper, ' "*There is none denies, / While Luti speaks of wrong*" ' (ll.171–2). When Nuleeni, in wondering innocence, softly asks why Luti would wish to defile a ' "bride-day" ' with a ' "word of *woe*" ' and a sinless child's ear with a ' "word of *wrong*" ', her fellow maiden cries out:

'Why?' Luti said, and her laugh was dread,
And her eyes dilated wild –
'That the fair new love may her bridegroom prove,
And the father shame the child!' (ll.174–85)

In 'A Romance of the Ganges' we begin to see the 'strong, angry heroine who dominates' most of Barrett Browning's ballads (Mermin 72). Indeed, Luti's cry for revenge registers an unrepentant excess that is formal as well as emotional, for her fierce declaration appears in four extra lines that spill over the limits of the eight-line ballad stanza employed throughout 'A Romance of the Ganges'. It is as if the river flowing in insistent monotone through the poem's constant refrain, 'The river floweth on' – resisting as well as marking each stanza's containment – has suddenly risen in angry overflow. As the refrain implies and the narrative makes clear, Luti's bitterness and grief flow from herself to Nuleeni. Thus the curious use of the female pronoun without a clear referent in the first stanza proves justified: 'The wave-voice seems the voice of dreams / That wander through her sleep: / The river floweth on.' (ll.7–9). The pronoun in the final line – 'She weepeth dark with sorrow' – is similarly ambiguous in its possible reference to both Luti and Nuleeni. Luti could be any woman, the poet implies, and her sorrow every woman's.

In the earlier 1836 ballad 'The Romaunt of Margret', the 'running river' in which the protagonist enounters the shadow of her own darkest fears murmurs a parallel story of betrayal and 'failing human love' (ll.39,240). The shade that rises from the river to confront Margret torments her with the thoughts that the love of her brother, her father, her sister, and her lover – all, all, will prove inconstant. The poem derives some of its power from the haunting effect of its relentlessly darkening images: the sound of 'silent forests' growing between the pauses of the shade's voice (68); the recurrent trembling of the shade's movement on the grass 'with a low, shadowy laughter'; the shadows falling 'from the stars above, / In flakes of darkness' on Margret's face (ll.204–6). Margret finally drowns herself in despair, fusing with her dark double and, ironically, with the inconstancy of the river in death.

The spell-binding effect of 'The Romaunt of Margret' is deepened by the ambiguities that Barrett Browning subtly develops. Were Margret's dark doubts justified or not? Does she suffer from the inconstancy of others' love, or the inconstancy of her own faith in love? Is the love of the knight who has given her no sign but an apparently heartfelt 'look' a 'transient' love because he is unfaithful or because he is dead (ll.197,210)? ' "The wild hawk's bill doth dabble still / I' the mouth that vowed thee true" ' (ll.211–12), the shade whispers with grisly relish. Lines such as these give 'The Romaunt of Margret' 'the true sadness of the old ballads' and their 'genuine cold grue' (Hayter 32).

The narrative frame of the poem, presenting an anonymous minstrel singing the 'wild romaunt' of Margret to the accompaniment of a harp, suggests how closely and consciously Barrett Browning was writing within the tradition revived by Percy's *Reliques*. Indeed, she may have felt particularly drawn to the minstrel tradition because, although Bishop Percy declared in the first edition of the *Reliques* that no 'real Minstrels were of the female sex', by the fourth edition if not before, the preface acknowledged that there were women minstrels who accompanied their ballads with the music of the harp.[12] In 'The Romaunt of Margret', the minstrel's sex is not revealed. But the intensity of the narrator's response to Margret's fate – 'Hang up my harp again / I have no voice for song' (ll.236–7) – may imply that the minstrel too is a woman.

Cooper suggests that the minstrel's apparent identification with Margret manifests the 'confused relationship of the narrator to her tale' (34) and her inadequacy to conclude her story. The minstrel's cry is a conventional framing device, however. More importantly, it marks the poem's movement into a deliberately ambiguous coda in which Barrett Browning develops the *Doppelgänger* motif at a meta-narrative level. The minstrel concludes but is unable to resolve the tale of Margret's dark inner conflicts. Her final series of laments (ll.240–4) can be read either as her response to the 'failing human love' that has betrayed Margret, or as her condemnation of Margret's own failing love. In effect, then, the minstrel mirrors the division within Margret herself embodied in the refrain, 'Margret, Margret'. In its subtle double depiction of the dialogue of the mind with itself, 'The Romaunt of Margret' justifies Cornelius Mathews' observation that Barrett's handling of the ballad form is 'subjective' (*BC* 9:342).

'The Romaunt of the Page' is a less 'subjective' ballad than 'The Romaunt of Margret', yet ultimately a more complex one that achieves its effects by subtly adapting the conventional figure of the woman-page so prevalent in the drama, in ballads and in Romantic narrative verse. As Dianne Dugaw suggests in *Warrior Women and Popular Balladry*, the female page has many features in common with the transvestite heroine who appears in the 'Female Warrior' ballads popular throughout the seventeenth and eighteenth centuries,

in which a woman disguised as a man follows her lover
to war or to sea. Barrett Browning was undoubtedly
familiar with one of the most famous of the Female
Warrior ballads, the variant on 'Mary Ambree'
included in Percy's *Reliques*. By illuminating the social
and historical conditions that explain the immense
popularity of the 'Female Warrior' ballads among
diverse social classes, Dugaw's study indirectly
suggests why a literary ballad like 'The Romaunt of
the Page' had such a widespread appeal at a time
when popular ballads like 'Mary Ambree' were dying
out because of an increasingly inflexible 'semiotics of
gender'.[13]

Mitford revealed her critical acumen in making
'The Romaunt of the Page' the lead poem in the 1839
*Findens' Tableaux of the Affections: A Series of Picturesque
Illustrations of the Womanly Virtues*. She also singled it out
in the 'Preface' and praised it privately to Barrett as
'by far the finest thing that you have ever written' (*BC*
5:135). Reviews of the 1839 *Findens'*, with the exception
of *The Literary Gazette*, were equally laudatory, describing 'The Romaunt of the Page' as 'a poem with the
spirit of the elder and better day of poetry in every line
of it', 'dipped in the hues of ballad minstrelsy' and 'full
of the early spirit of English poetry' (*BC* 4:405–6).

As these comments suggest, readers clearly linked
'The Romaunt of the Page' to the ballads recovered in
the Romantic revival. Henry Chorley was atypical in
relating the poem to the exclusively female tradition of
'Records of Woman' by Hemans and other 'song-
stresses' in his reviews of *Findens'* (*BC* 4:409) and of
the 1844 *Poems* (*BC* 9:320). Chorley's association of
'The Romaunt of the Page' with Hemans is justified in
one respect: the poem's conclusion does echo certain
details in Hemans' ballad 'Woman on the Field of
Battle' (which appeared in *Songs of the Affections*, not

Records of Woman). But the differences between Hemans' ballad and 'The Romaunt of the Page' are much more striking than the parallels, and again they help to reveal the distinctive features of Barrett Browning's ballad-writing.

Whereas Hemans presents a static, sentimental tableau of womanly sacrifice in 'Woman Slain on the Field of Battle', showing no interest in the narrative that leads up to it, Barrett Browning develops an ironic series of narrative conflicts in which a knight and a lady are both victimized by a system of gender relations treating women as objects of exchange. Much as Barrett Browning's woman-page is slain by the Saracens, Hemans pictures a 'gentle and lovely form' with 'golden hair' slain on the battlefield: an image that appears in the manuscript version of 'The Romaunt of the Page', though not in the published version. In Hemans' ballad, however, only one motive could have led a woman to such a death, the poet declares: not glory, but love, which 'Woman's deep soul too long / Pours on the dust'.[14]

Love is also a force contributing to the fate of Barrett's heroine, but in this case it is only one element in a subtle mix of circumstances, motives, and passions. 'The Romaunt of the Page' begins *in medias res*, with a knight and a page returning from 'the holy war in Palestine' (l.2), where the page has saved the knight's life 'once in the tent, and twice in fight' (l.ll). As thoughts of home fill the minds of both, the page recalls the dying prayer of his mother, while the knight points out to the page that, although he has proven himself in battle, he is too silent to serve well in the bower of the knight's lady. The page leads the knight to speak more of his lady: is she 'little loved or loved aright' (l.100)? Gloomily, the knight explains that he doesn't even know what his lady looks like since he married her in haste and darkness before leaving for Palestine. Moreover, he makes it clear that he married her out of a sense of obligation to his friend Earl Walter, who lost his life in avenging the honour of the knight's own dead father. On her deathbed, the Earl's wife sent for the knight and asked him to marry her daughter, the 'sweet child' made 'an orphan for thy father's sake' (ll.162–3). Bitterly the knight recalls how his bride rose from the ceremony '[a]nd kissed the smile of mother dead, / Or ever she kissed me' (ll.180–1).

In revising the *Findens'* version of 'The Romaunt of the Page' for its reissue in her 1844 *Poems*, Barrett Browning made the narrative fuller, more complex, more ironic, and more conflicted in developing the psychology of the knight and the page. Most notably, she greatly expanded the knight's inset narrative of the marriage forced on him by circumstance and the chivalric code – a narrative reversing the conventional plot in which a knight or a 'stranger (to all save the reader)', as Robert Browning facetiously remarked, wins a bride because the father owes his life or some other debt to him (*RB–EBB* 2:881). Barrett's additions create sympathy for the knight and develop his passions with psychological depth as he declares that it would have been better if he had avenged his own father and died, rather than have 'murdered friend and marriage-ring / Forced on [his] life together' (ll.146–7).

Responding with tears of grief to the knight's tale, the page explains that his own sister was married as the knight's lady was, but that she 'laid down the silks she wore' and followed her new husband to the 'battle-place', '[d]isguised as his true servitor'. The knight reacts with a 'careless laugh':

> 'Well done it were for thy sister,
>   But not for my ladye!
> My love, so please you, shall requite
> No woman, whether dark or bright,
>   Unwomaned if she be.' (ll.191–6)

In this case again, Barrett's revisions intensify the conflict between her two characters. In the manuscript the knight simply laughs 'loudly'; while in *Findens'* his laugh is 'gay', not 'careless', and the last three lines of his declaration are briefer and less unequivocal.

As the page passionately defends his hypothetical sister's actions to the scornful knight, Barrett presents her ironically paradoxical vision of the 'womanly virtues' the 1839 *Findens'* was meant to celebrate:

> 'Oh, womanly she prayed in tent,
>   When none beside did wake!
> Oh, womanly she paled in fight,
>   For one beloved's sake! –
> And her little hand, defiled with blood,
> Her tender tears of womanhood
>   Most woman-pure did make!' (ll.207–13)

Such a combination of heroic valour 'in fight' and womanly devotion is also quite typical of the 'Female Warrior' ballads that Dugaw explores, but in early nineteenth-century variants on these, as in 'The Romaunt of the Page', insistent 'gender-markers' like Barrett's phrase 'little hand' became much more common.[15]

Little hand or not, such a woman-servitor is wholly unacceptable in the eyes of Barrett's knight, who reiterates his belief in a more conventional type of womanly virtue that hides behind a veil. ' "No casque shall hide her woman's tear" ' (l.220), he declares in an ironically prophetic, punning line that does not appear in the manuscript. According to the knight, womanly virtue is ' "[s]o high, so pure, and so apart" ' from the world that it shines like ' "a small bright cloud / Alone amid the skies!" ' (ll.230–3). If his own lady so ' "mistook" ' his mind as to follow him disguised into battle, the knight asserts that he ' "would forgive" ' her, and ' "evermore / Would love her as my servitor / But little as my wife" ' (ll.223–9). As the little cloud that provokes the knight's comparison disappears behind a blacker one, the page sees the Saracens approaching. But while 'the page seeth all, the knight seeth none' (l.241), presumably because his eyes are still dazzled by what Barrett Browning scornfully referred to as the 'cloud-minding theory' of idealized womanhood (*LMRM* 3:81). As Stephenson notes (29–32), Barrett thought this chivalric theory was as perniciously confining for women as the 'pudding-making and stocking-darning' theory. 'Twas a stroke of policy in those ranty-pole barons of old to make their lady-loves idols, and curb their wives with silken idleness', another Victorian woman astutely remarked.[16]

Barrett Browning dramatically reveals the sterility of the chivalric ideal of womanhood in the hauntingly anticlimactic ballad, 'The Romance of the Swan's Nest', in many ways the counterpart of 'The Romaunt of the Page'. In this depiction of a young girl's fantasies, the female who opts for the conventional lady's role of inspiring rather than following her knight – of being his idol rather than his disguised page and 'servitor' – is as bitterly betrayed as her more active opposite. As Cooper observes (97), Little Ellie's fate in 'The Romance of the Swan's Nest' shows how 'dreaming courtly fantasies . . . gnaws at women's energy, sexuality, and identity' as insidiously as the rat gnaws at the reeds surrounding the empty swan's nest in the poem's ending.

'The Romaunt of the Page' concludes with the page sending the blind knight on before to safety, while the loyal 'servitor' drops her disguise, and the embittered wife exclaims,

> 'Have I renounced my womanhood
>   For wifehood unto *thee*,
> And is this the last, last look of thine
>   That ever I shall see?
>
> Yet God thee save, and mayst thou have
>   A lady to thy mind,
> More woman-proud and half as true
>   As one thou leav'st behind!' (ll.276–83)

Disillusioned by earthly love, Earl Walter's daughter turns to God's love and faces the Saracens, a ' "Christian Page" ' who taunts the enemy as boldly as any knight might do (l.301). 'False page, but truthful woman' (l.227), she dauntlessly dies beneath the scimitar, meeting its downward sweep '[w]ith smile more bright in victory / Than any sword from sheath' (ll.225–6).

Mermin observes of this conclusion that the protagonist of 'The Romaunt of the Page' 'succumbs to an ideal of "womanly virtues" that the poet both scorns and shares' because her page chooses 'a woman's fate – unrecognizing, self-sacrificing death' (91–2). Hickok similarly views the poem as 'a sentimental tale of extreme wifely devotion and self-sacrifice' (173). What such readings do not address, however, is the fact that Barrett Browning's heroic page never acts more like a man, in conventional terms, than when she is 'truthful woman'. Even her smile flashes like a sword. Moreover, her motives are mixed rather than 'pure' in that, like so many folk ballad heroines, she is driven as much by revenge as by devotion.

In revising 'The Romaunt of the Page' Barrett Browning intensified the woman-page's more vindictive motives. For example, in the manuscript, the page wishes her knight may find another lady 'More woman-proud, yet all as true / As one thou leavest behind'. In *Findens'* she wishes he may find a lady 'More woman-proud, not faithfuller / Than one thou leav'st behind!' The change from 'all as true' to 'half as true' is startling, bringing out the anger in the page's comment to her departing master, 'ride on thy way' (l.250), altered from the more tender address of 'my master dear' in the *Findens'* version. The page's pledge to be near to her master as 'parted spirits cleave / To mortals too beloved to leave' (ll.259–60) has a rather ominous note to it as well. Does the outraged wife plan to bless him from above, like the dying Catarina in 'Catarina to Camoens'? Or does she plan to haunt him? Perhaps the thought of her will indeed haunt him when he arrives home and realizes that the page who sacrificed himself for him was also the wife he so fiercely resented – a quite probable narrative extrapolation that is not considered in interpreting the page's sacrifice as unrecognized. He may be 'a knight of gallant deeds' (l.1), but how will he feel when he discovers, as the reader already has, that in this particular 'romaunt', the page and not the knight performs with greatest gallantry?

The ironies permeating 'The Romaunt of the Page' are intensified when Barrett Browning's representation of the lady-page figure is read against its prototypes in ballads like 'Child Waters' and 'A Not-browne Mayd' and in Scott's *Marmion*. The immediate inspiration of 'The Romaunt of the Page' was the illustration Mitford supplied Barrett with, picturing a woman disguised as a page, wearing a very short skirt and hiding behind a tree in the foreground, while a knight rides away from her in the background (*BC* 4:192). But it is clear that the conventions of the old ballads and 'Child Waters' in particular were in Barrett's mind when she composed the poem. Apologizing to Mitford for the length of her 'long barbarous ballad', she quips, 'I ought to blush – as ladyes always do in ballads – "scarlet-red" . . . By the way, the pictured one pretty as she is, has a good deal exaggerated the ballad-receipt for making a ladye page – Do you remember? – "And you must cut your gown of green / An *INCH* above the knee"! She comes within the fi fa fum of the prudes, in consequence' (*BC* 4:33, 38). The 'receipt for making a ladye page' Barrett cites is Child Waters' own, in the ballad of the same title in Percy's *Reliques*.

The frankly physical treatment of the heroine's ordeals in 'Child Waters' supplies an interesting subtext to the declaration of Barrett Browning's knight that, if his lady followed him as his page, he would love her as his 'servitor' but not as his wife. Hardly the conventional model of chivalry, Child Waters instructs his female companion Ellen, swollen with child by him, to cut off her skirt and her hair and run barefoot as his foot-page by his side. In this state, she must run to the north country, swim a swollen river, stable and feed his horse, find him a paramour to spend the night with (while she lies at the foot of the bed), and then feed his horse again. Finally, as she is moaning with labour pains in the stable, Child Waters' mother hears her, the gallant knight arrives to see the babe born, and like Griselda, Ellen is rewarded. Child Waters tells her to be of good cheer: he will marry her. But the ballad ends before the marriage takes place.

'The Romaunt of the Page' clearly echoes 'Child Waters' but also reverses its plot by making marriage the beginning and cause of the page's ordeals, not the end. Moreover, Barrett Browning shifts the focus of her ballad, both in its title and its narrative perspective, to the woman-page rather than the knight. In her ballad, it is the knight who is tested and found wanting, not the woman who is tested and rewarded. A testing of woman's devotion similar to that in 'Child Waters' appears in another Percy ballad Barrett Browning particularly liked, 'The Not-browne Mayd' (*BC* 7:266). The revisionary narrative of 'The Romaunt of the Page' is therefore written against a standard ballad plot of 'plausible' female constancy, as much as against a particular ballad.

Several textual echoes and parallels also connect 'The Romaunt of the Page' to Scott's epic romance *Marmion*, which more directly suggests the perils that attend the woman who proves her love by following her knight as his page.[17] When Constance breaks her religious vows to follow Marmion disguised as a horse-boy in his train, he treats her as such, making her not only his servitor but also his whore. Betraying his promise to marry her, he pursues the wealthy young Clara instead, while Constance is buried alive in the walls of a monastery dungeon for breaking her religious vows. *Marmion* indicates why, in the more prudish 1830s, Barrett was careful to have her heroine marry her knight before following him as her page, and like 'Child Waters', it illumines the narrative innovations in 'The Romaunt of the Page'. Whereas Scott depicts the old story of women suffering from male falsehood, Barrett Browning's ballad shows both sexes suffering from an oppressive ideology.

Barrett Browning's adaptation of elements in

Marmion is also apparent in the long Gothic ballad-romance, 'The Legend of the Brown Rosarie', retitled 'The Lay of the Brown Rosary' in her 1844 *Poems*. Anticipating Charlotte Brontë in *Villette*, Barrett appropriates the figure of the buried nun popularized by Scott's *Marmion* and other works to represent intense psychic conflicts. Whereas Scott's central focus in *Marmion* is male and military, Barrett Browning's, like Brontë's after her, is on the conflicts of female desire with institutionalized repression that speak so powerfully in the interstices of his narrative. The *Doppelgänger* motif linking Onora, the heroine of 'The Lay of the Brown Rosary', with the defiant cursing nun who is buried alive for her sins makes this poem a 'subjective' ballad like 'The Romaunt of Margret', but it is a more daring work, too complex in its play of intertextual allusions to consider fully here. Along with *Marmion*, 'The Lay of the Brown Rosary' also seems to draw on *Faust*, 'Christabel', Gottfried Bürger's 'Lenora', and possibly some of the Percy ballads, fusing elements from these texts in a highly original way with Barrett's own innovations, among them the heroine's dream, which she herself thought of as 'rather original in its manner' (*BC* 6:276). Any analysis of 'The Lay of the Brown Rosary' is further complicated by the extensive revisions made in the poem after its initial publication in the 1840 *Findens'*, including the change of the heroine's name from Lenora (a direct link with Bürger's ballad) to Onora.

'Rhyme of the Duchess May' also reflects Barrett's adaptation of motifs from Bürger's 'Lenora', in this case, as we have seen, creating a connection readily detected by the *Westminster* reviewer Sarah Flower Adams. By echoing Lenora's swift, dark gallop to the bridal bed of the grave with the ghost of her slain lover, Barrett subtly foreshadows the fate of the orphan Duchess May and her newly wed husband Sir Guy of Linteged as they flee to his castle, evading her guardian, the Earl of Leigh and the cousin whose hand in marriage she spurns: 'Fast and fain the bridal train along the night-storm rod [sic] amain' (l.89). Reminiscent of 'Lenora' too, 'The Duchess May' depicts what one reviewer aptly described as a 'dark bridal' concluding with a 'double death-ride'.[18] Facing certain defeat after a fourteen-day siege by the Leighs in which his castle has 'seethed in blood' (l.43), the anguished Sir Guy seeks to save the lives of his loyal men by riding from his castle tower to a sacrificial death. Against his will, he is accompanied by his young bride, who leaps into the saddle with him at the last minute. Reviewers were especially taken by this spectacular and novel climax, which Mermin astutely interprets as 'in effect a bold, bizarre sexual consummation' (93) – even if it does occur three months after the Duchess' actual marriage to Sir Guy.

'Rhyme of the Duchess May' adapts situations and scenes from the old Scottish ballad 'Edom o'Gordon' as well as Bürger's 'Lenora', although its sacrificial death leap was probably suggested by Benjamin Haydon's painting, 'Curtius Leaping Into the Gulf' (*BC* 6:208–9). The hero of 'Edom o'Gordon' is not the brutal border-raider referred to in the title, but the fiercely loyal wife of a Scottish lord who takes a stand on the castle walls and valiantly resists Gordon and his men in her husband's absence. The traces of 'Edom o'Gordon' in 'Rhyme of the Duchess May' thus once again reveal Barrett Browning's interest in the 'warrior women' heroines of the 'old burning ballads'. As in the case of 'The Romaunt of the Page', however, she once again significantly revises the ballad plot she most conspicuously echoes in 'Rhyme of the Duchess May'. Most notably, she rejects the futile and passive

sacrifice that occurs in 'Edom o'Gordon' when the
Scottish lord's daughter is lowered over the walls in a
sheet and spitted on Gordon's spear. Instead, she
depicts a more active and heroic sacrificial leap on the
part of the Duchess May, whom she made more
forceful and wilful in revising the manuscript draft of
the poem. Other significant revisions in the draft
intensify and complicate the psychological and narrative conflict between the Duchess May and Sir Guy in
ways that make Sir Guy a prototype of Romney in
Aurora Leigh.

Deborah Byrd suggests that Victorian women poets
like Barrett Browning turned to the Middle Ages
because it was envisioned 'as a time in which at least
some women had control over their property and
destiny and the courage to venture into the "male"
arenas of war and politics' (33). There is much truth
in this. The women Barrett Browning encountered in
the Percy ballads and even in Scott's romances were
not yet confined by what Mary Poovey identifies as
the cult of the 'proper lady'.[19] In fact, in its frankly
physical depiction of strong, heroic, passionate
heroines, the traditional ballad, that 'Cinderella'
among the Muses, very often was not the bashful
maiden Hales and Furnivall quaintly imagined.

Nevertheless, Barrett Browning was no celebrator
of the often brutal and violent gender and human
relations that prevailed in the Middle Ages when a
'black chief' was 'half knight, half sheep-lifter' – like
Edom o'Gordon and his kind – and a 'beauteous
dame' was 'half chattel and half queen' (*Aurora Leigh*
5:195–6). In medieval ballads like 'The Romaunt of
the Page', and 'Rhyme of the Duchess May', she
dramatizes the crudely overt power structures of the
society that also produced the chivalric idealization of
women. Thus the younger Lord Leigh threatens to

take the Duchess May in marriage over the 'altar' of her husband's corpse, seizing her hand and the gold it brings just as he seizes the sword in order to prevail.

Barrett Browning's ballads after 1844 represent contemporary rather than medieval scenes. Her often noted progression from medieval to modern subjects is manifested not only in 'Lady Geraldine's Courtship', but also in the unfinished ballad, 'The Princess Marie' in the 'Sonnets Notebook' in the Armstrong Browning Library. 'The Princess Marie' focuses on the daughter of King Louis Philippe of France. Phillip Sharp, who supplies a helpful account of this ballad's historical context, along with a rather unreliable transcription of the manuscript, describes 'The Princess Marie' as a 'domestic poem about a head of state' (169). But what really seems to have aroused Barrett Browning's interest in the Princess Marie was not her relation to Louis Philippe, but her skill in sculpture and the human cost of her devotion to her art. 'The Princess Marie' is thus not only a ballad in which Barrett turns to contemporary subjects, but also one anticipating her focus on the woman-artist in *Aurora Leigh*.

Although they move farther away from their proto-types in the old English and Scottish ballads and the narrative verse of the Romantic revival, most of Barrett Browning's later ballads continue to exhibit the distinguishing features I have dwelt upon in this chapter: the ironic manipulation of traditional ballad plots and motifs (often through narrative reversals or doublings); the focus on female subjectivity and on the conflicts created by female desire; and the exploration of connections between the 'female plots' shaping women's lives and the gender plots of encompassing ideologies. The female perspective, complicated by lingering ironies, is apparent in the deceptively simple 'Amy's Cruelty', for instance, where Barrett Browning explores female as well as male possessiveness in love. The manipulation of traditional ballad conventions is perhaps most evident in the often praised 'Lord Walter's Wife'. Like 'The Not-browne Mayd', 'Lord Walter's Wife' contains elements of the traditional debate or flyting match concerning female constancy. Yet typically, Barrett Browning subverts conventional expectations by dramatizing the contradictions and sexual double standard in male perceptions of women and by showing a man tested and found wanting, not the woman he flirts with and condemns.

In their representation of strong, transgressive women and their paradoxical combination of the medieval and the modern, Barrett Browning's ballads contributed to the nineteenth-century ballad tradition in ways that remain largely unexplored today. Several Victorian critics noted the impact of her medieval ballads on Pre-Raphaelite poets like D. G. Rossetti. In 1900, Charlotte Porter and Helen Clarke similarly observed that 'Rossetti and others of the pre-Raphaelite brotherhood' had followed Barrett Browning in writing 'modern ballads', 'archaic in diction and suggestion' yet striking 'new themes'. 'But her ballads were first', Porter and Clarke remind us. 'They are miracles of sympathetic reproduction of an old *genre* in new substance' (*CW* 2:xiii). Hayter suggests one reason why the influence of Barrett Browning on the Pre-Raphaelites was 'forgotten' in noting how critics after 1900 repeatedly apologized for or dismissed the many traces of Mrs Browning in the works of D. G. Rossetti and William Morris (231–2).

As long as this subtle work of cultural 'forgetting' remains unanalysed and unresisted, and as long as Barrett Browning's ballads continue to be excluded from standard anthologies and surveys of Victorian poetry, there will be a missing link in the history of the ballad revival – that movement that continues to shape the work of many poets and singers in our own century. Bob Dylan, whose 'Desolation Row' is now studied alongside T. S. Eliot's 'The Waste Land', seems very unlike Elizabeth Barrett Browning. Yet Dylan and his many followers seem drawn to the ballad form for some of the same reasons she was. Like Barrett Browning, Dylan recognizes the power of ballad stories with the people. Like her, he has often written in the tradition of the politicized broadside ballad. Like her, he exploits ironic twists in plotting ('twists of fate') as sites for exploring psychological and ideological conflict. And like Barrett Browning, Dylan – as 'Desolation Row' evinces – transforms the ballad form into a cultural palimpsest by intensifying its intertextuality. All of these features of Barrett Browning's balladry helped to prepare her for the writing of *Aurora Leigh*.

4 Juno's Cream: *Aurora Leigh* and Victorian Sage Discourse

'A dropped star / Makes bitter waters, says a Book I've read' (5: 917–18), Aurora Leigh comments midway through the text in which she writes her identity as both woman and poet. The 'Book' Aurora alludes to in this pivotal passage is Revelation, the Biblical book most frequently invoked in *Aurora Leigh* as in Emily Dickinson's poetry and H.D.'s *Trilogy*. The 'dropped star' is the 'great star from heaven' called Wormwood that flames down 'burning as it were a lamp' to embitter a third part of the earth's waters in the final Judgment (Revelation 8). In Aurora's book, however, this ominous star primarily signifies not God's wrath, but the destructive power of the woman artist who abandons her vocation for the material security of marriage.

The dropped star metaphor is prompted by a marriage proposal received by Aurora seven years after she emphatically rejects her cousin Romney Leigh's proposal that she share his philanthropic work and his fortune. Unlike Romney's, this second proposal is a ' "stereotyped" ' one brought to Aurora by her friend Lord Howe from Eglinton of Eglinton: a man ' "[k]nown chiefly for the house upon his back" ' (5:866) who is ' "so little modest" ' as to want ' "a star upon his stage" ' (5:915–16). It is ' "[t]he same he wrote to, – anybody's name, / Anne Blythe the actress

when she died so true" ', to ' "Pauline the dancer" '
after her ' "great *pas*" ', and to ' "Baldinacci, when her
F in alt / Had touched the silver tops of heaven itself" '
(5:899–906). Barrett Browning uses Eglinton's proposal to connect Aurora to her other sisters in art, in
keeping with her intent to present a representative
'artist woman' in her novel-epic (*LEBB* 2:112). But
the 'dropped star' of Revelation also traces a path
linking Barrett Browning's heroine to similar 'artist
women' in Charlotte Brontë's works before *Aurora
Leigh* and George Eliot's after. Unlike the 'Alcharisi',
the great opera singer in *Daniel Deronda* who marries
suddenly when she believes she is losing her voice only
to mourn her decision in embittered fallen splendour,
Aurora does not make the mistake of accepting
Eglinton's proposition – despite Lord Howe's warning
that ' "it is hard to stand for art" ' without ' "some
golden tripod" ': ' "To be plain, dear friend, / You're
poor" ' (5:939–49). Yet neither does she burn herself
out in solitary self-consuming absorption in her art
like the actress Vashti in *Villette*, whom Brontë
figuratively represents in terms of the same flaming
star in Revelation.

Instead, Aurora sells her English father's books,
along with the 'long poem' (5:1213) that is the most
mature fruit of her seven-year apprenticeship in a
London third-floor flat, to finance her relocation to her
motherland of Italy – the Italy that, as Sandra Gilbert
suggests, was both a nurturing *matria* and the 'home of
art' to a succession of nineteenth- and twentieth-
century women writers (196). 'And now I come, my
Italy, / My own hills!' '[D]o you feel tonight / The
urgency and yearning of my soul', Aurora asks, 'As
sleeping mothers feel the sucking babe / And smile?'
(5:1266–71). On the way to Italy, she rediscovers
Marian, the working-class woman whom Romney

unsuccessfully sought to marry for 'social ends' after proposing to Aurora for 'charitable ends' (5:1091–4). Betrayed, sold to a French brothel, raped, and now the mother of a 'sucking babe', Marian, finally embraced by Aurora as a 'sister', helps her to discover the 'sleeping mother', the common woman, and, more fully than before, the poet in herself.[1] When Marian finally proposes that Aurora and Romney marry, and Aurora finally declares her love to Romney, not once but three times over (9:607–13, 713–14), all signs suggest that the artist will not become a dropped star buried in the bitter waters of a wife. On the contrary, as Romney suggests, Aurora will be a radiant ' "morning-star" ' (9:908) speaking her revelation to the world. Fittingly, then, the book she writes for her 'better self' (1:4) takes her own name: the name which she first calls herself by in the moment of vocation generated by her girlhood encounter with 'the poets' (1: 854–5), and which she does not surrender even in finally marrying Romney Leigh.

Since Ellen Moers' recovery of *Aurora Leigh* in 1976, Barrett Browning's 'poetic art-novel', as she herself described it (*LEBB* 2:228), has most often been approached as a portrait of the woman writer closely paralleling Barrett Browning's own development. It has been described as a 'verse-novel on the growth of a poet' (Rosenblum, 1983, 321); the first 'properly female *Kunstlerroman*' in 'English letters' (Freiwald 414); a 'bildungsroman' depicting Barrett Browning's struggle to overcome the 'antifeminine biases' she had internalized as a woman poet (Gelpi 36); and a '*Kunstlerroman*' recording her 'own personal and artistic struggle for identity' and the 'insurrection-resurrection' of her marriage to Browning and journey to Italy (Gilbert 194–200). Even those who have emphasized the generic hybridization of *Aurora Leigh* still treat it

primarily as a portrait of the woman writer.[2] Rachael
DuPlessis' influential distinction between 'the love
plot and the *Bildungs* plot' in *Aurora Leigh*, like Alison
Case's similar distinction, does not mark a departure
from the *Kunstlerroman* approach so much as an
elaboration of it, designed to accommodate the conflict
between love and art, vocation and marriage, that
many have made a focus for discussion.[3] In encapsul-
ating this conflict, the 'dropped star' metaphor accords
with prevailing interpretations of *Aurora Leigh*. At the
same time, however, in foregrounding the pervasive-
ness of Barrett Browning's allusions to Revelation,
it points to another way of conceptualizing her
greatest work and the cultural work it carried out in its
age.

We leave out less in Barrett Browning's representation of the Hero as a Woman of Letters if we approach
the teeming, heterogeneous text of *Aurora Leigh* not
simply as a *Kunstlerroman*, but rather as a portrait of
the artist embedded within one of the Victorian
period's most notable works of sage discourse: in
short, as a work offering nothing less than a revelation.
Or more accurately, given the new light cast on the
composition of *Aurora Leigh* by Margaret Reynolds in
her annotated edition, it might be described as a
Kunstlerroman generating the sage discourse that
surrounds and completes it. For Barrett Browning's
purpose, according to an unpublished letter cited by
Reynolds (*AL* 85), was to show how 'in life, morals, or
art', the movement is always '*from inner to outer*'. True
to this principle, Barrett Browning shows how Aurora's
sage discourse grows out of her development as a
'prophet-poet' to her age.

Recent criticism has started to explore the importance of women writers such as Harriet Martineau,
Charlotte Brontë, and Christina Rossetti in the

tradition of Victorian sage writing previously constructed as almost entirely male: a tradition composed
of Carlyle, Mill, Ruskin, Newman, Disraeli, Arnold,
and a George Eliot uncomplicated by any considera-
tions of gender. Yet Barrett Browning has had a
surprisingly low profile in this critical recovery to
date. Most notably, the writers in *Victorian Sages and
Cultural Discourse: Renegotiating Gender and Power* make
only passing mention of *Aurora Leigh* (2–5, 116). This
neglect is surprising because *Aurora Leigh* is vitally
concerned with the nexus of gender and power, and it
exhibits in abundance the characteristic features of
sage writing identified not only in *Victorian Sages* but
also in earlier studies by George Landow and John
Holloway.[4]

Most obviously, *Aurora Leigh* enters the tradition of
Victorian sage writing through its representation of a
prophetic speaker, its pronounced Biblical allusions
and typological patterning, its polemical sermonizing
on the times, its argumentative intertextuality, its
exploitation of metaphor and definition as strategies of
persuasion, its quest for a sustaining 'Life Philosophy',
and its vision of a new social and spiritual order. As I
hope to show, however, Barrett Browning also transforms the sage tradition through her gynocentric
adaptation of its characteristic strategies, and her
subversion of the authoritative stance so strenuously
asserted by Victorian prophets like Carlyle. In keeping with her belief that the subjective is 'the nearest
approach to a genuinely objective view' (*AL* 28), she
employs a narrative perspective in *Aurora Leigh* that
has strong affinities both with the dramatic monologues
she experimented with throughout the 1840s and with
the experimental first-person form of novels like
Charlotte Brontë's *Villette*.

Nevertheless, despite this novelistic perspective,

Aurora Leigh was clearly read by many mid-Victorians as a work of sage discourse. Indeed, up to the end of the century it was viewed less as an epic of the literary woman than as a modern epic that philosophically addressed some of the most urgent issues of the age. Since no enumeration of textual properties can adequately convey the most vital dimensions of any dynamically polemical work of sage discourse, this chapter draws on contemporary reader response in order to reconstruct the cultural work that *Aurora Leigh* carried out in the mid and late Victorian periods. In effect, then, my analysis attempts to reverse the movement from 'inner' to 'outer' reflected in the genesis, form and philosophy of *Aurora Leigh* itself. The Victorian reception of Aurora's book helps to illumine the ideological transformations and conflicts it both manifests and addresses as sage discourse; and a better understanding of the political, philosophical, and aesthetic stakes involved in these may promote a fuller understanding of Barrett Browning's motives and methods in the book she described in the Dedication as 'the most mature' of her works, and the one embodying her 'highest convictions upon Life and Art'.

Accounts of the Victorian reception of *Aurora Leigh* are often distorted by two complementary fallacies. One – that the poem's appearance was marked by a 'comedy of critical extravagance' – has been ably discredited by Tricia Lootens (211–12). The other – that it was actually greeted by an 'avalanche of negative criticism' in the serious reviews – is equally inaccurate (David, *Intellectual Women*, 114). As Mermin's overview suggests (222–4), critical responses to Barrett Browning's most audacious work were as diverse as the conflicting ideological agendas readers brought to it.

Ideological concerns are particularly apparent in the response to *Aurora Leigh* because many Victorian readers clearly approached it less as a *Kunstlerroman* than as a work of sage discourse as polemical and philosophical as Carlyle's *Past and Present* or Arnold's *Culture and Anarchy*. This is the case in harsh critiques of *Aurora Leigh* like John Nichol's, as well in laudatory assessments like George Eliot's, both published in the *Westminster Review*. Nichol explicitly challenges Ruskin's praise of *Aurora Leigh* in *The Elements of Drawing* as 'the greatest poem of the century'. But the very force and energy with which he mounts an attack on the coarseness of the work, its mixture of poetry and prose, its disregard for classical unities, the repelling and unfeminine 'self-consciousness' of its heroine, and, above all, Barrett Browning's political and philosophical views, indicates how much *Aurora Leigh* dialectically engages some of the most controversial political, social, aesthetic and philosophical issues of the time. Moreover, in pointing to the parallel between *Aurora Leigh* and Ruskin's 'mistake of exaggerating the effect of Art', while expressing a comparative 'contempt of material wants and depreciation of political struggles', Nichol directly links Barrett Browning to one eminent Victorian sage. In explicitly challenging Ruskin, Nichol was also implicitly challenging Eliot, whose earlier, briefer review of *Aurora Leigh* in the *Westminster* had asserted that no poem of the day 'embraces so wide a range of thought and emotion'. By emphasizing the thought of *Aurora Leigh*, Eliot implies a view that it embodies the wisdom of the sage: its 'poetical *body*' is 'everywhere informed by *soul*', she observed.[5] But her anonymous review was conveniently forgotten by literary history (Lootens 226), while Nichol's was frequently cited. Nevertheless, like Ruskin's, Eliot's response to

Aurora Leigh was by no means atypical in its time.
Ruskin's description of Barrett Browning's novel-epic
as the 'perfect poetical expression of the Age' in a
letter to Browning coincides with Charles Hamilton
Aidé's similar view of *Aurora Leigh* in a private letter as
'the Poem of the Age'. In public, Aidé wrote that
' "Aurora Leigh" has been called "a modern epic" and
a "a three-volumed novel" '; it is 'an epic, inasmuch as
it treats of the passionate struggles, and the half-
conquest, half-failure, of two heroic natures in their
life-battle'; and a novel in that 'the fable is of our own
time'. But he emphasized the epic and philosophic
elements embodied in the representation of Romney
and Aurora, 'one ministrant to the physical, the other
to the spiritual wants of their fellowmen, each
acknowledging the failure of their self-reliant
schemes'.[6]

The *British Quarterly Review* similarly described
Aurora Leigh as a work embodying 'the result of much
reflection on some of the most anxious issues of our
time', notable for its 'sound philosophy' and the many
'wise and large-minded thoughts, vigorously expressed
in felicitous and glowing language'. Morever, the
reviewer speaks of Barrett Browning in terms clearly
marking her as a sage:

> Our generation scarcely numbers more than one or
> two among its master minds from whom we could
> have looked for a production at all to rival this in
> comprehensiveness – a poem with so much genuine
> depth and so free from obscurity. The results of
> abstract thinking are here, and yet there is no heavy
> philosophising or set purpose. A warm human life
> meets us everywhere. There are no broad levels of
> prosaic reflection, such as sometimes test the
> patience even of true Wordsworthians. Men and

women are introduced who learn philosophy by
actual life.[7]

Such views are not simply the product of an initial
rash of enthusiasm greeting *Aurora Leigh*. They persist
up to the end of the nineteenth century. Edmund
Clarence Stedman described *Aurora Leigh* as a 'versatile,
kaleidoscopic presentment of modern life and issues',
noting how 'Mrs. Browning, with finer dramatic
instinct' than Tennyson, 'entered into the spirit of
each experiment' in the 'social and intellectual phases'
of the era (141); while Lewis E. Gates observed of
Aurora Leigh that it 'is really an interpretation and
criticism of the entire age in which it was written'. For
the French critic Joseph Texte in 1898, *Aurora Leigh*
was still a work of intense relevance to 'contemporary
idealism' – indeed 'the poem of a century', written by
the most philosophical poet of the age.[8]

It is not hard to see why mid-Victorians saw *Aurora
Leigh* as a 'modern epic' philosophically addressing
contemporary concerns. Topical references jostle on
every page, reflecting Barrett Browning's aim of
taking her material 'from the times, "hot and hot" '
(*AL* 85). Among much else, we encounter references to
the 'Tracts' for and '*against*' the times (1:394),
Parliamentary committees (3:612), the educational
catechism of the middle-class girl of the period
(1:392–446), crystal balls and spirits (6:169), the
exploration of the Nile (6:166), the Irish potato famine
and the political fortunes of Guizot and Louis Napoleon
in France (4:398–406), the controversy over the
authorship of the Homeric works (5:1246–57), and
contemporary scientific controversies like that
surrounding the 'od-force' of the German scientist
Reichenbach – a mesmeric force that, oddly enough,
supposedly flamed from the fingertips of healthy men,

whereas female fingers emitted only a feeble light (*AL* 654). *Aurora Leigh* is also notable for its modern cityscapes of London, Paris and Florence, which Barrett Browning paints with swift strokes praised by more than one of her contemporaries for their Turneresque quality. The London fog is described with Dickensian metaphoric gusto in Book 3, while skeletal teeth grin at Aurora and the reader from dentists' signs on the streetcorners of Paris in Book 6. In an often cited passage (7:395–452), the railway journey from Paris to Marseilles is conveyed as vividly as Dickens conveys the train that crushes Carker in *Dombey and Son*. Fleeing southward on 'the roar of steam', Aurora watches as the landscape of France falls away behind and the train sweeps into the tunnels under the Alps, its 'fierce denouncing whistle wailing on / And dying off smothered in the shuddering dark'.

At a deeper level, however, the intense modernity of *Aurora Leigh* for mid-Victorians sprang less from its topical allusions and contemporary scenes than from the social issues it engaged. 'It sings of our actual life, embodying the schemes and struggles, the opinions and social contrasts of our day', as one reviewer put it.[9] Reflecting the growing activism of mid-Victorian feminist reformers, Barrett Browning confronts the pressing questions associated with women's work, women's education, women's property rights, battered wives and systemic prostitution in their complex interactions with 'the social question' (*AL* 85). The 'social question' includes the gulf between social classes, the threat of class warfare, the reforms it precipitated, and French and English political developments between 1846 and 1853. Allusions to French politics in *Aurora Leigh* make it clear that Romney's Fourieristic schemes reach a peak in the period when

Chartist and socialist agitation culminated and collapsed in England and America. In France, where socialist reform was less politically marginalized, the early 1850s brought a similar setback with the crowning of Louis Napoleon as Emperor. These developments spawned a host of works addressing the 'condition of England': among them, the novels of Benjamin Disraeli, Elizabeth Gaskell and Charles Kingsley, as well as Carlyle's *Latter Day Pamphlets* and Tennyson's *Maud*.

Although *Aurora Leigh* is seldom included in discussions of this 'condition of England' discourse, its representation of the 'social question' reflects many of the same concerns. Influenced in part by Kingsley, Barrett Browning further portrays the 'social question' in conflict with what might be termed the 'art question' in the prolonged, complex debate between Romney and Aurora, who represent what she described as 'the practical and the ideal' lives (*AL* 85). This debate is inflected at every turn by the persistent 'woman question', which expands into a systematic exploration of gender ideologies.

Although these dimensions of *Aurora Leigh* interpenetrate each other, Barrett Browning's representation of the 'woman question' generated the most innovative and iconoclastic elements in her sage discourse and also provoked the strongest response among her contemporaries. Peter Bayne aptly described *Aurora Leigh* as a 'modern epic' singing '[n]ot of arms and the man, but social problems and the woman' (107). But Barrett Browning's singing had a discordant sound to many of her male reviewers. The greatest source of controversy was not, as she had feared, her depiction of Marian's rape and illegitimate motherhood. The feminist views of her heroine were the features that led the Roman Catholic *Tablet* to condemn 'brazen-faced Aurora', and the *Dublin University Magazine* to blame Mrs Browning for assuming 'the gait and garb of a man' and writing a book that should be 'almost a closed volume for her own sex'; while the *Spectator* liked the book best when 'Aurora forgets she is a poetess, or, still better, when she herself is forgotten' (Lootens 212–14; 231–2).

Aurora is not easily forgotten, however. Indeed, Barrett Browning most overtly enters the tradition of Victorian sage discourse through representing a woman who unabashedly aspires to become a 'prophet-poet' (5:355). Aurora is repeatedly affiliated with Biblical, classical, and even Muslim prophets and figures of wisdom, at times in a spirit of parody, at times in complete seriousness. The opening line of Book 1 echoes Ecclesiastes the preacher, but allusions to various Biblical figures are even more pervasive in the opening of Book 3, originally the introduction to the entire work (*AL* 671–5). In earnest emulation, Aurora compares her struggle to realize her ideals in the world to the martyrdom of Simon Peter and the other apostles after the zealous 'first girding of the loins' in youth. Soon after, with one of those mercurial shifts to self-mocking irony that characterize her narrative, she notes that one of her fans, Kate Ward, sees her as Elijah – in hopes of becoming ' "Elisha to [her]" ' (3:54). She also playfully compares the opening of letters from her critics and readers to the opening of the seven seals in Revelation 5: 'A ninth seal; / The apocalypse is drawing to a close' (3:98–9). Aurora does not directly set herself up as Elijah or John of Patmos, but subsequent allusions link her to the 'prophet-poets', including Mahomet (5:354); to the Pallas of the Vatican – a classical and, significantly, a female figure of wisdom (5:799); to Dante with his 'prophet-breath' (7:936); and to Aaron in his priestly robes (7:1303; 9:252). Aaron might seem atypical in this company, but when Aurora actually speaks as Aaron does in the Ninth book, she compares herself to the Levite at the moment when he divests himself of his priestly robes to die – to an Aaron, in other words, who is less priest than prophet.

The focus on Aurora as a prophetic rather than a priestly figure points to the importance of Romantic paradigms both in Barrett Browning's mature works and in Victorian sage writing generally. Janet Larson observes that Victorian sage discourse, like Romantic poetry, reflects the historical displacement of the 'longstanding Protestant view of the prophet as the obedient interpreter of Mosaic law' by a new 'prophetic type, independent and creative' (Morgan, *Victorian Sages*, 67–8). *Aurora Leigh* incorporates Romantic paradigms not only in its representation of poets as prophets – 'the only truth-tellers now left to God' (1:859) – but also in its defence of individualism (Reynolds *AL* 16), its embodiment of the Coleridgean organic form it defends (5:223–9), its Wordsworthian and Carlylean metaphysics of Natural Supernaturalism (7:821), and its free-wheeling social satire, which blends Byronic wit and ironic self-reflexiveness with Carlylean moral purpose.

The Romantic transformation of the priestly interpreter into the independent prophet opens the way for Barrett Browning's iconoclastic project of depicting a female sage whose prophetic aspirations are both undisguised and explicitly challenged on the grounds of her sex. ' "[You] measure to yourself a prophet's place / To teach the living. None of all these things, / Can women understand" ' (2:181–3), Romney roundly asserts to the twenty-year-old Aurora on her youthful ' "mountain-peaks of hope" ', where she stands ' "All glittering with the dawn-dew, all erect / And famished for the noon" ' of poetic greatness (2:534–6). Romney obviously hadn't read that other visionary and searing social critic William Blake, who said 'To generalize is to be an idiot', because his chief ground for scorning Aurora's aspirations is the generalization that women can ' "generalise / Oh, nothing, — not even grief!" ' (2:183–4). Like Carlyle, who poetically denounced poetry and spoke at great length in defence of silence, Romney also stresses the virtues of labour and action over poetry and song. Tormented by the ' "social spasm / And crisis of the ages" ' (2:273–4), the high-minded Romney dedicates himself to the social and political reform the desperate condition of England calls for. ' "Who has time" ', he asks Aurora impatiently,

> 'to sit upon a bank
> And hear the cymbal tinkle in white hands?
> When Egypt's slain, I say, let Miriam sing!
> Before – where's Moses?' (2:168–72)

To which Aurora scornfully ripostes, ' "Ah, exactly that, / Where's Moses? – is a Moses to be found?" '

Without exactly claiming to be *the* Moses who will deliver England out of the 'Egypt' of social injustice into the promised land of Fourieristic socialism, Romney nevertheless sets himself up as a type of Moses, meanwhile casting Aurora as Miriam, the female adjunct who will sing his victories. In his typological role casting, he forgets, as Aurora and Barrett Browning do not, that Miriam is identified as 'the prophetess' as well as 'the sister of Aaron' in Exodus 25:20. Romney also proves to be a poor prophet in asserting of '[m]ere women, personal and passionate', that ' "We get no Christ from you, – and verily / We shall not get a poet" ' (2:221–5). For, after much aspiration, struggle, and self-doubt, Aurora becomes a veritable 'prophet-poet' – even in Romney's eyes – singing the revelation of a new social order at his urging: ' "Now press the clarion on thy woman's lip / . . . And blow all class-walls level as Jericho's" ' (9:929–33). In Barrett Browning's recasting of the Exodus story, Miriam's singing does not follow and celebrate the triumph of Moses. Quite the reverse, it is Miriam's prophetic singing that creates the possibility of the new spiritual and social order that Moses envisions.

The typological structuring evident in the allusions linking Romney to Moses, Aurora to Miriam, and the 'condition of England' to the state of the Israelites in Egypt is another characteristic of *Aurora Leigh* identifying it with the Victorian sage tradition. This structuring is further manifested in the complex narrative palindrome of the plot analysed by Cooper (153–4) and Reynolds (*AL* 32, 50), in which repetition creates the opportunity for revision and reinterpretation, much as New Testament figures and events echo and reveal the significance of Old Testament types. Most notably, the debate in Book 2 between Romney and Aurora over the relative merits of art and social action is replayed in Book 8, where the allusions to Miriam and Moses recur (8:334, 1144). In between, we hear Marian's first and second stories of sexual victimization, terrified flight, and redemption: the first, an incomplete redemption to be passively achieved through Romney, the second a more complete redemption that she achieves through her own evolving strength.

The extended debates between Romney and Aurora provide ample opportunity for the sermonizing on the 'signs of the times' and the call for social and spiritual change that the sage typically engages in before

presenting his vision of a redeemed society, according
to the paradigm of sage writing proposed by Landow
(Morgan, *Victorian Sages*, 34). In *Aurora Leigh*, however,
the characteristic activities of the sage are initially
split between Romney and Aurora. He is the bleak
prophet warning of catastophe, while she sings the
vision of a new world. In her succinct terms, 'he
marked judgment, I, redemption-day' (4:428). Yet
they are not the only sages in this text, we gradually
realize. Both Aurora and Romney have much to learn
from the graphically conveyed and particularized
suffering of Marian, and from the wisdom she
acquires. Through Marian's means, the split focus on
judgment and redemption fuses in the conclusion with
its revisionary interpretation of Revelation, just as
Romney and Aurora fuse in a mystical Swedenborgian
vision of ' "the love of wedded souls" ' (9:882). Barrett
Browning's representation of a raped, fallen woman as
a source of wisdom indicates how radically she
subverts the phallocentric discourse of the prophetic
and wisdom traditions. For Marian is in effect the
priest who brings Aurora and Romney together,
'permitting, not through law, but from a feminine
and specifically outcast position, Aurora's desire and
marriage' (Reynolds *AL* 46).

The tendency to approach *Aurora Leigh* as a
Kunstlerroman has led to a focus chiefly on Aurora's
development as a woman and artist. But Barrett
Browning actually presents three interconnected
spiritual autobiographies – Aurora's, Romney's, and
Marian's – which together embody the quest for a
sustaining 'Life-Philosophy' that Holloway finds at
the heart of Victorian sage writing. Such a Philosophy
cannot be simply propounded. As the *British Quarterly
Review* puts it, Barrett Browning depicts 'men and
women . . . who learn philosophy by actual life'. The

wisdom they acquire must be learned and conveyed through individual experience because it involves what Holloway describes as a transformation in perception, 'seeing new things in old ways'.[10]

In *Aurora Leigh*, the search for a Life-Philosophy centres on the question of how best to be of use in the world. ' "Of use! . . . there's the point / We sweep about for ever in argument" ' (4:1169–70), Aurora says as she meets with Romney approximately seven years after his marriage proposal, when they resume their protracted debate between the relative merits of social activism and art. The conflict that divides them is still very much with us. Should one write, paint, study? Or should one march, open a home for battered women, work in the inner city or the tellingly named 'Third World'? At a 1977 conference, the Marxist-Feminist Literature Collective observed of the conflict between the ideological and the practical in *Aurora Leigh*, 'On this Moebius strip we too as Marxist-feminist critics and writers inscribe ourselves' (201). ' "Make bread or verses, (it just came to that)" ', as Vincent Carrington the painter, the mutual friend of Aurora and Romney, aptly says of their conflict (7:636).

That the disjunction between bread and verses is a false one is something *Aurora Leigh* in its entirety demonstrates. In the eucharistic imagery that expresses 'the double action of the metaphysical intention' in *Aurora Leigh* (*LEBB* 2:243), 'verses' are metamorphosed into 'bread', just as the bread of daily existence is transformed into poetry. As Aurora's books become stronger in art, taking in more of others' actual lives and embodying ' "something separate" ' from herself (8:606), they begin to live and move within Romney. Ten years after Romney dismissed Aurora's 'verses' because her 'sex is weak for art'

(2:372), and she rejected his marriage proposal because he asked not for a wife but for a 'helpmate' in his social programmes (2:402), he testifies of her 'long poem' (5:1213), ' "My daily bread tastes of it, – and my wine" ' (8:267).

Again, however, it is Marian who most reveals some of the essential similarities between Aurora the poet and Romney the social activist in revealing how the projects of both are excessively abstract and intellectual. It is too often overlooked that Romney is chiefly criticized in *Aurora Leigh* not because he is a pragmatic reformer of class inequities, but because he is an ideologue, wedded as Fourier was to rigid blueprints of reform. ' "You have a wife already whom you love, / Your social theory" ' (2:409–10), Aurora sarcastically observes to Romney, meanwhile not recognizing how much she herself is wedded to poetic theories. In part through Marian, Aurora and Romney eventually learn that neither the ideal nor the practical can suffice in itself. Marian's rape and victimization 'shows what can and will occur to a woman when the body is treated purely as body, divorced from spirit. . . . and both Aurora and Romney are guilty of that separation', Joyce Zonana rightly observes (256). At the same time, the opposition Zonana posits between Romney's materialistic focus on the body and Aurora's 'disembodied' pursuit of poetic ideals is too schematic to convey the paradoxes and ironic contradictions Barrett Browning explores in suggesting how alike these two highminded, idealistic cousins are. '[T]he practical & real (so called) is but the external evolution of the ideal & spiritual', Barrett Browning said of her chief argument in *Aurora Leigh* (*AL* 85). Aurora makes a similar assertion as a naïve young poet, but she as much as Romney needs to appreciate the application of this truth to her mission in life.

If Barrett Browning's condensed statement of her argument in *Aurora Leigh* seems disappointingly trite, we should remember that, put simply, the summarized teaching of any sage never seems particularly original or impressive. In sage discourse, nothing can take the place of the reader's experience of the 'life and meaning' in the sage's actual creative use of argument, figure, and narrative.[11] Philosophical and moral truth are grounded in the process of discovery and transformation which individual characters undergo, as it is brought to life in the minds of individual readers. In George Eliot's words, 'we learn *words* by rote, but not their meanings; *that* must be paid for with our life-blood, and printed in the subtler fibres of our nerves'.[12] Thus Marian, as Barrett Browning observed, 'had to be dragged through the uttermost debasement of circumstances to arrive at the sentiment of personal dignity' (*LEBB* 2:242). Only then does she acquire the strength, like Alice Walker's Celie in *The Color Purple*, to claim and take pride in her essential humanity and individuality by asserting, ' "a woman, poor or rich / Despised or honoured is a human soul" ' (9:328–9). Thus Romney's attempts to establish a Fourierite phalanstery collapse in disarray before he recognizes that he was too ' "absolute in dogma" ' (8:370) to acknowledge the importance of the individual soul or to anticipate the actual social conditions that sabotage his ' "abstract willing" ' (8:800). Thus Aurora, at the zenith of her artistic success, feels her self dissolving at the core 'like some passive broken lump of salt' dropped in 'a bowl of oenomel' (7:1308–9) because her abstract poetic idealism is not enough to sustain the 'poor, passionate, helpless blood' of the body's need she confesses to on the pavement of a Church in Florence (7:1271).

Like other Victorian sages, Barrett Browning

embodies the process of discovering sustaining life philosophies in a text that is dynamic, heterogeneous and insistently intertextual – a text constantly 'dialogized' by the interplay of conflicting social voices, and engaged in a 'dialectical process' of persuasion and rebuttal (Morgan, *Victorian Sages*, 2–3). Critics have frequently emphasized the intense inter-textuality that led Cora Kaplan to compare *Aurora Leigh* to a 'collage' in the groundbreaking 'Introduction' to her 1978 Women's Press edition (14). Kaplan's remains the single most dynamic and comprehensive analysis of the 'overlapping sequence of dialogues with other texts, other writers' in *Aurora Leigh* (16), although others have joined her in exploring Barrett Browning's intertextual debates with Wordsworth's *Prelude*, Tennyson's *The Princess*, Carlyle's 'hero-worship', Clough's *The Bothie of Tober-na-Vuolich* and Kingsley's *Alton Locke*.[13] As I note below, Barrett Browning's letters and the response of reviewers also point to her strategic revisioning or questioning of Thomas DeQuincey's and Coventry Patmore's views on women, Richard Hengist Horne's 'penny epic' *Orion*, Dickens' *David Copperfield*, Richardson's *Clarissa*, Bryon's *Don Juan* and Hawthorne's *The Blithedale Romance*.

Barrett Browning's transformations of a whole range of texts by modern male writers suggest the aptness of Reynold's reference to her 'art of *bricolage*', the use of 'a magpie form which steals fragments of a tradition or language, from which women have been alienated, to rewrite or invert them' (*AL* 50). Indeed, the dropped star allusion strikingly reveals that Barrett Browning not only 'steals' fragments from the classical and Christian fathers who establish her authority. She also submits these fragments to a gynocentric metamorphosis, anticipating the textual practice of modern women poets like Muriel Rukseyer, Adrienne Rich and Margaret Atwood as Alicia Ostriker and others have described it.

The boldness of Barrett Browning's famed use of the 'woman's figures' (8:1131) is particularly apparent in her use of metalepsis – the troping of a precursor's trope. Thus the 'dropped star' retains traces of its symbolic reference to God's wrath, while simultaneously signifying the thwarted woman-artist's ominous power. Metalepsis is a feature that Harold Bloom associates with Milton's 'transumptive allusion' and the culminating phase of the 'strong poet'.[14] As any reader of Carlyle recognizes, however, it is also a prominent feature of Victorian sage discourse: indeed, one of the chief tools Carlyle uses to refashion traditional Christianity – 'Hebrew old clothes', in the terms of *Sartor Resartus* – into a new life philosophy.

The 'transumptive allusions' of *Aurora Leigh* draw on classical as well as Biblical texts, combining them in a textual palimpsest with densely interwoven allusions to her more immediate precursors and contemporaries. The adaptation of the story of Io from Aeschylus' *Prometheus* to figure Aurora's torment as an artist (7:829–33) and Marian's victimization as a raped woman is one among many examples of 'revisionist mythmaking', to use Ostriker's term (211). Zonana and Beverly Taylor have shown how Barrett Browning subtly adapts both the story of Io and the story of Danaë in representing the complex process whereby Aurora comes to terms with her own sexuality, in part through Marian's experience. Aeschylus and Homer are the classical authors most frequently visible in the textual palimpsest of *Aurora Leigh*. But in almost every case the play of allusion decentres the phallocentrism of these two Greek precursors, both described by Victorian critics in insistently masculine terms. Thus, while Aeschylus marginalizes the story of Io's torment in representing the Titanic suffering of Prometheus, it is Io, not Prometheus, who most prominently figures in *Aurora Leigh*. This is the tactic of 'revisionary mythopoesis' that DuPlessis describes as 'displacement': telling the story from the other side in order to give 'a voice to the muted' (108).

A similar 'displacement' of the rugged and masculine Aeschylus occurs in Barrett Browning's mock-epic allusion to the bizarre death he met when his bald head, mistaken for a rock, was crushed by a tortoise dropped by a hungry eagle. The shepherdess that Aurora is forced to embroider to fulfil her aunt's educational regimen has 'pink eyes' where she 'mistook the silks', and a 'head uncrushed by that round weight of hat / So strangely similar to the tortoise shell / Which slew the tragic poet' (1:451–5). Like so many of the metaphors in *Aurora Leigh*, this apparently playful allusion indirectly activates deeper and graver concerns. Graphic images of death and torture frequently strike out obliquely from the play of Aurora's figures, as in the reference to the Roman 'smeared with honey', bitten by insects and 'stared to torture by the noon' (2:890–1), and to the 'water-torture' suffered by the Marquise of Brinvilliers (1:467), executed for poisoning her father and brothers. Tormented by the water-torture of the young lady's education forced down her throat, 'prick[ed] . . . to a pattern' by her aunt's pin (1:381), and trapped like the tortured Roman in the death-in-life of a young girl's English countryhouse existence, Aurora is yet able to preserve the poet 'uncrushed' within her mind and grow beyond a shepherdess by marking her feminine difference from the fathers, in this case the great 'tragic poet' who so dominated Barrett Browning's initial artistic endeavours.

According to Bloom's paradigm of poetic influence, the metalepsis or transumptive allusion practised by the strong poet is a means of expressing his mastery over his precursors and rivals. Victorian sage discourse has been similarly viewed as a discourse motivated by the drive for mastery. In Thaïs Morgan's words, 'the sage always aims to establish her or his worldview as the right, true, and authoritative one' (*Victorian Sages* 3). While Barrett Browning questions this stance of monological authority in significant ways, a drive for mastery is nevertheless discernible in the gynocentric metalepsis that makes Aurora's book a subversively female textual body even when it most overtly pays homage to the poetic fathers of Western literary tradition.

One of the more dramatic examples of such metalepsis is the Homeric allusion to Juno's 'cream' prompting the title of this chapter. Expressing her scorn for Friedrich Wolf's theory that the *Iliad* and the *Odyssey* were composite texts created by a number of writers, Aurora employs one of the most overtly Titanic female figures in *Aurora Leigh*. 'Wolf's an atheist', she declares. The man who 'writes above' Homer's works ' "The house of Nobody!" '

> floats in cream, as rich as any sucked
> From Juno's breasts, the broad Homeric lines,
> And, while with their spondaic prodigious mouths
> They lap the lucent margins as babe-gods,
> Proclaims them bastards. (5: 1246–54)

The long, widemouthed vowels, followed by the murmuring meeting of lips in 'lap the lucent margins', combine with the syntax of this passage (the inter-polated hanging appositive of 'the broad Homeric lines') to recreate in the reader the very action of drinking in Juno's cream that Aurora describes. Even more striking are the implications of the compressed, interfused metaphors, as Aurora embodies Homer's artistic creativity in the cream from Juno's breasts and the fruit of her womb, defending his works against the same charge of illegitimacy that subsequently afflicts Marian.

'Juno's cream' seems an apt metaphor for Barrett Browning's own 'unscrupulously epic' (5:214) sage discourse in the work in which she carries out, in the full confidence of her mature powers, her girlhood dream of becoming 'the feminine of Homer' (Mermin 183). Deirdre David, the only critic thus far to emphasize Barrett Browning's affinities with the Victorian sage tradition, overlooks this transformative, gynocentric energy in her influential reiterated claims that Barrett Browning is a 'profoundly conservative' writer whose intellectual practice is '[u]nambiguously affiliated with a male poetic tradition . . . [and] hierarchical male supremacy' ('The Old Right', 201; *Intellectual Women*, 157–8). Granted that the other texts and writers explicitly named in *Aurora Leigh* are almost exclusively male: Homer (5:146), Aeschylus (1:455, 5:291), Plato (7:746); John of Revelation, Dante (5:494; 7:935), Shakespeare (5:246, 316), Keats (1:1003); and, in two rarer references to contemporary authors, Carlyle (5:156) and 'the poet of our day', Browning (7:810). Nevertheless, one cannot assume that because Barrett Browning so royally invokes the founding texts of the epic and the Christian sage traditions, she therefore acknowledges the supremacy of their patriarchal assumptions. On the contrary, in the Homeric allusion to 'Juno's cream', we encounter the emancipatory, emphatically female energy that led one contemporary reviewer to discern in *Aurora Leigh* 'the old anarchic nature of the Titaness'.[15] The same Titanic spirit is dramatically apparent in the more often discussed image of the 'double-breasted age' (see Stone, 'Taste', 751–2). Little wonder that Barrett Browning's 'choice of language, imagery, and metaphor' was the element in *Aurora Leigh*, along with its representation of an assertive, female poet-heroine, that Victorian critics clearly found most iconoclastic (Lootens 238). In Hélène Cixous's words, once a woman allows her body 'to articulate the profusion of meanings that run through it', she 'will make the old single-grooved mother tongue reverberate with more than one language'.[16]

Barrett Browning's appropriation of the character-istic rhetorical strategies of sage writing in *Aurora Leigh* turns them into the 'emancipatory strategies' identified by Patricia Yaeger in Mary Wollstonecraft, the Brontës, and other 'honey-mad' women writers. Thus, the use of figurative language as 'a half-covert but powerful form of argument', which Holloway discerns in Carlyle's writing in particular, becomes the eman-cipatory strategy of engendering new gynocentric epistemologies through new metaphors.[17] The 'inter-textuality characteristic of sage writing' (Morgan, *Victorian Sages*, 2) operates with a subversive *différence* when it becomes the circulation of 'male bodies and texts' through a female textual body (Yaeger 161). The 'control of meaning' through strategies of definition (Holloway 41) becomes a tool for 'confronting and appropriating, destroying and reconstructing the sociolect' of gender (Yaeger 83), most noticeable in Barrett Browning's paradoxical play with the con-tradictory conventional meanings of words like 'womanly'. 'To see a wrong or suffering moves us all / To undo it though we should undo ourselves', Aurora observes of herself in lines that apply equally well to

Romney's chivalric socialism – 'Ay, all the more, that we undo ourselves, – / That's womanly, past doubt, and not ill-moved' (7:215–18).

Although 'not one woman author is named or quoted directly' in *Aurora Leigh* (Reynolds *AL* 50), the influence of women writers, and especially women novelists from Madame de Staël to Charlotte Brontë, is everywhere felt. The textual echoes and revisions of De Staël's *Corinne*, several of George Sand's novels, Gaskell's *Ruth*, and Brontë's *Jane Eyre* have been frequently discussed.[18] There were many reasons why Barrett Browning affiliated herself with women novelists in planning to write, as early as 1845, a 'novel-poem. . . as modern as "Geraldine's Courtship," running into the midst of our conventions, & rushing into drawing-rooms & the like . . . & so meeting face to face & without mask the Humanity of the age' (*LEBB* 1:31). No doubt, 'the novel served as a model for contemporary narrative that released her from imitating the masters of the past' (Friedman 209), and gave 'her the confidence of writing for the first time in a strong female tradition' (Mermin 185). But her description of her projected novel-poem suggests that she was also drawn to the novel because, as Yaeger suggests, it is a more dialogical, 'disruptive' form than most poetic modes, providing a 'multivoicedness' that enables 'the woman writer to interrogate and challenge the very voices that tell her to conform' (59). By writing a novelized epic, in short, she could more easily address the subject matter and assume the manner of the Victorian sage.

Wollstonecraft's polemical prose, Gaskell's *Mary Barton* and Brontë's *Villette* have been less often mentioned in discussions of *Aurora Leigh*. But they provide particularly important precedents for Barrett Browning's entry into the male realm of sage discourse.

The 'abruptness and energy' with which Wollstonecraft 'seizes the role of speaking subject and constructs fictive dialogues with silent male interlocutors' (Yaeger 161) is manifested throughout *Aurora Leigh* – along with Wollstonecraft's strong Enlightenment feminist interest in women's education and employment. As for *Mary Barton*, though Barrett Browning criticized it as a 'class book' defective in its art when it first appeared (*LEBB* 1:472), she follows Gaskell and other female predecessors such as Harriet Martineau in representing class conflict: ' "rich men make the poor, who curse the rich" ' and there's ' "nought to see, / But just the rich man and just Lazarus" ' (2:271, 276–7), Romney says, sounding very much like an upper-class version of Gaskell's working-class hero John Barton.

The parallels with *Villette*, a novel which Barrett Browning thought 'very powerful' (*LEBB* 2:142), run at a deeper level. Janet Larson has perceptively analysed Charlotte Brontë's most mature and sophisticated work as a 'sage narrative' of '*la vie d'une femme*' incorporating a 'combat narrative of encounters with male religious texts . . . on the plane of figure and allusion' (Morgan, *Victorian Sages*, 78, 81, 86). The same might be said of *Aurora Leigh*, where Barrett Browning's recurrent metalepsis clearly enacts a liberating struggle on 'the plane of figure and allusion'. A more direct connection can be traced in Aurora's pyschological and spiritual breakdown on the pavement of a Florentine Catholic Church in a scene recalling Lucy's similar confession and breakdown in the alien church of a foreign land.

Less obviously, the parallels between *Villette* and *Aurora Leigh* include the narrative method. Most critics to date have assumed that Aurora is either a fictionalized version of her creator, or a character who is always reliable in what she says about art, politics,

and metaphysics, if not in what she initially assumes
about Marian and her feelings for Romney.[19] Yet
Barrett Browning's 'Autobiography of a poetess'
whom she emphatically identified as 'not me' (*AL* 85)
presents a first-person narrator remarkably like Lucy
Snowe in *Villette*. If Aurora is less duplicitous and
evasive than Lucy, her narrative is nevertheless
similarly permeated by repressed desires and conflicts,
and fissured by chronological ruptures.

The narrative perspective of *Aurora Leigh* develops
less out of Barrett Browning's use of lyric forms in the
1840s, as Susan Stanford Friedman suggests (208),
than out of her experimentation with dramatic speakers
throughout the 1840s in poems like 'Bertha in the
Lane', 'The Runaway Slave at Pilgrim's Point', 'Lady
Geraldine's Courtship' and several unpublished or
unfinished works, most notably the 'monodrama' on
Aeschylus attributed to Browning for many years.
Reynolds subtly analyses Aurora's narrative discrep-
ancies, her constant revisions of the past, the 'split'
between her roles as actor and narrator, the 'multi-
plicity of voices' her text incorporates, and the
increasing 'self-consciousness' it registers as a 'text-in-
process' (*AL* 32–8). All of these features point to the
traits *Aurora Leigh* shares both with Victorian dramatic
monologues and with the narrative perspective of
novels like *Villette*. Significantly, *Aurora Leigh* was not
only prompted by Barrett Browning's success in 'Lady
Geraldine's Courtship', which can be best described
as a framed dramatic monologue in the epistolary
mode. Her first mention of her novel-epic to Browning
also appears in a letter much concerned with the new
kind of drama he should write, immediately after her
description of her projected Aeschylus monodrama
(*RB–EBB* 1:30–1).

Barrett Browning's choice of narrative perspective

in *Aurora Leigh* has significant implications for many of her heroine's utterances. Since Aurora begins writing her story in *medias res* at the age of twenty-seven, throughout much of the poem she speaks not as a sage and prophet, but as a sage-in-formation whose wisdom is in process of revision and often contradicted by her own actions. The textual ironies thus generated call in question the authoritative stance so strenuously asserted by some male Victorian sages. If the woman-artist's power is expressed more overtly in *Aurora Leigh* than in *Villette* because Aurora is a much less 'reluctant prophet' than Lucy, to use Larson's term (Morgan, *Victorian Sages* 84), this does not mean that Aurora is presented throughout as a sage of un-questionable authority, or that Barrett Browning endorses the possibility of such infallibility.

An incomplete appreciation of the narrative ironies in *Aurora Leigh* has resulted not only in a general undervaluation of Barrett Browning's narrative sophistication, but also in the misrepresentation of her social and political vision. Ever since Kaplan con-demned Barrett Browning for her 'vicious picture of the rural and urban poor' (11) and her 'bourgeois rejection of working-class consciousness', critics have abstracted Aurora's opinions on the 'people' and on women's rights from their ironic contexts and objected to the 'constriction' or weakness of Barrett Browning's views on socialist and feminist activism (Gelpi 35; Lootens 223). Even Reynolds' astute analysis of Aurora's narrative unreliability does not question the view that Barrett Browning's 'condemnation of socialist endeavour . . . can be an embarrassment to some twentieth-century readers' (*AL* 16).

In many cases, this 'embarrassment' or unease is prompted by Aurora's description of the poor invited to attend Romney's aborted marriage with Marian. In

order to stage his symbolic marriage between the
classes, Romney takes his wife ' "[d]irectly from the
people" ' (4:369), inviting 'Half St. Giles in frieze . . .
to meet St. James in cloth of gold', and afterwards
share a marriage feast (4:538–9). Undeniably, Aurora's
response to the crowd that enters the church is graphic
and disturbing. In her horrified eyes, 'the people'
appear like the 'humours of a peccant social wound',
oozing 'into the church / In a dark slow stream, like
blood' – crawling 'slowly toward the altar from the
street / As bruised snakes crawl and hiss out of a hole' –
raising 'an ugly crest / Of faces' – faces that usually
'hid in cellars, not to make you mad / As Romney
Leigh is'. 'Faces? . . . phew / We'll call them vices,
festering to despairs, / Or sorrows, petrifying to vices':
'twas as if you had stirred up hell / To heave its lowest
dreg-fiends uppermost' (4:544–88).

This scene has typically been read as an expression
of Barrett Browning's own bourgeois revulsion for the
people, reflecting the limitations of her sheltered
existence in Wimpole Street. Yet such figurations of
the poor were common in the mid-Victorian period,
even among those with much more experience of the
London slums than Barrett Browning. Similar tropes
appear not only in novels by Dickens, Kingsley and
others, but also in the Parliamentary Reports on the
living and working conditions of the poor. Indeed,
the latter 'consistently employ a language of the
inferno: bodies tumble together in crowded hovels,
dunghills dominate the landscape, and all is festering
and pestilential', even though the observers are
sympathetic (David, *Intellectual Women*, 125). Aurora's
figuration of the poor thus registers a collective
discourse of the poor as much as a personal response
on Aurora's or Barrett Browning's part.

More importantly, Aurora's middle-class figuration

of 'the people' as a demonic mass appears at a relatively early stage in her artistic development, and is gradually and subtly undermined both by the representation of the poor elsewhere in her own text, and by the ironies pervading her attempt to develop an art that confronts and incorporates the realities of her age. In other words, Barrett Browning strongly embodies representative middle-class assumptions about the lower classes in Aurora's consciousness not in order to endorse them, but in order to question them, much as she subsequently represents and discredits Aurora's initial priggish and conventional assumptions about Marian's illegitimate pregnancy.

Aurora Leigh offers little to compare to Gaskell's full and variegated representation of working-class voices and perspectives in *Mary Barton*. Yet when Barrett Browning does represent the actual voices of working-class people, what we hear exposes the limitations of Aurora's initial lurid and blurred impressions of the masses. When Romney's wedding ceremony is broken off because of Marian's disappearance, the first sound that fills the pause is 'a baby sucking in its sleep / At the farthest end of the aisle' (4:814–15). The natural hunger the baby expresses finds a more threatening voice in the working-class man who first speaks, primarily concerned that ' "all the beef and drink / Be not filched from us" ' (4:816–17). But the woman who cries out next and at much greater length reveals her concern not for 'beef and drink', but for Marian: ' "I've not stomach even for beef, / Until I know about the girl that's lost" '. Significantly, the crowd is swayed not by the man's voice, but by hers, as it joins in her expression of class solidarity:

'We'll have our rights.
We'll have the girl, the girl! Your ladies there

Are married safely and smoothly every day,
And *she* shall not drop through into a trap
Because she's poor and of the people: shame!
We'll have no tricks played by gentlefolks;
We'll see her righted.' (4:841–7)

The snobbish, idle, superficial chat of the majority of
the 'gentlefolks' prior to this outburst – ' "These
Leighs! – our best blood running in the rut!" '(4:685) –
makes the people's expression of solidarity all the
more admirable. Yet Aurora, who participates at this
point in many of the prejudices she satirizes in the
fashionable St James folk, exhibits little recognition of
the people's collective concern for Marian's fate.
Instead, she perceives the people as a pack of hungry
hounds falling on their Actaeon-like huntsman Romney
and then faints away struggling to rescue him much as
Margaret Hale flings herself forward to rescue
Thornton in Gaskell's *North and South*.

Similar limitations in Aurora's blurred and feverish
perceptions of the poor are apparent when she first
enters the slum of St Margaret's Court to seek out
Marian. Cursed by a 'rouged' woman with 'angular
cheek bones' and a 'flat lascivious mouth', who asks,
' "What brings you here / My lady? is't to find my
gentleman / Who visits his tame pigeon in the
eaves?" ', Aurora states that she did not 'flinch' in
saying to the woman, ' "The dear Christ comfort you
. . . you must have been most miserable, / To be so
cruel" ' (3:764–82). But she does not pause to consider
the causes of the woman's bitterness, which the reader
might see as not unmotivated: her 'angular cheek-
bones' bespeak starvation (Reynolds' note indicates
that the manuscript here initially read 'starved to
the bone'), her words indicate that her mother is dying
of cholera, and she is absolutely right in inferring

that Aurora comes into her court 'close-veiled' not out of concern for the poor's suffering but because of her interest in a 'gentleman'. Ironically, Aurora's 'unflinching' first encounter with a working-class individual ends with her hastily emptying out her purse upon the stones, then fleeing as she imagines hideous sounds all about her in the slum: 'a hideous wail of laughs / And roar of oathes, and blows perhaps . . . I passed / *Too quickly for distinguishing*' (3:786–8, my emphasis).

Aurora first seeks out Marian because she has been informed of Romney's interest in this ' "drover's daughter" ' by Lady Waldemar (3:659), the fashionable lady who falls in love with Romney and who completes Barrett Browning's tryptich of working-class, middle-class and upper-class womanhood. Lady Waldemar is linked to Aurora through a complex series of plot and character parallels and contrasts that bring into relief both Aurora's limitations and her growing strengths. Thus Aurora climbs up to Marian's garret for much the same reason that Lady Waldemar has climbed up to her third-floor Kensington flat. Both love Romney for his Quixotic nobility while simultaneously criticizing his chilly absorption in abstract ideals. Both think of marrying him to 'save' him: Lady Waldemar professedly acts to save him from marrying Marian, the vulgar seamstress (3:502); and Aurora briefly considers that she might have saved Romney from Lady Waldmar's wiles by marrying him (7:186), though she quickly rejects such foolish female 'knight-errantry'. In direct contrast to Aurora, Lady Waldemar confesses her physicality and her desire for Romney with a startling frankness: ' "We fair fine ladies, who park out our lives . . . have hearts within / Warm, live, improvident, indecent hearts / As ready for outrageous ends and acts / As any distressed seamstress" ' (3:456–64). But her 'warm' heart does not extend to geniune sympathy for the poor, despite her short-lived attempt to act as Romney's helpmate in his phalanstery. Whereas Aurora's perception of 'the people' is profoundly altered by her sympathetic intimacy with Marian and her quest for greater social realism in her art, Lady Waldemar manifests a fairly callous disregard for Marian's fate, for distressed seamstresses (she disdains to wear gowns made by the Ten Hours movement), and for the lower classes generally. She is not so vicious as to be directly responsible for Marian's kidnapping, as Aurora mistakenly assumes. But Lady Waldemar indirectly contributes to Marian's victimization by persuading the girl of her own unworthiness, and by placing her in the hands of the maid who sells her into prostitution.

When Aurora first meets Marian, she marks her off as different from the mass, amazed that such a flower could appear from 'such rough roots' – 'the people, under there, / Can sin so, curse so, look so, smell so . . . faugh! / Yet have such daughters?' (3:806–9). Ironically, at this stage in her artistic development, Aurora bears out Romney's claim that she can respond only to the personal, although the limitation is not a consequence of her sex, as he assumes, but of her relative artistic immaturity. She reveals a related limitation as an artist when she submerges Marian's discourse in her own. Rather than respecting the otherness of Marian's story, Aurora decides to 're-tell' it with 'fuller utterance' (3:828), growing 'passionate' where Marian did not as she imposes her feelings upon the events described (3:847). Marian's account of her parents – her father, a drover and labourer who drinks between the 'gaps' of irregular work, and her mother, a battered wife who beats her child in turn and surrenders her to the squire's lascivious interest (3:858–70) – only confirms Aurora in her unexamined revulsion for the 'rough roots' of the people. But if we listen for Marian's own voice filtered through Aurora's and for the other voices of the poor that Marian conveys, the limitations of Aurora's general assumptions about the people emerge, much as they do in the aborted wedding scene. We can consider, for instance, the variegated expressions of the poor women around Marian in the hospital where she is taken by a kindly waggoner after her flight from her parents (3:1150–66). Such passages, like the marriage scene, call in question Kaplan's assertion that Barrett Browning represents 'the poor as a lumpen motley of thieves, drunkards, rapists and childbeaters' (12).

Significantly, Marián's account of her mother's attempt to prostitute her is pervaded, as the later account of her rape is, by imagery of animal drovers and of tramping/trampling that makes its first, veiled indirect appearance in Aurora's description of the common lane running by her aunt's country manor, '[o]ut of sight' and 'sunk so deep, no foreign tramp / Nor drover of wild ponies out of Wales / Could guess if lady's hall' existed behind the wall of shrubbery (1:588–91). As this textual connection suggests, Marian's story of her life as the daughter of a drover and itinerant labourer, and then as a seamstress, exposes Aurora to the rural and urban poverty her sheltered adolescence carefully fenced out. After Marian's disappearance, her 'memory moans on' within Aurora's mind (5:1097). But it isn't clear that the aesthetic philosophy Aurora expresses in her famous manifesto – the poet's work is to 'represent the age' – has been significantly informed by her encounter with the working-class girl, even though it results in the 'long poem' that Romney later praises for its transcendence of the merely personal (8:606). On the contrary, Books 6 and 7 (written not retrospectively but as a journal) indicate that Aurora's growth as a poet-sage must be completed by a more intimate confrontation with Marian's suffering and the urgent social issues it manifests.

The opening of Book 6 presents Aurora walking in the streets of Paris, resolving that the love of pastoral poetic beauty will not draw her backward from the 'coarse town-sights': 'I would be bold and bear / To look into the swarthiest face of things', she declares (6:141–7). Striving to contemplate 'the people in the rough' in her sphere of poetry as Romney does in his sphere of philanthrophy (6:202), she states her desire to 'pore upon / An ounce of common, ugly, human dust' rather than to 'track old Nilus to his silvery roots' (6:163–6). Aurora's ideals are laudable, like the political ideals of the French people which she earlier defends. But Barrett Browning signals the gap between her heroine's artistic theory and her practice through multiple textual ironies. Amidst the crowds of Paris, Aurora is 'musing' in a solitary state, 'pulling thoughts to pieces leisurely / As if [she] caught at grasses in a field' (6:229–30) – like the escapist pastoral poet she condemns. Her wandering thoughts reflect her own vagueness, not Barrett Browning's, given that her movement through Paris can be very precisely mapped (Reynolds *AL* 648). Although she shows a fuller appreciation now of Romney's vocation of philan-throphy, the 'larger metaphysics' Aurora imagines is still unduly dismissive of the need for 'bread' as she focuses chiefly and rather bombastically on the 'essential prophet's word': 'we thunder down / We prophets, poets . . . To inaugurate the use of vocal life' (6:204–20).

Just as Aurora asserts that 'a poet's word' is worth

more to any man than food or warmth, she is struck by
the sight of a face: 'God! what face is that? / O
Romney, O Marian!' (6:221–7). The doubling of
Romney's with Marian's face underlines the role
Marian plays in reconciling Aurora's life philosophy
or metaphysics with Romney's, the need for 'bread'
with the need for 'verses'. At this point, however,
when Aurora plunges into the crowd in pursuit, she
only runs into a 'gentleman as abstracted as' herself,
some 'learned member' of the French Institute,
'meditating on the last "Discourse" ' (6:261–6).
The abstracted and elitist Academician, pinching the
'empty air' as he takes his snuff, strikingly embodies
the dangers of the abstract, arid theoretical musing
Aurora herself has been absorbed in – ironically while
she meditates on a democratizing poetics. Aurora does
not begin to translate this poetics into practice until
she experiences the concrete and particularized story
of Marian's rape and degradation, '[s]tepping by her
footsteps, breathing by her breath / And holding
her with eyes that would not slip' (6:503–4). Seeing
alone is not sufficient, she gradually realizes, given
that her 'artist's eye' is '[h]alf-absent, whole-observing'
(6:427–9). ' "You feel? / You understand? no, do not
look at me, / But understand" ', Marian insists
(6:1204–5). Like Dante, Aurora has to journey
vicariously with Marian into the underworld (Mermin
217) before she can attain the vision and authority of
the sage who eventually finds in 'the despised poor
earth, / The healthy odorous earth' (9:652–3).

Like her utterances concerning the people, socialist
reform and her own aesthetic practice, Aurora's
comments on women's rights have often been interpreted without sufficient consideration of contextual
ironies. Moreover, the neglect of diachronic and
dialogical dimensions within Barrett Browning's

representation of her protagonist has been mirrored by a similar neglect of the ideological formations and transformations shaping the production of her novel-epic. Rod Edmond is a welcome exception to this tendency in exploring some of the ways in which *Aurora Leigh* 'became part of the wider political and social debate about the status of women' in 1856 (138). But helpful as his historically contextual survey is, it does not sufficiently acknowledge that *Aurora Leigh* became part of this wider debate precisely because it so directly addressed so many of the issues on the agenda of mid-Victorian feminists like Barbara Bodichon: particularly, women's employment and education.

The emphasis on women's employment permeates *Aurora Leigh*. Although Bayne saw it as a revision of Virgil's 'arms and the man', one might more accurately see it as a revision of Carlyle's earlier transformation of Virgil. Whereas Carlyle writes of 'tools and the man' in *Past and Present*, Barrett Browning sings of tools and the woman. Whereas Carlyle, like Romney, denigrates poetry and privileges silence, Aurora includes God's ' "singers" ' among ' "the workers for his world" ' (2:1233–4). ' "I too have my vocation, – work to do . . . Most serious work, most necessary work" ', Aurora declares to Romney (2:455,457). Later, hard at work in her London flat, writing for the periodical press in order to support herself in her 'veritable work' (3:328), Aurora's pen becomes a 'spade' in her hand (3:294).

Such passages convey the passionate belief in the importance of women's work that Barrett Browning expresses in an 1859 letter to Mary Hunter, where she simultaneously reveals the intense desire for a daughter reflected in many of her letters of the 1850s. 'Oh, if I had a daughter', she declares, 'she would be educated

to stand by herself and work; she should learn nothing
that she could not turn to use. I would rather have her
a good housekeeper & cheapener in the market, than a
fritterer away of time at the piano & painting &
reading ... in an amateur fashion. ... [W]omen
now-a-days (taking the mass) are educated for the
intellectual seraglio' (*AL* 63). As this letter suggests,
there is a vital connection between the penetrating
satire of the typical young lady's education in *Aurora
Leigh* (1:385–481) and Barrett Browning's focus
throughout on work.

Ironically, however, one of the strongest expressions
of the importance of women's work in *Aurora Leigh*
appears in a passage that has often been cited out of
context as evidence for Barrett Browning's contempt
for feminist activism.[20] In the extended conversation
between Romney and Aurora that takes up much of
Book 8 and 9, Aurora agrees with Romney that there's
' "too much abstract willing, purposing / In this poor
world" ', and sarcastically observes,

>   'Yes, we generalise
> Enough to please you. . . .
> A woman cannot do the thing she ought,
> Which means whatever perfect thing she can,
> In life, in art, in science, but she fears
> To let the perfect action take her part,
> And rest there: she must prove what she can do
> Before she does it, prate of woman's rights,
> Of woman's mission, woman's function, till
> The men (who are prating too on their side) cry,
> "A woman's function plainly is . . . to talk."
> Poor souls, they are very reasonably vexed;
> They cannot hear each other talk.' (8:808–24)

The apparent attack on prating of 'woman's rights'

in this exchange is permeated by double-edged contextual ironies, as Barrett Browning's satiric shafts characteristically fly in a number of different directions. First, we may note that Romney and Aurora are both talking compulsively and at great length as they denounce talking and abstract willing, largely in order to avoid dealing with their feelings for each other. Aurora herself implicitly acknowledges this strategic evasion in prefacing this speech to Romney by confessing that she was 'fain to throw up thought / And make a game of it' (8:806–7). But Aurora is also ironic at the expense of those prating men who are 'reasonably vexed' at woman's talk because *they* 'cannot hear each other talk'. This is the most obvious reading of the closing lines of her speech on prating, although the pronoun 'they' is calculatedly ambiguous enough in its context to refer to both women and men collectively. In other words, men are so busy talking on their side of the gender divide, and women's on theirs, that the two sexes – 'poor souls' indeed – are at an impasse in communication.

Interpretations of this passage as an attack on feminist activists overlook such ironies as well as two other important points. Aurora is not only talking lightly, for suspect reasons, of those who promote women's rights. She also dismisses those who prate of 'woman's mission, woman's function': in other words, the conservative women like Sarah Ellis who wrote that 'score of books on womanhood' which were anathema to the youthful Aurora – books preaching the 'general missionariness' of woman and her 'angelic reach / Of virtue, chiefly used to sit and darn, / And fatten household sinners' (1:427–40). Barrett Browning appears to be deliberately blurring the boundaries between feminist and conservative discourse here, just as she goes on to blur the boundaries between women and men talking. And of course, many Victorian men did talk, very loudly, about 'woman's function'.

At the same time, however, Barrett Browning states the case for women's work very strongly: women should be free to do the thing they can do best '[i]n life, in art, in science'. If we have any doubt that Barrett Browning is making a case here for the opening of the various professions to women, we can consider what Aurora goes on to stress: women should act according to their aspirations, claim their 'license' to work through action and achievement in various vocational fields. Like Harriet Hosmer, the celebrated sculptor whom Barrett Browning admired in Italy, they should speak through the power of their acts. Similarly, Aurora points out, ' "Whoso cures the plague, / Though twice a woman, shall be called a leech" '; while the woman who ' "rights a land's finances, is excused / For touching coppers, though her hands be white,– / But we, we talk!" ' (8:842–6). Here again, the ironic ambiguities multiply. The 'we' who talk are apparently women, but the phrase refers equally accurately to the long-winded Aurora and Romney, and indeed to all who belong to the age, as Romney goes on to point out.

However we interpret Aurora's talk in this instance, we should note the striking similarities between what Barrett Browning is implying about women and work, and what the 'Langham Place' group of feminist activists associated with Barbara Bodichon were saying in the pamphlets and essays brought together by Candida Lacey.[21] Bodichon provides two epigraphs for her groundbreaking 1857 pamphlet, *Women and Work*: the second comes from the recently published *Aurora Leigh*, the first from St Paul (Lacey 36). By quoting the passage in which Aurora asserts 'The honest earnest man must stand and work, / The woman also, – otherwise she drops / At once below the dignity of man' (8:712–14), Bodichon creates a subversive intertext converting St Paul ('there is neither male nor female, for ye are all one in Christ Jesus') into an apologist for women's right to enter the professions and find honest, remunerated employment. Bodichon subsequently weaves another quotation on women and work from *Aurora Leigh* (2:439–49) into the body of her argument, evidently assuming that the author and source will be obvious to her readers (Lacey 40).

Frances Power Cobbe's allusions to *Aurora Leigh* similarly indicate that Barrett Browning's ideological affiliations with the Langham Place feminists were closer than has traditionally been assumed. In 1860, Cobbe sought an introduction to Barrett Browning in Florence because she was 'bubbling over with enthusiasm for her poetry'.[22] Two years later, in her spirited and witty argument for women's vocational opportunities, 'What Shall We Do With Our Old Maids?', Cobbe took Aurora's argument about women claiming their 'license' to work one step further by using the example of Barrett Browning's achievement in poetry, along with Harriet Hosmer's in sculpture and Rosa Bonheur's in painting, to prove woman's creative powers in the arts. '*Aurora Leigh* is perhaps the least "Angelical" poem in the language', Cobbe remarks, and it bears the relation to the 'feebleness and prettiness' of conventional female poetry that 'a chiselled steel corset does to a silk boddice with lace trimmings. The very hardness of its rhythm, its sturdy wrestlings and grapplings, one after another, with all the sternest problems of our social life – its forked-lightning revelations of character . . . all this takes us miles away from the received notion of a woman's poetry' (Lacey 366).

Barrett Browning also refers to a third important member of the Langham Place group, Bessie Rayner Parkes, more than once in her letters, most revealingly in a letter of 1856 (*AL* 18):

> Bessie Parkes is writing very vigorous articles on the woman question, in opposition to Mr Patmore, poet & husband, who expounds infamous doctrines on the same subject . . . – Oh if you heard Bessie Parkes! – she & the rest of us militant, foam with rage – . . . I hear he is to Review in the North British my poor 'Aurora Leigh,' who has the unfeminine impropriety to express her opinion on various 'abstract subjects,' – which Mr. Patmore cant abide.

'The rest of us militant' suggests good reason to reconsider the view that Barrett Browning, in Catharine Stimpson's words, 'was fastidiously aloof from the organized women's movement' (Mermin xi), or that she rejected 'militant' feminism (Kaplan 27).

Barrett Browning's remarks about Patmore dramatically convey the embattled context in which some mid-Victorian women at least encountered *Aurora Leigh*, while simultaneously reminding us of the ideological axes many professedly impartial reviewers had to grind. Patmore's 'infamous doctrines' on the woman question had found an earlier expression in his 1851 *North British Review* essay, 'The Social Position of Women', in part a review of Margaret Fuller's *Woman in the Nineteenth Century*. This is an essay Barrett Browning is likely to have read, given her friendship with Fuller. We know, at least, that the *North British* was among the periodicals she was reading in the 1850 period (*LEBB* 1:467), and that many of the arguments Patmore advances for the natural and social subordination of woman are refuted in *Aurora Leigh*.

Like her differences with Patmore, many of the intertextual debates Barrett Browning carries on in *Aurora Leigh* are directly concerned with issues placed on the reform agenda by the Langham Place activists. This is true both of the intertextual arguments with Tennyson, Carlyle, Clough and Kingsley already explored in criticism on *Aurora Leigh*, and of other intertextual elements which remain largely uninvestigated. For instance, Barrett Browning carries out a multi-faceted revision of Byron's representation of women in *Don Juan* through a series of textual echoes too numerous to be considered here. As well, the *North British Review* obituary essay of 1862 saw *Aurora Leigh* as taking up a gauntlet thrown down by Thomas De Quincey on the subject of the 'woman question'. The review opens with the words from De Quincey's 1847 essay on 'Joan of Arc' which are almost certainly echoed in Romney's mistaken prophecy that there will never be a great woman poet: 'Woman, sister – there are some things which you do not execute as well as your brother, Man; no, nor ever will. Pardon me, if I doubt whether you will ever produce a poet from your choirs, or a Mozart, or a Phidias, or a Michael Angelo, or a great philosopher, or a great scholar.' Sounding very much like Francis Power Cobbe, the reviewer then proceeds to pay tribute to the amassing evidence for 'woman's powers' in literature and the arts.[23]

Another reviewer's comments point to Barrett Browning's strategic revision of Samuel Richardson in joining 'together the central incident of Clarissa Harlowe with the leading sentiment of Ruth – . . . The combination is striking and original, not to say courageous in a lady'.[24] The influence of Gaskell's *Ruth* is apparent in Barrett Browning's combining of 'the qualities of the Madonna and the Magdalen' in representing Marian (Cosslett 52). Yet she also significantly revises both *Clarissa* and *Ruth* in refusing to kill Marian off or ship her out to Australia. She explicitly noted 'that Marian should be permitted dignity and purity and that she should "triumph" over Clarissa in being allowed to live' (*AL* 44). She also alters Richardson and extends Gaskell's analysis by depicting Marian's rape in the economic and social context of systemic prostitution that makes it a sadly representative rather than an isolated act. As Angela Leighton observes, 'Barrett Browning constantly emphasizes the culpability of the system, and particularly . . . the class system' (1989, 112).

Despite their very different visions and priorities, both Aurora and Romney passionately indict the social and economic system in which 'all the towns / Make offal of their daughters' for man's 'use' (7:866). As Romney graphically puts it, prostitution 'slurs our cruel streets from end to end / With eighty thousand women in one smile, / Who only smile at night beneath the gas' (8:413–15). In such passages, *Aurora Leigh* anticipates the prominence of the attack on prostitution by British feminist activists in the 1860s; while, in its representation of Marian's abduction and drugging, it precedes by almost thirty years the attack on the white slave trade in 'The Maiden Tribute of Modern Babylon' (Hickok 190). The depiction of Marian among her fellow seamstresses underlines the economic causes of prostitution, but Barrett Browning is more actively concerned with its spiritual and philosophical causes, which seemed to her remediable. Tennyson's reading of *Maud* led her to declare that the Crimean War was 'terrible certainly', but that mass prostitution was a greater evil. '[T]here are worse plagues, deeper griefs, dreader wounds . . . What of the forty thousand wretched women in this city? The violent writhing of them is to me more appalling than the roar of the canons' (*LEBB* 2:213).

In asserting Marian's right not only to live, but also to mother *and* father her fatherless child, Barrett Browning may have furthermore been critiquing the conventional fates allotted to Little Emily and Martha, the fallen women in Dickens's *David Copperfield*. She associated her deliberate use of contemporary scenes in *Aurora Leigh* with walking on Dickens' 'ground' (*AL* 86); and a passage deleted by Frederic Kenyon in the typescript of an 1851 letter indicates that she read *David Copperfield* soon after it was published and regarded it as Dickens' 'most beautiful' novel.[25] It is not Dickens' portrait of fallen women, however, but his portrait of the writer that she most obviously revises in *Aurora Leigh*. Thus, in place of Dickens' representation of the young David reading his father's books in an attic room 'as if for life', she represents the young Aurora reading her father's books to preserve her inner life: 'Books, books, books! / I had found the secret of a garret-room / Piled high with cases in my father's name', Aurora recalls as she describes herself 'creeping in and out' among the 'giant fossils' of her past like 'some small nimble mouse between the ribs / Of a mastadon' (1:832–8).

Richard Hengist Horne's 'penny epic' *Orion*, inspired in part by Keats' *Endymion* and Nicholas Poussin's painting, 'Blind Orion hungering for the Dawn', is another male portrait of the artist that Barrett Browning echoes and alters in *Aurora Leigh*. She accurately described *Orion* as a 'Spiritual epic' of the growth of a poet's mind in her 1843 *Athenaeum* review, but privately criticized it for fading 'off into a mist of allegorism' (*BC* 7:205, 219, 173). While she adapted elements of Horne's epic in her depiction of the blinded Romney staring at the sun in the conclusion of

Aurora Leigh, she replaced his focus on a male poet 'hungering for the dawn' with her focus on a female poet symbolically associated with the dawn herself who – like Emily Dickinson after her – is 'famished for the noon' (1:536). Despite the transcendental metaphysics of her own 'spiritual epic', she was also careful to avoid Horne's excessive 'allegorism' by firmly contextualizing Aurora's development as a woman writer within a modern setting and contemporary debates concerning the 'woman question' and the 'social question'.

Kaplan has shcwn how Barrett Browning's emphasis on Aurora's artistic vocation radically critiques Kingsley's representation of women, art and socialist reform in *Alton Locke*, where Eleanor Lynedale gives up her dilletantish pursuit of the beautiful in poetry and art to engage in socially useful tasks (33). Several textual echoes suggest that Barrett Browning was simultaneously responding to Hawthorne's depiction of the failed socialist experiment at Brook Farm in *The Blithedale Romance*, a work that she had read by the summer of 1853 (*LMRM* 3:392). The *Athenaeum* review indicates that Victorian readers were quick to link Romney's failed socialist experiments with Hollingsworth's in Hawthorne's novel. But Barrett Browning's subtle recasting of the love triangle in *The Blithedale Romance* and the ideological work her revision carried out remain unexplored.

To a greater extent than either *Alton Locke* or *The Blithedale Romance*, *Aurora Leigh* foregrounds some of the complex ways in which feminist reform intersected and conflicted with socialist reform in the midnineteenth century. As Barbara Taylor points out in *Eve and the New Jerusalem*, the conflict was more pronounced than the points of intersection after the demise of Owenite and associated socialist movements in the late 1840s, when 'the political location of feminism began to shift' from working-class socialist groups to the middle class (276). Taylor's study of British socialism and feminism indicates that the essentially middle-class perspective so many critics have objected to in *Aurora Leigh* is as much a reflection of broader historical and cultural developments as it is of Barrett Browning's own social formation and her limitations as a writer. Several passages in *Aurora Leigh* indicate that she was certainly aware of some of the progressive ideas socialists such as Fourier expressed concerning woman's position and potential. Yet, like the Langham Place activists, she strategically distanced herself from the socialist reform movements that had collapsed in disarray by mid-century, among them the British Owenite movement. That she was far from alone in her scepticism of the abstract idealism of socialists like Fourier is furthermore indicated by the differently motivated critiques of such visionaries in Marx and Engels' 1848 *Communist Manifesto*, and in the periodical literature of the period. These critiques remind us that Fourier's theories were by no means consistently informed by enlightened, progressive ideals, as modern readers tend to assume. Indeed, certain elements in Fourier's thinking, as in Robert Owen's, were autocratic or systematically bizarre.

Even as she distanced herself from the more discredited aspects of socialist reform, however, Barrett Browning appropriated the millenarian discourse of the British Owenites, French Saint-Simonians, and other socialist movements to convey her own vision of a woman-engendered new Jerusalem. The affinities between the revelation Aurora and Romney share in the conclusion of *Aurora Leigh* and socialist millenarian visions of a female messiah described by Taylor (161–80) are particularly apparent in Barrett

Browning's symbolic allusions to the 'woman clothed with the sun' in Revelation 12 – a prominent figure in Owenite and socialist feminism in the first half of the nineteenth century. Mary Wilson Carpenter is surely right in interpreting Aurora the 'prophet poet' as a type of this apocalyptic figure (Morgan, *Victorian Sages*, 116). Like the visionary woman in Revelation 12, the golden-haired Aurora metaphorically stands with the moon beneath her feet in her final passionate embrace with Romney (9:842), as both '[g]aze on, with inscient vision toward the sun' (9:913).

In the context of Aurora's artistic development, the woman clothed with the sun emerges as a countertype to the 'dropped star' of the woman-artist buried in the waters of domestic life. In the context of the spiritual evolution that is inseparable from Aurora's artistic development, this visionary figure affiliates *Aurora Leigh* with a tradition of Protestant iconoclasm in which, as Carpenter notes, the woman clothed with the sun exemplifies 'the activity, change and even violent revolt of the Protestant Reformation' (113). Within this tradition Swedenborg's works, with their emphasis on divine 'dawnism', an androgynous deity, and love fulfilling itself in useful works, had a particularly important influence on *Aurora Leigh*, as they did on some of the socialist feminist movements that preceded it. But as James Borg notes, Barrett Browning developed Swedenborg's 'gloss' on the woman clothed with the sun into a 'core' element in articulating her own revisionary revelation (122–7, 137).

Nevertheless, in presenting Aurora as a type of the woman crowned with the sun, Barrett Browning does not exalt her 'prophet poet' into an infallible source of authority. Aurora's final vision of Revelation is presented in the context of a number of earlier,

contradictory interpretations, thereby reinforcing the
hermeneutical instability generated throughout *Aurora
Leigh* by the poet-protagonist's narrative unreliability.
These contradictory interpretations of Revelation
include, on the one hand, the radical young Mr
Smith's critique of Romney's conservative Christian
socialism and his call for a 'new church' free of
'marriage-law' (5:714,706); and on the other, the
conservative Sir Blaise Delorme's castigation of
Romney as one of the 'dogs' outside the gates of the
heavenly city in Revelation 22 (5:749), a judgment
echoed in the vicar's association of Romney not with
the dogs but with the 'frogs' or unclean spirits of the
false prophet in Revelation 16 (8:903–5). In explicitly
contrasting Aurora's 'book' with the vicar's discourses,
Romney calls attention to the contradictions between
their interpretations of Revelation. Thus we are left
with little doubt that the vicar would denounce
Aurora too as one of the unclean 'frogs'.

Another particularly complex set of allusions to
Revelation, this time on Marian's part, suggests to the
contrary that Aurora's limitations as a prophet lie not
in her uncleanness, but in her excessive preoccupation
with purity. When Aurora priggishly and wrongly
rebukes Marian for taking delight in her illegitimate
child, Marian compares her to the pure and speckless
angels who walk ' "up and down the new Jerusalem" '
holding up their trailing lutestrings from ' "brushing
the twelve stones, for fear of some / Small speck as
little as a needle-prick" ' (6:711–16). Later, comparing
herself to the dying Aaron, Aurora takes a stand on
her speckless purity in sanctifying Marian as a fitting
wife for Romney (9:265). But in a sudden reversal, it is
the fallen Marian who emerges as the enabling priest
and intermediary in this scene. Marian is the necessary
angel of earth who redeems Aurora by reminding her

of her own humanity, and who leads her towards the revelation of a new order based not on purity but on love, focused not on the afterworld but on this world. This may explain why Barrett Browning divides the features associated with the woman clothed with the sun between Aurora and Marian, in presenting the latter as a Madonna figure who bears a 'man-child', who flees into the wilderness, and who is persecuted by the dragon of ' "man's violence" ' and inequity (6:1226).

The subversive hermeneutics of Barrett Browning's revisionary mythopoesis have not been adequately considered by those critics who fault the conclusion of *Aurora Leigh* for its conservative and otherworldly rhetoric and agenda.[26] Such readings typically overlook not only Barrett Browning's focus on the woman clothed with the sun, but also the extent to which millenarian discourse was interpreted and mobilized by nineteenth-century reformers in pragmatically political ways. In Rita Felski's words, 'the political value of literary texts from the standpoint of feminism can be determined only by an investigation of their social functions and effects in relation to the interests of women in a particular historical context', and not by 'an abstract literary theory' of ' "subversive" and "reactionary" forms'.[27] Barbara Taylor emphasizes that 'the language of prophecy and apocalypse' in nineteenth-century socialist discourse often 'expressed not a literal faith in millenarian change' but 'commitment to the construction of a new heaven on earth' (160–1). Aurora's clarion call for '[n]ew churches, new oeconomies, new laws' (9:929–47) seems to have been read in this light by many nineteenth-century activists. In carrying *Aurora Leigh* with her as she travelled through America campaigning for women's rights, Susan B. Anthony clearly interpreted it not as a vision of a new heaven, but as a vision of a new woman and a new earth.[28]

At the same time, critics are surely right in emphasizing that *Aurora Leigh* does not offer any blueprints for reform. Barrett Browning emphatically rejects any 'mapping out of masses to be saved, / By nations or by sexes' (9:867–8). Similarly, as Kaplan points out, the critique of female education is not accompanied by an 'alternative system' (21). Kaplan attributes the absence of 'alternative systems' in *Aurora Leigh* to the fact that Barrett Browning 'has no answer to the misery of the poor except her own brand of Christian love – and poetry' (12). But the provision of such 'systems' would contradict the most fundamental philosophical premises of Barrett Browning's textual enterprise. The manuscript jotting 'System against instinct' was central to Barrett Browning's thinking from the start, as Reynolds emphasizes. 'Her project, formal as well as political, was to privilege instinct and development as process, over the ordering limits of education and system' (*AL* 25). This project is embodied in the complex series of textual and intertextual processes that *Aurora Leigh* traces and generates. Any text is a practice rather than 'an archive of structures', Julia Kristeva reminds us.[29] But her description of textual practice as involving 'the sum of unconscious, subjective, and social relations in gestures of confrontation and appropriation, destruction and creation – productive violence' seems particularly applicable to Barrett Browning's dynamically intertextual representation of a sage representing her own formation.

Although the 'productive violence' of *Aurora Leigh* sometimes seems to resolve into static philosophical touchstones contradicting Barrett Browning's project, her overall textual practice avoids such reifications of process. ' "Subsist no rules of life outside of life" ' (9:870), Romney declares, apparently echoing Barrett Browning's privileging of instinct over system. Such a maxim clearly risks exalting 'instinct' itself as a rule. As Rachael DuPlessis observes, revisionary mythopoesis is 'fraught with some irony' since the critique of traditional legitimating narratives often results in the creation of alternative narratives that claim a similar privileged status (107). Yet the rule that there is no rule, like the assumption that the subjective is the only approach to the objective, can have the radical effect which DuPlessis describes as 'breaking the sequence' of narrative legitimation (108), even though DuPlessis herself does not associate this effect with the conclusion of *Aurora Leigh*.

In her view, on the contrary, Barrett Browning succumbs to traditional narrative patterns in making 'her hero's work facilitate the romance to be achieved' (6) and in aligning Aurora's artistic work with the 'feminine ideology' of self-sacrifice (87). Ironically, however, DuPlessis' reading may reflect her own totalizing narrative pattern concerning the irresolvable conflict between vocation and marriage in nineteenth-century plots, without capturing the textual complexities of the work it purports to describe. For Romney clearly intends his marriage to Aurora to facilitate her work, not the other way round, as he first urges her to ' "work for two" ' while he ' "for two, shall love" ', then revises his rhetoric of gender complementarity to emphasize that love and work are inseparable: ' "let us love so well, / Our work shall still be better for our love" ' (9:911–12; 925–7). Nor does such an ethic of work merely reinscribe the conventional ideology of feminine self-sacrifice, given that women and men are equally urged to work, and that Barrett Browning's conception of women's work throughout *Aurora Leigh* is analogous to Barbara Bodichon's.

Because DuPlessis' project involves a metanarrative contrasting nineteenth-century and twentieth-century women writers, she does not consider the parallels between *Aurora Leigh* and twentieth-century strategies of revisionary mythopoesis. Nevertheless, her suggestive reading of H.D.'s transformative appropriation of Revelation suggests the affinities between Barrett Browning's emancipatory sage practice as I have described it and H.D.'s poetic practice in her epic *Trilogy*. If John declares 'that there shall be no other prophet after him', but H.D. 'demurs, proceeding to recast not only John's misogynistic interpretations but also his authoritarian voice' (DuPlessis 119), so too does Barrett Browning. 'For more's felt than is perceived / And more's perceived than can be interpreted', Aurora learns (7:891–2); and, given that, no vision of revelation, not even John's or Aurora's, can be definitive. If H.D. transforms the iconography of the Madonna by presenting her as a Lady with 'none of her usual attributes', so too Barrett Browning transforms the iconography of both the Madonna and the woman clothed with the sun in her representation of a raped woman and a woman writer. Finally, if H.D.'s apocalyptic Lady carries a book that 'resists assimilation into the past' because its text is 'blank, unwritten ... complete potentiality', one might similarly find in the conclusion to *Aurora Leigh* not a lack of alternative systems but an open-ended apocalyptic potentiality generating the reader's inscription of meaning.

Critics have rightly celebrated Aurora's strong opening assertion, 'I write', though without noting how it contrasts with Marian's initial submission to Romney's authority – 'let him write / His name upon her . . . it seemed natural' (6:911–12) – or how it relates to the general dangers of writing for or upon others in *Aurora Leigh*. Barrett Browning reveals a keen awareness of how we are 'written' by dominant ideologies, how we become the texts of others, yet at the same time she retains faith in the individual's potential to write 'for' a 'better self' – that is, in order to call a better self into existence. Clearly there are inescapable contradictions in this ideology of individualism, which Reynolds describes as 'a Romantic and liberal position' (*AL* 18). But as Alice Walker's Celie observes, change has to begin somewhere and our own self is what we have at hand. If, as Barrett Browning believed, life, morals and art develop from within, then the prophet-poet's task is not to write a programme of reform for others, but rather to create a space for each to 'write' the self and the future:

> She carries a book but it is not
> the tome of the ancient wisdom,
> the pages I imagine, are the blank pages
>
> of the unwritten volume of the new. . . .[30]

5 A Handmaid's Tale: The Critical Heritage

Reception histories of an author's work typically privilege the opinions of reviewers and critics: they present 'the critical heritage', to cite the title of one well-known series. Like literary histories in general, such collections and surveys do not record the responses of the culturally marginalized. Nor do they include responses expressed in pyschological and social transformations rather than in writing. Ironically, however, the socially marginalized and/or socially mobilized often dramatically alter history in ways that official histories obscure. In Frederic Jameson's words, history is a 'process of the reappropriation and neutralization . . . of forms which originally expressed the situation of "popular", subordinate, or dominated groups', with the result that there are innumerable silenced 'utterances scattered to the winds, or reappropriated' by the hegemonic order.[1] Yet it is precisely these silenced utterances that constitute the seeds of historical change and the sites of historical struggle.

Since no reception history can hope to reap the 'winds' that Jameson invokes, this one begins by emphasizing what it will inevitably exclude: the transformations Barrett Browning's works produced in the minds and lives of those who did not write because they were immersed in action, or who spoke and wrote privately but were not heard or recorded. 'Could there be a slenderer, more insignificant thread in human history than this consciousness of a girl . . .?', George Eliot asks of Gwendolyn Harleth in Chapter 11 of *Daniel Deronda*. Yet the most compelling half of her last and greatest novel explores that very terrain, while the earlier *Middlemarch* begins – like the history of Herodotus, Eliot pointedly observes – with the story of a woman.

Like Eliot, Barrett Browning is vitally concerned with the ways in which the historical process is shaped by dramatic or subtle movements of consciousness in the minds of apparently insignificant girls. For Aurora Leigh, the conversion is as cataclysmic as St Paul's – 'Life calls to us / In some transformed, apocalyptic voice'(1:673–4) – when she first encounters 'the poets' among her dead father's books. 'As the earth / Plunges in fury, when the internal fires / Have reached and pricked her heart', Aurora recalls, her soul '[l]et go conventions and sprang up surprised' (1:845–52). Yet books can also lead to silent invisible refigurations of consciousness, as Romney testifies when he tells Aurora that her poems have 'moved' him

> 'in secret, as the sap is moved
> In still March-branches, signless as a stone:
> But this last book o'ercame me like soft rain
> Which falls at midnight, when the tightened bark
> Breaks out into unhesitating buds. . . .' (8:593–7)

We cannot hope to trace even a fraction of the shifts in consciousness, 'signless as a stone', that *Aurora Leigh* and Barrett Browning's other works produced as they were reissued in edition after edition from the 1860s on, with over twenty editions of *Aurora Leigh* alone before 1900. As the root metaphors permeating *Aurora Leigh* imply – the roots of conviction (2:894), the roots of 'the fibrous years' (4:598), the roots of motives

(7:2), the roots of days (8:492), the roots of vision (2:944; 9:914) – action is transformed into art and art into action in myriad subtle ways. We do know, however, that a 'new American edition of Barrett Browning's work could sell ten thousand copies' (Reynolds *AL* 149). And we do know how important *Aurora Leigh* in particular was to some young women who later embodied the 'roots' of their own vision in writing.

Looking back almost forty years, Elizabeth Stuart Phelps, who passed her girlhood in Andover, Massachusetts, recalled how *Aurora Leigh* entered and transformed her mind in 1860 when she was sixteen.

> There may be greater poems in our language than 'Aurora Leigh', but it was many years before it was possible for me to suppose it; and none that ever saw the hospitality of fame could have done for that girl what that poem did at that time. I had never had a good memory – but I think I could have repeated a large portion of it; and know that I often stood the test of haphazard examinations on the poem from half-scoffing friends, sometimes of the masculine persuasion. . . . [W]hat Shakespeare or the Latin Fathers might have done for some other impressionable girl, Mrs. Browning . . . did for me.[2]

'Masculine persuasion' is a nice touch – reflecting the influence of Aurora's satiric wit and her critique of essentialist gender ideologies. What 'the poets' were to Aurora, making her earth plunge and clear 'herself / To elemental freedom' (1:845–50), Barrett Browning's works were to Phelps. Her aspiration to become a writer was confirmed by *Aurora Leigh*, and she went on to produce the highly successful Civil War novel *The*

Gates Ajar (1868), making her one of Emily Dickinson's more famous contemporaries.

Dickinson's response to Barrett Browning's greatest work is not enclosed in a 'house of prose'. But she did leave a few marked passages in one of her two copies of *Aurora Leigh*, scattered references to Mrs Browning in her letters, and three cryptic poems including the powerful 'I think I was enchanted', testimony to the 'Conversion of the Mind' she first experienced on reading Barrett Browning's 'Tomes of solid Witchcraft'.[3] One can readily imagine the inner earthquake accompanying that conversion in the poet who identified herself as 'Vesuvius at Home'. Noting the many 'lines, images, and phrases' in Dickinson's poems that echo Barrett Browning, Betsy Erkkila points out that the period when Dickinson read *Aurora Leigh* – 'between 1857 and 1861' – was also the period in which 'her poetic output increased from about fifty poems written in 1858 to over 300 written in 1862' (72–3). In Dickinson's case too, one might say, Barrett Browning's poems and the few other 'Books' she lists in her letters – Keats, Robert Browning, Ruskin, Sir Thomas Browne, and Revelations – supplanted 'Shakespeare and the Latin fathers'.[4]

The dissemination of Barrett Browning's works among women readers in general in the nineteenth century – women without literary inclinations, yet with intense, individual aspirations of varying kinds – has yet to be explored. However, the educational reformer Alice Woods gives some sense of how important *Aurora Leigh* was to the generation of Victorian women activists inspired by the earlier example of Barbara Bodichon and others. Woods first encountered *Aurora Leigh* in 1873. For her the passage used by Bodichon as an epigraph for *Women and Work*, along with other passages in the same vein like

Aurora's declaration, 'get work, get work; / Be sure
'tis better than what you work to get' (3: 167–8),
gave 'living expression' to the longing for worthy
employment she shared with so many other young
middle-class women of her time.[5] In traces such as
these we glimpse the lines of transmission that made
Aurora Leigh a text of Revelation for Susan B. Anthony
as well as for Emily Dickinson.

It comes as no surprise, given the relative absence of
women's histories before 1970, that such connections
should have been buried. What is more difficult to
account for, given Barrett Browning's poetic stature in
the nineteenth century and her impact on a host of
other writers and thinkers, male as well as female, is
the virtual elimination of her major works from most
standard literary histories within fifty years of her
death – with the telling exception of the *Sonnets from the
Portuguese*. Only 'Elizabeth's' status as Robert
Browning's wife and the popular appeal of their
romantic story saved her from becoming one of the
'disappeared' altogether. At the same time, these very
circumstances helped to furnish the means of contain-
ing and co-opting the force of her emancipatory
example.

The story of the reception of Barrett Browning's
works from the time of her death in 1861 until the
beginning of the second wave of feminism is, in more
ways than one, a handmaid's tale. Mrs Browning –
the wife, the mother, the muse – remained in a variety
of supplementary roles. But Elizabeth Barrett
Browning the poet was erased, even as many of her
generic and technical innovations were appropriated
and in some cases even attributed to male writers
whom she had clearly influenced. Thus, like the
protagonist of Margaret Atwood's *The Handmaid's
Tale*, her creativity was assimilated by a hegemonic

discourse that denied her enabling agency – and that, outside the circles of feminist critical studies, often does so still. One of the pleasures of artistic creation for a woman, according to 'Guerilla Girls', subversive activists in the world of contemporary art, is seeing your ideas live on in the works of others – unacknowledged, of course. Barrett Browning, were she alive, might well agree.

A number of broad cultural transformations not necessarily related to ideologies of gender clearly contributed to the drastic decline in Barrett Browning's reputation within fifty years of her death. The anti-Romantic spirit of early Modernism led to a preference for qualities thought to be 'Classical', while Barrett Browning is a Romantic writer fired by Promethean aspirations. By 1900, Christina Rossetti, a poet of less range and audacity but more perfect technique, had displaced Barrett Browning as the greatest English 'poetess' in many anthologies and literary histories. The aesthetic movement of the 1890s with its cry of 'art for art' also led to condemnations of Barrett Browning's politically or ethically engaged poetry, condemnations revived in the neoformalism of the 1950s and 60s. Those readers who were politically engaged in the 1890s, and in the Georgian and World War I periods, often endorsed a jingoistic patriotism that made them hostile towards Barrett Browning's Italian sympathies and her strong critique of English parochialism in *Casa Guidi Windows*, *Aurora Leigh*, and *Poems before Congress*. The final poem in *Poems before Congress*, 'A Curse for a Nation', had been interpreted by some outraged English reviewers and subsequent critics as Mrs Browning's 'hysterical' curse on her own country when the collection was published in 1860. By the turn of the century, such descriptions of Barrett Browning's political poetry as 'hysterical' were increasingly common.[6] Finally the Edwardian reaction, which led to a slump in the reputation of Victorian writers generally, undoubtedly contributed to Barrett Browning's decline in reputation. Taken together, however, all of these cultural transformations do not suffice to explain the burial of Barrett Browning's unprecedented achievement. As E. K. Brown observed in 1942, 'no other Victorian of comparable talent . . . suffered so steep a decline in public admiration and critical interest'.[7]

The questions I address here are straightforward then. How, when, and where was England's first major woman poet erased from literary history? Who buried her and why? In her study of the reception of Barrett Browning's works up to 1900, Tricia Lootens observes that the poet crowned as England's 'Queen of Song' in 1850 soon came to fit the profile of Marge Piercy's 'Token Woman', who ' "serves a season / then is ritually dismembered" ' (179). As Lootens suggests, 'absurd though it would be to presume a monolithic conscious conspiracy, it would be equally foolish to presume that a monolithic unconscious innocence underlies the suppression of Barrett Browning's work' (17–18). Nevertheless, Lootens' own emphasis falls more on unconscious innocence, as she demonstrates how the narrative paradigms of 'conventional literary historiography' obscured Barrett Browning's achievement by casting her as a series of 'stock romantic figures': a sister-saint, a Queen of song, a domestic heroine (8).

While these narrative paradigms undoubtedly contributed to the myths that concealed Barrett Browning the poet, the reception history of her works also embodies a remarkably overt conflict between competing ideological agendas. Certainly the substitution of Christina Rossetti for Barrett Browning as

England's new Queen of Song was not motivated merely by aesthetic concerns or the unconscious perpetuation of fictional conventions. In 1915, for example, Arthur Waugh praised Rossetti's poetry as the best produced by her sex because 'it accepts the burden of womanhood', whereas Mrs Browning's fails 'because she is trying to make a woman's voice thunder like a man's'.[8]

The assumption that history is marked by 'progress' – a concept that we castigate as 'Victorian' yet often implicitly endorse – might suggest that twentieth-century critics were somehow more enlightened than their Victorian precursors and therefore less likely to object to women who rejected 'the burden of woman-hood'. Margaret Reynolds reflects the general view of the reception of women writers in the Victorian period in observing that they were effectively silenced 'through the undervaluing of "women's" subject matter' and poetic forms, through 'professional scorn' for their mediums of publication (the *Annuals*), through 'the dismissive pigeon-holing' of a diffusive feminine style, and above all through 'the overriding assumption . . . that only men could be the producers of "true" poetry' (*AL* 4). Although there is much truth to these claims, the case of Barrett Browning suggests that the mid-Victorian era was a less repressive period for women writers than the 1890s and the early twentieth century. Because the transformations generated by women's entry into various fields of literary discourse were occurring so quickly in the mid-nineteenth century, at a time when the institutions of criticism were themselves undergoing metamorphosis, critical discourse about women's writing was markedly dialogized in the period.

By the 1890s, however, the reaction to the mid-Victorian women's rights movement had set in, a reaction now amply documented in studies like Bram Dijkstra's *Idols of Perversity*, Gaye Tuchman and Nina Fortin's *Edging Women Out*, and Elaine Showalter's *Sexual Anarchy*.[9] This reaction, comparable in some ways to the 1990s backlash to second wave feminism, is reflected in the reception of Barrett Browning's works. Turn-of-the-century and early modern critics were more actively, hostilely, and unanimously involved than their mid-Victorian precursors in erasing the transformative presence of England's first major woman poet from the emerging canon of nineteenth-century literature.

Nevertheless, I begin with the obituary assessments of 1861–2 here because they prefigure many of the ideological strategies subsequently deployed to domesticate, diffuse or deny the subversive potential of Barrett Browning's example. The obituaries also form a fascinating site of ideological struggle because the gender debate they reflect is so overt and so marked by internal contradictions and clashing perspectives. Almost all of the critics retrospectively assessing Barrett Browning's achievement are intensely preoccupied with the manifestations of 'Woman's Powers' in literature, to use the running title that appears in the *North British Review* essay. But they interpret these 'Powers' in very different ways.

Gerald Massey, the author of the *North British Review* essay, responds positively to 'Woman's Powers', taking issue with Thomas De Quincey's prophecy that there will never be a great woman poet, and pointing to the great strides of woman writers 'during the last twenty years'. Despite the cultural obstacles that in effect mean 'a woman-Shakespeare would really have to be doubly as great as the man Shakespeare', women have run 'almost abreast' of their brothers in 'more than one department of literature, Massey observes, instancing 'fiery little Charlotte Brontë', George Eliot laying hold of life 'with a large hand', and Mrs Browning, 'the greatest woman-poet of whom we have any record', Sappho included. Even in the *North British Review* obituary, however, there is a note of defensiveness: Eliot is 'almost a prose Shakespeare', and 'De Quincey himself would have admitted that in Mrs. Browning we have woman's nearest approach to a great poet'.[10]

Other reviewers are more divided and, in some cases, much more hostile to the signs of 'Woman's Powers' and what they see as the unhealthy feminin-ization of literary genius. Several of the obituary writers are still willing to grant Mrs Browning the status of the greatest English poetess or even of a great poet, but only after elaborate ideological manoeuvres producing startling contradictions. Employing what was to become the most common strategy for contain-ing Barrett Browning's empowering example, the *North American Review* obituary domesticates her as a womanly woman and her husband's handmaid: 'inasamuch as she was a great woman, she was greatly a woman; and if she exceeded her sex in strength and aspiration, it was only to foreshow what a woman may gain in her proper sphere, – not in another, – and to assure us that no soul of man, however high, need lack a companion to strengthen and complete, as well as beautify, his life.' Mrs Browning sought intellectual equality with men and, with 'beautiful insanity', imagined a state of sexlessness in heaven in her sonnet 'To George Sand: A Recognition', the reviewer observes. But her 'great success is in her failure', which illustrates what woman is and what she may do in her own sphere. Predictably, the writer observes that Mrs Browning's life came to a climax when she wrote *Sonnets from the Portuguese*, a statement he fails to reconcile with his acknowledgement of *Aurora Leigh* as her 'greatest work'. The gender ideology informing this assessment of Barrett Browning is undisguised. 'The moral difference between the sexes is not an accidental or unessential matter . . . It is necessary, radical, and most unchangeable.' Mrs Browning remained a woman and 'only a woman' and therefore not a 'monstrosity in God's creation'.[11]

More overtly hostile reviewers employ what may be called the double-stick strategy in their obituaries on Barrett Browning: that is, they use her as a yardstick to measure the achievement of other women writers, and as a stick to beat down any new women aspiring to scale Parnassus. The *Edinburgh Review*'s comprehensive critique of her works up to and including *Poems before Congress* is a case in point. After a savage critique of Barrett Browning's poetical ambition, 'grotesque ideas', 'intolerable conceits', and 'coarsely masculine' tone, the writer faintly praises her more conventionally feminine and slight poems (for example, 'My Doves'), and then concludes: 'Considering the great capabilities she possessed, her career may be accepted as some proof of the impossibility that women can ever attain to the first rank in any imaginative composition.' The *Saturday Review* is even blunter: 'no woman can hope to achieve what Mrs. Browning failed to accomplish.'[12]

In the *Saturday Review* obituary, we also encounter the increasing insistence on Barrett Browning's imitation of other male writers – including Poe (who clearly was influenced by her) and her own husband. The related assumption that a woman writer can be no more than a simulacrum of a male writer appears frequently in mid- and late Victorian responses to Barrett Browning. For instance, the writer of the *North American Review* obituary cited above observes: 'Ther is no philosophy in "Aurora Leigh." It is rather a playing with philosophy, – an acute and imitative handling of the tools of the masculine workman' (345). Similarly, in keeping with his theory that women writers 'put on the earthly feminine likeness of some favourite of the other sex', Leigh Hunt defined Barrett Browning as 'an ultra-sensitive sister of Tennyson'; while George Barnett Smith's earnest lucubrations on whether Mrs Browning could better be described as Shakespeare's daughter or Tennyson's sister produced Henry James' apt sarcasm, 'it might do better to try "Wordsworth's niece" or "Swinburne's aunt" ' (Lootens 151, 330).

Most insistently, however, she was cast as Browning's wife in her poetry as in her life by many reviewers. Shortly after her marriage, when Barrett Browning's fame still completely eclipsed Robert's, she was amused to find one reviewer complaining that her husband had started to imitate her defects, while another reviewer simultaneously and independently complained she was imitating his. But by the time of her death, the emphasis was principally on her imitation, not his. Thus the writer of the *Saturday Review* obituary referred to above condescendingly observed: '[T]he only considerable poetess who ever married an original poet may well be excused for copying, and perhaps exaggerating, his casual peculiarities' (492). A subsequent article on 'Poetesses' in the *Saturday Review* indicates that women poets were damned if they did 'imitate' male writers and damned if they didn't. According to this writer, Mrs Browning missed greatness because 'women, in writing poetry, draw their style from other women, and thus miss that largeness and universality which alone compel attention'.[13]

The references to Browning in the obituaries

marking Barrett Browning's death raise some interesting questions about the interconnections between the
reception of his works and the reception of his wife's.
Editions of her works frequently included advertisements for his throughout the 1850s. Browning also
quite consciously used his wife's name on occasion to
encourage publishers to accept work from him
(Reynolds *AL* 84). It seems very likely, therefore,
that Barrett Browning's international reputation at
the time of her death in 1861 significantly contributed
to Browning's growing public recognition in the
1860s. The emphasis in the reviews of the 1860s on
Barrett Browning's womanly role as Browning's wife
and the inferiority of her poetry to his furthermore
suggests that the lionizing of Browning may have been
related to the ideological work of domesticating his
wife's audaciously female genius. By acknowledging
Browning's genius or, at the very least, his originality,
as the *Saturday Review* does, critics could more easily
put his wife in a suitably subordinate position.

As the *North British Review* indicates, however, not
all male critics in the 1860s were unprepared to
acknowledge female literary genius. Nor did they
consistently reduce Barrett Browning to a figure
ancillary to Browning. Indeed, up to the turn of the
century, she was categorized and approached as a
major poet not only by numerous British and American
critics, but also by French, Italian and Russian critics.
In his detailed analysis of *Aurora Leigh* as 'le poème d'un
siècle', Joseph Texte notes that his admiration for
Barrett Browning's works is shared by Hippolyte
Taine; while Patrick Waddington documents the
considerable praise of Barrett Browning's works (and
the dismissal of Browning's) in Russian criticism up to
the 1890s.[14]

Among British and American critics, H. Buxton

Forman and Edmund Clarence Stedman are representative of late Victorians who accord Barrett Browning
the status of a major poet. Forman, who engages in an
eloquent defence of women writers, takes several of his
chapter epigraphs from her works in *Our Living Poets*
(1871) and pairs her suggestively with Walt Whitman
in the epigraphs facing his title page. He also offers
astute and high praise of various works in her canon in
his analyses of Jean Ingelow, Augusta Webster,
Christina Rossetti and George Eliot; and, contrary to
those critics who see Mrs Browning as imitating male
writers, he points to the echoes of her works in poets
such as Coventry Patmore.[15] Stedman's essay on
'Elizabeth Barrett Browning' in his often reprinted
Victorian Poets is a work of criticism more mixed with
sentimental hagiography, as Lootens emphasizes
(324–34). Nevertheless, he provides a comprehensive
and often perceptive analysis of her works, allotting a
full chapter to her, and only a third of a chapter to
Matthew Arnold by comparison. Moreover, although
Stedman judges *Aurora Leigh* a 'failure' considered
merely 'as a poem' by 'accepted standards', he
simultaneously pays tribute to its 'audacious, specula-
tive freedom'. It contains 'enough spare inspiration to
set up a dozen smaller poets', he observes; and its verse
is 'flexible', 'noticeably her own', and 'terser than her
husband's'. He further praises *Aurora Leigh* as 'the
metrical and feminine complement to Thackeray's
"Pendennis" ': '[n]owhere in literature is the process of
culture by means of study and passional experience so
graphically depicted' (141–2).

Forman and Stedman are far from alone in their
consideration of Barrett Browning as a major
nineteenth-century poet, as the examples of William T.
Herridge, Thomas Bradfield, and Lewis E. Gates
indicate. Gates, who ranks Barrett Browning with

Arnold and above Arthur Hugh Clough, perceptively counters the stereotypical picture of her as a secluded visionary invalid, still apparent in some current criticism. One might have expected her to be a 'dreamer', he observes. 'Yet in truth in reading her poetry we are taken . . . into the thick of the tumult of living . . . She belonged vitally to her age.'[16] I cite these critics in some detail because their often laudatory assessments disappeared from literary history, as opposing and more hostile or dismissive views of Barrett Browning prevailed.

One index of the hostility that the author of *Aurora Leigh* aroused in some Victorian men appears in a letter written by Edward Fitzgerald on hearing of her death in 1861. 'Mrs. Browning's death is rather a relief to me', Fitzgerald confided to a friend; 'no more Aurora Leighs, thank God! A Woman of real Genius, I know: but what is the upshot of it all? She and her Sex had better mind the Kitchen and their Children; and perhaps the Poor: except in such things as little Novels, they only devote themselves to what Men do much better, leaving that which Men do worse or not at all.'[17] When the letter was published in Fitzgerald's *Letters and Literary Remains* in 1889 and came to Browning's attention, he was understandably outraged, and it was deleted from subsequent editions of the *Remains*. But the opinions privately expressed by Fitzgerald in 1861 came to be expressed more openly in the ensuing decades, as articles in the notoriously conservative *Saturday Review* indicate. The evaluations of Mrs Browning in its 1861 obituary, and in a subsequent 1868 essay on 'Poetesses' are mild and not uncomplimentary compared to the denunciation in its pages in 1888 of 'the endless gush and the sickening sentimentality, the nauseous chatter about "womanhood" and "woman's heart", and all the rest of it, which she almost invented, but of which the secret by no means died with her'.[18]

Opposition to the author of *Aurora Leigh* and the 'secret' which 'by no means died with her' is also indirectly discernible in Frederic Kenyon's indication that there was some talk on Browning's death in 1889 of transferring Mrs Browning's remains from Italy to England, 'to lie with his among the great company of English poets in which they had earned their places. But it was thought better, on the whole, to leave them undisturbed in the land and in the city which she had loved so well . . . In life and death she had been made welcome in Florence' (*LEBB* 2:452). In other words, Kenyon implies, there were those (and no doubt he had Fitzgerald in mind) who had not welcomed or would not welcome her in England 'in life and death'.

Indeed, when Kenyon's carefully prepared edition of *The Letters of Elizabeth Barrett Browning* appeared in 1897, Edmund Gosse joined Fitzgerald in expressing relief over her early death: but he expressed his relief publicly, not privately. In *A Short History of Modern English Literature*, he claimed that Mrs Browning's 'late work was formless, spasmodic, singularly toneless and harsh, nor is it probable that what seemed her premature death, in 1861, was a real deprivation to English literature'. As for her readers, '[t]heir nerves were pleasurely [sic] excited by the choral tumult of Miss Barrett's verse, by her generous and humane enthusiasm, and by the spontaneous impulsiveness of her emotion. They easily forgave the slipshod execution, the Pythian vagueness and the Pythian shriek.' This assessment contrasts strongly with Gosse's earlier enthusiasm for the 'broader and robuster spirit' of poetry reflected in the 'stupendous epic-satire' of *Aurora Leigh*.[19]

Gosse's image of the 'Pythian shriek' associates

Barrett Browning with the demonic figures of the witch and the sorceress so prevalent in fin-de-siècle representations. Susan Casteras notes that 'personifications of positive feminine knowledge' were increasingly rare in the images produced 'from the 1860s' onwards, displaced by 'the negative side of female sapientia or wisdom, namely, witchcraft' (Morgan, *Victorian Sages*, 145). Given this, it is hardly surprising that the woman who had been read as a sage, and who had created in Aurora Leigh a positive and powerful figure of female wisdom, began to be portrayed as a witch-like figure.

Notwithstanding the misogyny of Gosse and Fitzgerald, it would be erroneous to conclude that only men participated in the critical devaluation of Barrett Browning, in opposition to critics like Stedman and Forman. The ideological clash between opposing views was also apparent among women. It emerges with particular starkness in two editions of Barrett Browning's collected works published in 1900: Harriet Waters Preston's Cambridge edition and the scholarly edition prepared by Charlotte Porter and Helen A. Clarke. Preston's highly critical view of Barrett Browning is readily apparent both in the Preface to her edition, and in an essay which had appeared the previous year in the *Atlantic Monthly*.[20] Casting Mrs Browning as a writer whose later works were 'hysterical', she joins Gosse in echoing and endorsing Fitzgerald's relief that the poet's death meant no more Aurora Leighs could be written. Porter and Clarke, on the contrary, present Mrs Browning 'as one of the great poets of the Victorian era, her work standing comparison with the most original among the men of the age' (*CW* 6:xv). Moreover, they analyse her works with illuminating detail in the successive 'Critical Introductions' to the volumes of their carefully annotated edition, noting, among many other points, those 'signs of the sibyl' in her works condemned by critics such as Gosse – the same signs 'against which the sober-suited critics of her own day pompously admonished her' (*CW* 2:xii). They also acutely summarize the absurdities and contradictions of the criticism accusing Barrett Browning of 'imitating' male writers like Tennyson, Poe and Shelley (*CW* 2:xx).

Given its scholarly annotation, one might have expected Porter and Clarke's edition to consolidate Barrett Browning's position in the canon of major nineteenth-century poets, and to provide a resource for subsequent studies. But this edition is almost never cited in criticism after 1900. It seems to have virtually disappeared until the 1973 reprint, along with the laudatory analyses of Barrett Browning's poetry by critics such as Stedman and Taine, whom Porter and Clarke cite in support of their interpretations on more than one occasion. The hostile and disparaging views of critics like Preston and Gosse carried the day, along with the related, though apparently more benign approaches to Barrett Browning as either an append-age to her husband or one of a group of 'poet-esses'.

The transition to the 'appendage' approach is apparent in Mrs Margaret Oliphant's *The Victorian Age of English Literature*, one of the first literary histories to treat Barrett Browning's poetry in a supplementary section of a chapter on her husband's works rather than in a separate and prior chapter. Oliphant pauses over the 'question in chronology whether the other poet whose name is for ever linked with that of Robert Browning, the first of women-poets in her own race, perhaps in the world, should not have come before his in the record, the beginning of her work, preceding his by a few years, and the end of it by many. But it seemed undesirable to separate the great Twin Brethren of our generation from each other', she explains, alluding to Tennyson. 'Why it is that no woman (except in fiction) ever attains the highest rank in poetical literature, it is probably quite impossible ever to determine', Oliphant continues. The suppression of Barrett Browning's name throughout these ponderous speculations is symptomatic, like the claim that the *Sonnets from the Portuguese* represent 'the highest tide' of Barrett Browning's poetic genius.[21] At the same time, however, the doubt Mrs Oliphant expresses is revealing.

Later critics had no second thoughts about the chronological violation in treating Barrett Browning as a supplement to her husband. Indeed, it became standard practice in literary histories for a discussion of her life and works (increasingly the former) to appear as a sort of conventional tailpiece to the section on Browning. How different such representations are from the image of the Brownings as poetical peers and equals we find in Harriet Hosmer's famous sculpture of 'The Clasped Hands' of the Brownings made in 1855. Although Robert's slightly larger hand partially encloses Elizabeth's, her hand is in the foreground, granting the two a visual equality.

Ironically, Barrett Browning's objections to Richard Hengist Horne's treatment of Mary Howitt in *A New Spirit of the Age* provide a prophetic prefiguration of her own fate as the female half of a literary couple. 'I wish in this second edition of yours you would give Mary Howitt room to take her full stature', she wrote to Horne. 'She appears in the book simply as Mrs. Howitt, William's wife, whereas his reputation has grown from the stem of hers' (*LRHH* 2:25–6). As she wryly observed of the conventional comparisons of the poet John Gower to Chaucer, 'He who rides in the *king's* chariot will miss the people's *"hic est"*' (*CW* 6:246). In her case, it made no difference that she had once been the 'Queen of Song' and that she had at one point overshadowed Browning in her own chariot – so much so in fact, that in the 1899 essay cited above, Preston observes: 'I myself have heard, as late as the early eighties, a well-connected and presumably well-instructed Englishman, of the military caste, stoutly deny that there were *two* poets of the name of Browning, – a man as well as a woman!' (822).

A further phase in the reduction of Barrett Browning to a mere supplement or handmaid of Browning is reflected in critical assessments by John W. Cunliffe and Laurie Magnus appearing in 1908 and 1909.[22] 'Elizabeth Barrett Browning was not a great poet, but she was the ideal counterpart of a great lover', Magnus observes in his survey of nineteenth-century literature. 'Literature owes her a great debt for *Aurora Leigh* and *Sonnets from the Portuguese*, but the indirect debt is larger for her influence on Robert Browning's life and work' (287). Cunliffe more dramatically converts Barrett Browning into a handmaid to her husband's genius:

Browning's influence upon his wife is written large on the surface of all her later works, the best thing she ever did, the *Sonnets from the Portuguese*, being directly due to his inspiration. Her influence upon him is subtler, deeper – the influence of the weaker and finer upon the stronger nature. Richly as her ardent spirit developed under the emotional and intellectual stimulus she received from him, I am inclined to believe that her most enduring contributions to literature were not direct but indirect – through the influence she exerted on her poet-husband. Her best work is to be found not in her own writings, but in his. (169–70)

This interpretation is remarkable for the way in which, in Robert Graves' well known words, it translates Barrett Browning into a 'muse or nothing'. Browning's role as muse, on the contrary, is translated into an inscription 'written large' on all his wife's works: he is presented as a muse and everything else, one might say. Cunliffe's article indicates the ideological context in which edition after edition of the *Sonnets from the Portuguese* came to be published. Meanwhile, Warner Barnes' bibliography indicates that no new edition at all of *Aurora Leigh* appeared between 1905 and Cora Kaplan's 1978 Women's Press edition.

Hugh Walker's magisterial survey of Victorian literature (1910) reflects the other common approach to Barrett Browning among literary historiographers after the turn of the century. Walker is a literary monarchist bent on constructing a male line of king poets. Accordingly, he discusses Browning and Tennyson in a chapter entitled 'The New Kings' that makes no mention of Elizabeth Barrett. Nor does he include more than a passing reference to her in the preceding chapter on 'The Interregnum', dealing with the period between the Romantic 'kings of thought' and 'The New Kings' – though she was one of the most important poets in this period. At last we find her, in the seventh and last subsection of a third chapter on 'The Minor Poets: Earlier Period', in a separate ladies' compartment entitled 'The Poetesses'. The first six subsections in 'The Minor Poets', on such subjects as 'The Balladists', 'The Philosopher Poets', and 'The Political Poets' are almost exclusively concerned with male writers. The fact that Barrett Browning wrote important works in all of these categories calls in question the assumption that Barrett Browning was dismissed by mainstream male critics because she did not 'fit with the periodization and concerns of male literature' (Cooper 4). On the contrary, Walker explicitly acknowledges Mrs Browning's 'sex' as his justification for placing her in the seventh subsection of 'The Minor Poets' of *The Literature of the Victorian Era*.[23] His strategy of ideological quarantine is particularly ironic because it so grossly distorts the ideal of historical comprehensiveness he strives to achieve.

Because Walker was such a formidable authority, his pronouncements regarding Mrs Browning proved to be very influential. But rather than offering any original analysis of her works, he simply consolidated the critical commonplaces tirelessly recirculated after 1900. For example, he emphasizes her imitation of her husband, identifying the 1844 *Poems* as 'the point where the influence of Browning begins'. Unlike some critics, he saw this influence as largely negative: 'She was thoroughly feminine; but under the impulse from him she unconsciously adopted a more masculine tone. She imagined herself a thinker; in reality she *felt*, and in the attempt to translate her feeling into thought she fell into numerous mistakes.' Predictably, he pronounces the *Sonnets from the Portuguese* her greatest work because they are 'the genuine utterance of a woman's heart'. He pronounces upon her deficiency in art. 'She will not restrain herself', he complains, criticizing her for the carelessness of her rhymes and ignoring the explanations of these as deliberately experimental in the letters published by both Richard Hengist Horne and Frederic Kenyon. *Aurora Leigh* he dismisses as an 'ambitious metrical romance' suffering from excessive expansiveness. 'He who has read it once shrinks for travelling again through many flats of commonplaces', despite the 'beautiful oases of poetry' it offers (367–70). Walker bears out Lootens' observation that the 'most damaging attacks' on Barrett Browning's greatest work 'would deny rather than condemn its audacity' through strategic use of the 'politics of boredom' (248, 233). The ideological agenda underlying his apparently aesthetic assessment of mere monotony is more visible in an earlier study, where he bluntly asserts that 'always the thought, the social discussions' of *Aurora Leigh* 'are wrong'.[24]

Between *The Literature of the Victorian Era* in 1910 and the 1950s, I have discovered no significant critical assessments of Barrett Browning that question the views articulated by Walker and the growing body of professional academic critics – with two notable exceptions. The first is the voice of G. K. Chesterton, saltily testifying in the critical wilderness like some irreverent prophet; the second is Virginia Woolf. Chesterton eschews gender-inflected essentialist distinctions between Barrett Browning and other Victorian writers. On the contrary, he explicitly rejects the 'false sex philosophy' that would see her strengths as masculine and her weaknesses as feminine: 'we remember all the lines in her work which were weak enough to be called "womanly", we forget the multitude of strong lines that are strong enough to be called "manly"; lines that Kingsley or Henley would have jumped for joy to print in proof of their manliness.' Chesterton also trenchantly dismisses the idea that Barrett Browning imitated her husband: 'As to the critic who thinks her poetry owed anything to the great poet who was her husband, he can go and live in the same hotel with the man who can believe that George Eliot owed anything to the extravagant imagination of Mr. George Henry Lewes' (179–81).

Chesterton is particularly refreshing in emphasizing

Barrett Browning's cosmopolitanism, rather than her 'hysterical' un-English sympathies with Italian libera-tion. Browning, with 'all his Italian sympathies and Italian residence . . . was not the man to get Victorian England out its provincial rut', Chesterton suggests. 'His celebrated wife was wider and wiser than he in this sense . . . She is by far the most European of all the English poets of that age; all of them, even her own much greater husband, look local beside her. Tennyson and the rest are nowhere' (178). He also praised her wit and the 'powerful concentration' of her rhetoric (181), in contrast to the conventional critical emphasis on her diffuse and feminine expansiveness: 'She excelled in her sex, in epigram, almost as much as Voltaire in his. Pointed phrases like: "Martyrs by the pang without the palm" . . . came quite freshly and spontaneously to her quite modern mind' (177–8). Chesterton's own strength in the epigram makes his witty survey of Victorian literature engaging reading. Yet, despite the fact that his study was reprinted at least twelve times between 1913 and 1931, his evaluations of Barrett Browning are never cited by subsequent critics.

Virginia Woolf's 1931 reassessment of *Aurora Leigh* was similarly disregarded during the middle decades of the twentieth century. Since the 1970s, however, feminist critics have repeatedly quoted her sardonic description of Mrs Browning's assignment to 'the servants' quarters' in the 'mansion of literature . . . where, in company with Mrs Hemans, Eliza Cook, Jean Ingelow, Alexander Smith, Edwin Arnold, and Robert Montgomery, she bangs the crockery about and eats vast handfuls of peas on the point of her knife' (134). While the appreciation of Woolf's grotesquely apt metaphor for literary hegemonies is understand-able, the focus on this graphic passage in her essay on

Aurora Leigh has tended to foreground her defensive distancing of herself from 'Mrs Browning'. As a result, critics have less adequately appreciated both the daring iconoclasm of Woolf's critical revisionism and her tribute to Barrett Browning as one of her own literary 'grandmothers'.

Like Chesterton's views on Mrs Browning, Woolf's were those of a voice crying in the wilderness. What she had to say about *Aurora Leigh* and Barrett Browning may have been true, but it was not 'in the true', to use Foucault's well-known formulation. 'Speed and energy, forthrightness and complete self-confidence', combined with the spell-binding narrative powers of the Ancient Mariner (135): these were hardly qualities that critics like Walker or Gosse or Cunliffe had associated with the author of *Aurora Leigh*. Nor did they dwell on Aurora's satire of women's education, as Woolf did, or the fact that she 'was blessed with a little room' of her own in which to read and write (136). In the face of the demure domestic handmaid or the diffusive, emotional poetess constructed by the prevailing critical tradition, Woolf stressed as Chesterton did that 'the mind of Elizabeth Barrett was lively and secular and satirical', passionately engaged with 'the arguments, the politics, and the strife of the modern world'. If *Aurora Leigh* was not 'the masterpiece it might have been', the circumstance was not due to the quality of Barrett Browning's genius or to her sex, according to Woolf, but to the 'irreparable damage' of her long years as a cloistered invalid and to the social conditions of Victorian woman writers for whom 'the connexion between a woman's art and a woman's life was so unnaturally close' that it was 'impossible for the most austere of critics not sometimes to touch the flesh when his eyes should be fixed upon the page' (137–9). This comment is typical of Woolf's subtle indirectness in revaluing *Aurora Leigh*. She introduces this comment in her essay by stating that 'Mrs. Browning could no more conceal herself than she could control herself', then attributes this circumstance to historical conditions, and finally ends by implying that male critics, with their eyes 'fixed' on a woman writer's 'flesh', were in fact those in danger of losing control.

Although Woolf does not see Barrett Browning's attempt to mix poetry with the novel in *Aurora Leigh* as a success, her own views on this point are themselves strikingly mixed and developed at length, with the result that she pays tribute to the work even as she seems to dissect its weaknesses.

> [I]f Mrs Browning meant by a novel-poem a book in which character is closely and subtly revealed, the relations of many hearts laid bare, and a story unfalteringly unfolded, she failed completely. But if she meant rather to give us a sense of life in general, of people who are unmistakably Victorian, wrestling with the problems of their own time, all brightened, intensified, and compacted by the fire of poetry, she succeeded. Aurora Leigh, with her passionate interest in social questions, her conflict as artist and woman, her longing for knowledge and freedom, is the true daughter of her age. . . . The aunt, the antimacassars, and the country house from which Aurora escapes are real enough to fetch high prices in the Tottenham Court Road at this moment. The broader aspects of what it felt like to be a Victorian are seized as surely and stamped as vividly upon us as in any novel by Trollope or Mrs Gaskell. (143)

As in the case of her earlier essay on George Eliot, the originality of Woolf's revaluation of *Aurora Leigh* can only be appreciated when we consider the critical current she was writing against in 1931, to use one of her own metaphors. For thirty years, critics concerned for their reputations had only felt safe in praising the *Sonnets from the Portuguese*. Yet Woolf not only focuses on *Aurora Leigh*, excluding any consideration of the *Sonnets*. She also asserts that *Aurora Leigh* is a work that 'still commands our interest and inspires our respect' (140).

Aside from opposing the orthodox views established by critics like Gosse and Walker, Woolf was also swimming against the current created by the spate of books (at least eight) popularizing Barrett Browning as the heroine of a romance appearing between 1928 and 1931, *The Barretts of Wimpole Street* and *The Immortal Lovers* conspicuous among them.[25] 'Passionate lovers, in curls and side whiskers, oppressed, defiant, eloping – in this guise thousands of people must know and love the Brownings who have never read a line of their poetry' (133). This is Woolf's point of departure in her essay, and it is not a promising one for initiating a reassessment of Barrett Browning and a forgotten work that she views as almost a 'masterpiece'. Woolf's difficulties were compounded by the fact that the elopement making the Brownings such a popular symbol of defiance against Victorian parents ironically co-existed with the denigration of Barrett Browning's poetry as dreadfully, earnestly 'Victorian'. The patronizing tone of Irene Cooper Willis' *E. B. Browning* (1928) in the 'Representative Women' series illustrates this attitude. Characterizing the Victorians as 'oppressively rigid and moral', indeed as 'hideously moral', Willis presents Mrs Browning as a 'true mid-Victorian . . . inspired by piety as well as ruled by it': a woman who articulated a 'dreary gospel of suffering and sacrifice', and who presented in *Aurora Leigh* an 'absurd picture of English social life' because she 'did not know what she was writing about'.[26]

Such responses become more understandable, in the general public's case if not in Willis', if we consider the contexts in which many readers no doubt encountered *Aurora Leigh*: in the excerpted ' "vallooable thoughts" ' recalled by Paul Landis, which included, 'It takes a soul / To move a body' (cited Lootens 405). Nevertheless, we should not overlook the complicity of scholarly academic criticism as well as school texts and popular biographies in promoting the construction of Barrett Browning as the rescued naïve heroine of a sentimental romance. As Lootens astutely observes, 'the very literary historiographers who scorned the presumed sentimentality' of Mrs Browning's works, of women readers, and of the Victorian public generally 'continued to develop Miss Barrett of Wimpole Street as a sentimental heroine of their own'. The 'poet's works were increasingly (and retroactively) consigned to a sentimental public, while her life provided literary historians with an opportunity to indulge their own sentimentality by writing the woman's biography as romantic or comic relief from accounts of the "real" development of literary tradition' (410–11).

The 'real' development of the Victorian literary tradition as it was constructed in the 1930s, 40s and 50s could not accommodate the conceptualization of *Aurora Leigh* as a work of transformative gynocentric sage discourse, an approach that Woolf's analysis implies in focusing on the work's dynamic engagement with vital social problems and its generic heterogeneity. In these decades, as Carol Christ observes, the body of Victorian prose sage writing was gathered together from the various disciplines into which it had been dispersed (for example, history and philosophy) and consolidated as 'a heroic masculine bulwark set up against a democratized and feminized novel' (Morgan, *Victorian Sages*, 26). Victorian poetry was similarly constructed as a predominantly or exclusively male discursive space. Thus the first edition of Walter E. Houghton's and G. Robert Stange's widely used *Victorian Poetry and Poetics* (1959) included no women writers at all, while the second edition (1968) added Christina Rossetti as the single woman among its roster of nineteen poets.

By the 1950s, then, Barrett Browning, the candidate for Poet Laureate in 1850 and the author of *Aurora Leigh*, had effectively disappeared from literary history, except in her capacity as the romantic heroine who laid bare her heart in the *Sonnets from the Portuguese*. In a categorization perhaps suggested by Gosse, Jerome Buckley included a brief consideration of Elizabeth Barrett's 'feverish lyricism' and of *Aurora Leigh* in his chapter on the Spasmodic poets in *The Victorian Temper*, but he gave much more sustained attention to poets like Philip James Bailey and Sydney Dobell who never approached Barrett Browning's fame or critical success in the mid-Victorian period.[27] Buckley's comments on *Aurora Leigh* are not without his usual insights: at least he acknowledged that there were many anti-Spasmodic elements in the work. The bald summary of Elizabeth Browning's works by John D. Cooke and Lionel Stevenson in 1949 is more representative of the critical consensus in this period:

Her poetry was fluent and copious, with emphatic rhythms. She was always motivated by generous enthusiasm: in her early work it was aroused chiefly by literary and historical subjects; later her husband's influence directed it towards contemporary events. Her narrative poems were inclined to slip into sentimentality, and her political poems were sometimes hysterically violent. Carried along by the flow of obvious rhythm, she often wrote too much, and was careless with the meaning of words and the accuracy of rhymes. . . . The discipline of the sonnet was good for her, and artistically as well as emotionally, the *Sonnets from the Portuguese* rank with her best work, whereas the diffuse *Aurora Leigh* is no longer read. . . . Both the charm and the weakness of her poetry reside in the impulsive naïveté which originated in her bookish girlhood and was never subjected to the abrasions of everyday life.[28]

Typically, Cooke and Stevenson devote far more words to describing 'Elizabeth's' life than her poetry.

This is also the principal focus of Gardner Taplin's *The Life of Elizabeth Barrett Browning* (1957), the most comprehensive study to appear in the thirty years following Woolf's 1931 essay. No reader of Barrett Browning's works in the 1970s can fail to be indebted to the thoroughness of Taplin's scholarship, still a resource for critics today. At the same time, the biases and omissions of his study are equally striking and all the more insidious in their effects because Taplin seemed to be, and in many respects was, so meticulous and authoritative. The biases are most evident in Taplin's surveys of contemporary reviews of the 1844 *Poems* and of *Aurora Leigh*, which often suppress the more positive criticism, creating the impression that Barrett Browning was merely a popular rather than a critical success.

Taplin's study is also informed by a persistent attitude of condescension, accompanied by and perhaps even producing some startling contradictions. Thus he criticizes Elizabeth for reading the classics 'largely as an escape' and failing to 'assimilate much of what she read', with the result that her poetry was 'lawless' (70); meanwhile his own documentation elsewhere reflects the speed and thoroughness of her reading of Greek texts (29), and the deliberately experimental rather than merely 'lawless' nature of her verse technique (134). He also suggests that she abandoned Greek and Latin in order to read 'much that was merely ephemeral: newspapers, periodicals, travel books, memoirs, and romances, none of which could be considered serious literature' (94). As we read down the page, however, we find that this 'ephemeral' material included journals like the *Athenaeum*, *Blackwood's*, and the *New Monthly Magazine*; and 'almost all of the fiction and poetry published in England from about the middle of the thirties to the middle of the forties'. To this should be added, the 'ephemeral' novels of France by authors like Balzac and George Sand – novelists Elizabeth Barrett was ahead of her time in appreciating according to Henry James in a review of her correspondence with Horne that Taplin was certainly familiar with (419). Barrett's scholarly articles and reviews on the Greek Christian poets, the history of English poetry, and contemporary authors (in her contributions to Horne's *A New Spirit of the Age*) are described by Taplin as the output of 'her brief career in journalism' (105). Meanwhile, the male authors who wrote on her works in the pages of the same periodicals are referred to as 'professional critics' (163).

Throughout his biography, Taplin creates a picture of an emotional, impulsive, undisciplined woman and writer: Elizabeth's approach to social problems was 'idealistic and emotional' (116); she had 'only a hazy idea of what she was trying to express' in *A Drama of Exile* (126); most of the 1844 poems 'now seem diffuse, sentimental, and trite' (132); 'Elizabeth's approach to the problems of the *Risorgimento* . . . was based on emotion rather than logic' (218). This last point has remained an enduring critical commonplace despite the strong evidence to the contrary provided by Julia Markus in the 'Introduction' to her edition of *Casa Guidi Windows*, and by Flavia Alaya's spirited dissection of the misogynist criticism concerning Barrett Browning's political views. After very little analysis of her actual poetry, Taplin concludes that, because Elizabeth's 'ability to create failed to keep pace with her abundant thoughts and feelings', '[i]t is the quality of her life even more than her artistic achievements which will live' (424).

Unlike Taplin's biography, Alethea Hayter's *Mrs. Browning: A Poet's Work and its Setting* (1962), focuses on Barrett Browning's poetry, not her life. Indeed, Hayter's is the most detailed analysis of her poetry published in more than fifty years. One cannot help wondering about a woman critic's work and its setting in sensing the dominant paradigms that constrain Hayter at various points, as in her defensive dismissal of Barrett Browning's ballads. Yet her critical analysis is often astute, and her chapter on 'Experiments in Poetic Technique' remains the best treatment to date of Barrett Browning's experiments with assonantal double rhymes, metrical variations, play with the pause, enjambement, artfully varied refrains, and differing forms of syntactical ellipsis and compression, including the use of adjectives as nouns. Together with Fred Manning Smith's largely forgotten *PMLA* article of 1939, suggesting how Barrett Browning anticipated the technical innovations of poets like Emily Dickinson, Archibald MacLeish, and W. H. Auden, Hayter's work bears out the truth of Woolf's oblique observation that Mrs Browning had 'some complicity in the development of modern poetry' (Hayter 47).

A decade after Hayter's scholarly study appeared, the publication by the Feminist Press of Mary Jane Lupton's *Elizabeth Barrett Browning* (1972) marked the recovery of *Aurora Leigh* that Woolf's 1931 article had failed to bring about in an earlier, more alien environment. This was the beginning of the period when feminist students began passing around 'pirated photocopies' of the out-of-print *Aurora Leigh*, as if it were a 'scurrilous tract or a new underground newspaper instead of the most ambitious, controversial work of nineteenth-century England's most famous woman poet' (Lootens 1). Imagining the controversy some of these students may have stirred up themselves in seminars on Victorian literature may help to explain the peculiar intensity with which some established male critics now sought to dismiss *Aurora Leigh* and its author.

In their 1974 biography of Browning, for instance, William Irvine and Park Honan summarize his wife's novel-epic in terms reminiscent of Gosse and those conservative Victorian reviewers for whom a woman writer was always already an inferior simulacrum of some prior male writer. 'Nothing if not serious and didactic, Elizabeth began with a load of themes', they observe of *Aurora Leigh*, and then proceed, with rhetorical guns blazing, to discharge their volley of condemnations.

The narrative first person is based on a thinly disguised inward autobiography, which in the First Book is a pious and conventional *Prelude*, and thereafter a record of travel and literary composition told in an inflated, overelaborate variant of her letter-writing style, with suggestions of Tennysonian

music, Byronic satire, and Browningesque stream-
of-consciousness. The result is frequently vivid and
frequently mawkish. At any rate the 'Pythian
shriek' is seldom heard. Mounted on this rather
elaborate autobiographical structure is an entire
novel of intrigue ... drawn from the teeming
recollections of twenty years of compulsive novel-
reading.[29]

In the 1973 anthology of Victorian poetry and prose
he edited with Lionel Trilling, Harold Bloom adopts a
more minimalist approach than Irvine and Honan.
Categorizing Mrs Browning under 'Other Victorian
Poets', Bloom and Trilling observe that, despite her
'enormous contemporary reputation', she survives
'only in her husband's work and in a handful of lyrics'.
Aurora Leigh is dismissed with the bald and unsupported
assertion that it is 'very bad'. The ideological grounds
of this judgment are more visible in Bloom's *A Map of
Misreading* (1975). Here he revealingly remarks, 'I fear
to tell students that while I judge Ruskin to have been
the best critic of the nineteenth century, he did
proclaim *Aurora Leigh* by Mrs. Browning to be the best
poem of that century.' In the same chapter, he
expresses alarm at the way in which literary tradition
has 'become the captive' of the Romantic 'revisionary
impulse', expressed in the 'common garishness' of
' "black poetry" or the "literature of Women's
Liberation" '. He also assumes the oracular mantle –
writing, we may note, in the tradition of sage discourse
so powerfully transformed by the gynocentric energy
of *Aurora Leigh* – to 'prophesy ... that the first true
break with literary continuity will be brought about in
generations to come, if the burgeoning religion
of Liberated Woman spreads from its clusters of
enthusiasts to dominate the West'[30]

Rather than making any 'break with literary continuity', three landmark studies, Ellen Moers' *Literary
Women* (1976), Elaine Showalter's *A Literature of Their
Own* (1977) and Gilbert and Gubar's *Madwoman in the
Attic* (1979), demonstrated that there were other
traditions than the phallocentric one Bloom had in
mind. Along with Cora Kaplan's 1978 edition of
Aurora Leigh and Other Poems, sections of these books
began the process of contextualizing Barrett Browning's
works in the matrix of women writers explored in my
first chapter. Again, the reactions of older, more
established Victorian scholars help to illumine the
ideological currents shaping and shaped by these acts
of reconstruction. In a more sympathetic 're-hearing'
of *Aurora Leigh* in 1979, Taplin opened his review of the
new feminist criticism by citing, first, Fitzgerald's
'misogynist' response to Barrett Browning's death in
the letter quoted above, and then a letter to him from
the Browning biographer who had savaged *Aurora
Leigh* in 1974: 'Park Honan . . . has written to me from
Birmingham to report upon Mrs. Browning's emergence as a leader in the feminist movement of the
nineteenth century. "I can't resist writing to you . . .
to report the delicious news that " 'Woman's Lib' " in
England are now espousing EBB with great fervor –
and at the expense of her husband's reputation!
She really is such a good poet (as I felt in super-
vising a Ph.D. thesis on her recently). So it's nice
that British ladies, at least, or some of them are
turning to her, don't you think?" ' (Taplin, *'Aurora
Leigh'*, 7).

Feminist critics turned to Barrett Browning in
increasing numbers during the 1980s, producing
dozens of articles (though still mainly on *Aurora Leigh*
in isolation from her other works) and several full-
length studies: most notably, those by Mermin,

Leighton, Cooper, Stephenson and Lootens that I have drawn on throughout this book. One is therefore tempted to think that Barrett Browning's works are now being 'rescued' in ways that make it impossible for them to be buried again. Yet the relative ghettoization of this recovery in women's series and feminist journals points to the dangers of complacency. 'The greatness of works of art lies solely in their power to let those things be heard which ideology conceals', Adorno observes.[31] As 'the handmaid's tale' of Barrett Browning's reception history suggests, however, the reverse very often occurs. Subversive works are themselves concealed by the hegemonic structures they challenge from within.

In Barrett Browning's case the latter pattern has persisted in the 1980s, as the recovery of her canon has remained largely unacknowledged in many quarters. Bernard Richards' 1988 survey of Victorian poetry, appearing in an influential critical series and in many respects providing a comprehensive overview, is one index of Barrett Browning's continuing marginalization in mainstream literary histories. In a welcome departure from previous surveys, Richards does briefly consider how *Aurora Leigh* participated in the important Victorian debate between past and present – a dimension of the text more fully treated by Kerry McSweeney in his 1993 edition.[32] But Barrett Browning's canon is otherwise completely excluded from Richards' survey of representative Victorian genres, themes and movements.

Among Browning scholars in the last decade there has been growing recognition of the need to explore Barrett Browning's artistic interaction with her husband, as Daniel Karlin's penetrating analysis of exchanges in the love letters indicates. Yet Barrett Browning still tends to be bracketed in literary history as a figure supplementary to her husband. The handmaid paradigm has also persisted. In *Robert Browning: His Poetry and His Audiences*, for example, Lee Erikson perceptively discusses Elizabeth's role as a discerning critic and 'ideal audience' of her husband's poetry. Yet he presents her not as a major poet in her own right, at least in the eyes of her contemporaries, but as the 'poet of some merit and popular acclaim' whom Browning claimed as ' "my Audience, my crown-bearer, my path-preparer" '.[33]

Even within the field that Showalter terms 'gyno-critics' there are startling gaps. For instance, there are no comprehensive studies of the ways in which feminist activists such as Barabara Bodichon, Frances Power Cobbe and Susan B. Anthony appropriated *Aurora Leigh* as a revolutionary text – although, as my previous chapter indicates, all three testified to its influence. The connections between Wollstonecraft and Barrett Browning also remain largely unmapped, like the connections beween Barrett Browning and Romantic women writers generally, among them Joanne Baillie, the woman she honoured as a poetical 'grandmother'. Modern feminist poets and critics like Adrienne Rich and Alicia Ostriker who have been quick to celebrate Dickinson as a foremother often overlook the ways in which Barrett Browning's emancipatory strategies made her a 'path-preparer' not for Robert Browning, but for subsequent women poets. Despite Betsy Erkkila's succinct overview of Dickinson's response to Barrett Browning in *The Wicked Sisters*, assimilating and adding to the work of earlier critics, the ways in which Dickinson emulated and resisted the formidable author of *Aurora Leigh* are still insufficiently appreciated. Surprisingly, even less attention has been given to Barrett Browning's impact on Christina Rossetti, although Antony Harrison's examination of Rossetti's 'Eve' as 'a minimalist sequel to *A Drama of Exile*' is a welcome exception to this rule (131).

In Margaret Laurence's classic Canadian novel, *The Stone Angel* (1964), the protagonist Hagar Shipley describes her futile search among her old school books for poetry to sustain her in the desert of an unfulfilling marriage: 'I'd thrown away my collected Browning, for when I left school I'd much preferred Robert's wife, with *Sonnets from the Portuguese*, which I found in the trunk, inscribed and annotated with violet ink – "n.b. *passion*" or "plight of women," scribbled there by a nincompoop who'd borne my Christian name.'[34] *Aurora Leigh* was non-existent for the aptly named Hagar and, one assumes, for Laurence herself in 1964. Nor did the *Sonnets from the Portuguese* revealed by Angela Leighton's revisionary reading twenty years later exist for Hagar. Otherwise, she might have found in the margins, along with 'plight of women', 'n.b. the *sexual-textual politics* of a woman reversing the conventions established by centuries of poets'.

In what light will Barrett Browning's works come before future readers, many of whom we might think of as Hagar's children? Will today's feminist reconstructions permanently transform the appreciation of her place in the history of English literature? Or will they go the way of Porter and Clarke's 1900 edition of her poetry? Will future readers be guided instead by summaries like the entry on Barrett Browning in the 1987 edition of the *World Book Encyclopedia*, written by J. Hillis Miller, one of the most influential critics of our time? Miller makes no mention of *Aurora Leigh*. Instead he writes about Elizabeth's son, her hospitality, and her complexion (Lootens 274).

In *Aurora Leigh* itself the heroine observes,

> What the poet writes,
> He writes: mankind accepts it if it suits,
> And that's success: if not, the poem's passed
> From hand to hand, and yet from hand to hand,
> Until the unborn snatch it, crying out
> In pity on their fathers' being so dull,
> And that's success too. (5:261–7)

Clearly, Aurora's Romantic aesthetic of the artist's transcendence over time and her opposition between success in one's own time or success in a future one do not adequately accommodate either the vicissitudes of Barrett Browning's own 'success', or her exploration of the intense struggle of competing ideologies in *Aurora Leigh*. What saves this passage from being merely a rearticulation of consoling Romantic ideology is Barrett Browning's emphasis on the drama and potential conflict of hand-to-hand textual transmission: hands that pass on texts, hands that obscure the distinctive features of texts, and hands that 'snatch' and discover texts anew.

Among the already born of the future Aurora alludes to, those of us living more than a century later than Barrett Browning, the snatching may persist for a time. To use Kristeva's words again, the 'productive violence' engendered by *Aurora Leigh* and Barrett Browning's other texts will no doubt continue to provoke the struggles that register their vitality, for this generation at least. On the one hand, the zeal of Barrett Browning's rescuers – sometimes exhibiting the inflections of what Reynolds describes as 'feminist folk-poetics' (10) – shows no immediate signs of diminishing. On the other, resisting critics will no doubt continue to disparage *Aurora Leigh*, or to write as if it never were published, or to imply that Elizabeth Barrett Browning was a Victorian who achieved popular success, but who now lives on only in her husband's works. Or, in a subtler manoeuvre, on a more ambiguous middle ground, some may argue that she was never a feminist in any sense of the term, that *Aurora Leigh* – the book that inspired Barabara Bodichon and Susan B. Anthony – is not a feminist work, and that it can therefore be appreciated even by those who reject feminist ideology. As for the 'unborn', what they will make of Barrett Browning lies in their own hands – to the extent that they recognize the role their own hands play in the textual transmissions that constitute literary history.

Notes

Note on Texts

Parenthetical documentation is used for all works listed in the Selected Bibliography. Other sources are identified in the footnotes. The following abbreviations are used:

AL   *Aurora Leigh*, ed. Margaret Reynolds (Athens, Ohio, Ohio University Press, 1992).

BC   *The Brownings' Correspondence*, ed. Philip Kelley and Ronald Hudson, 11 vols (Winfield, Kan., Wedgestone Press, 1984–).

CW   *The Complete Works of Elizabeth Barrett Browning*, ed. Charlotte Porter and Helen A. Clarke, 6 vols (1900; New York, AMS rpt, 1973).

Diary   *Diary by E.B.B.: The Unpublished Diary of Elizabeth Barrett Barrett, 1831–32*, ed. Philip Kelley and Ronald Hudson (Athens, Ohio, Ohio University Press, 1969).

HUP   *Hitherto Unpublished Poems and Stories*, ed. H. Buxton Forman, 2 vols (Boston, Bibliophile Society, 1914).

LEBB   *The Letters of Elizabeth Barrett Browning*, ed. Frederic G. Kenyon, 2 vols (New York, Macmillan, 1897).

LMRM   *The Letters of Elizabeth Barrett Browning to Mary Russell Mitford 1836–1854*, ed. Meredith B. Raymond and Mary Rose Sullivan, 3 vols (Winfield, Kan., Armstrong Browning Library of Baylor University, Browning Institute, Wedgestone Press & Wellesley College, 1983).

LRHH   *Letters of Elizabeth Barrett Browning, Addressed to Richard Hengist Horne, With Comments on Contemporaries*, ed. S. R. Townshend Mayer, 2 vols (London, Richard Bentley & Son, 1877).

RB–EBB   *The Letters of Robert Browning and Elizabeth Barrett Browning 1845–1846*, ed. Elvan Kintner, 2 vols (Cambridge, Mass., Bellknap Press of Harvard University Press, 1969).

Notes to Chapter 1

1. I am indebted to one of my former students, Dawn Henwood, for this example.

2. *The World Split Open: Four Centuries of Women Poets in England and America 1552–1950*, prefatory note by Muriel Rukeyser (New York, Vintage Books, 1974) pp. 29–30.

3. *The Romantic Ideology: A Critical Investigation* (Chicago, University of Chicago Press, 1983) p. 14.

4. 'Introduction: The Feminist Critical Revolution', *The New Feminist Criticism: Essays on Women, Literature, and Theory*, ed. Elaine Showalter (New York, Pantheon Books, 1985) pp. 5–8.

5. Judith Lowder Newton, 'History as Usual? Feminism and the "New Historicism" ', in *The New Historicism*, ed. H. Aram Veeser (New York, Routledge, 1989) pp. 152–3.

6. *New French Feminisms: An Anthology*, ed. Elaine Marks and Isabelle de Courtivron (New York, Schocken Books, 1981); 'Varieties of Feminist Criticism', in *Making a Difference: Feminist Literary Criticism*, ed. Gayle Greene and Coppélia Kahn (London, Methuen, 1985) p. 48.

7. Leighton's important study of Victorian women poets appeared when I was in the final stages of revising this book; I regret not being able to incorporate more of her insights.

8. *Engendering the Word: Feminist Essays in Psychosexual Poetics*, ed. Temma F. Berg, Anna Shannon Elfenbein, Jeanne Larsen and Elisa Kay Sparks (Urbana, University of Illinois Press, 1989) pp. xxi, 52.

9. Joanne Feit Diehl, *Dickinson and the Romantic Imagination* (Princeton, Princeton University Press, 1981).

10. Patricia Yaeger, *Honey-Mad Women: Emancipatory Strategies in Women's Writing*, Gender and Culture Series (New York, Columbia University Press, 1988).

11. Teresa de Lauretis, *Alice Doesn't: Feminism, Semiotics, Cinema* (Bloomington, Indiana University Press, 1984) pp. 12–36; Lynda E. Boose and Betty S. Flowers (eds), *Daughters and Fathers* (Baltimore, Johns Hopkins Press, 1989) pp. 19–74.

12. See DuPlessis, pp. 86–7 and Alicia Ostriker, p. 42 (in the Selected Bibliography); Rita Felski, *Beyond Feminist Aesthetics: Feminist Literature and Social Change* (Cambridge, Mass., Harvard University Press, 1989) pp. 54–5.

13. *The Nightingale's Burden: Women Poets and American Culture before 1900* (Bloomington, Indiana University Press, 1982) p. 36.

14. Berg Notebook 4 (entry D1400) in Kelley and Coley, *The Browning Collections*. Also see entry D468.

15. See Kelley and Coley, *The Browning Collections*, entries D1245, 1247, 1249, 1250, 1264 & 1397, and Sharp, pp. 80–103.

16. Susan J. Rosowski, 'The Novel of Awakening', in *The Voyage In: Fictions of Female Development*, ed. Elizabeth Abel, Marianne Hirsch, and Elizabeth Langland (Hanover, University Press of New England, 1983) pp. 49–68. See also 'Introduction', p. 11.

17. *Doing Literary Business: American Women Writers in the Nineteenth Century* (Chapel Hill, University of North Carolina Press, 1990); Robert W. Gladish, *Elizabeth Barrett and the 'Centurion': The Background to an Addition to the Elizabeth Barrett Browning Canon* (Waco, Armstrong Browning Library, Baylor University, Baylor Browning Interests, 23, 1973) p. 22.

18. George William Curtis, 'Editor's Easy Chair', *Harper's Magazine*, 23 (June–Nov. 1861) p. 555; Margaret Fuller, *The Woman and the Myth: Margaret Fuller's Life and Writings*, ed. Bell Gale Cevigny (Old Westbury, NY, Feminist Press, 1976) p. 203.

19. *The Complete Works of Algernon Charles Swinburne*, ed. Sir Edmund Gosse, C.B. and Thomas James Wise, (London, Heinemann, 1929) vol. 6, pp. 3–8; *The Works of Ruskin*, ed. E. T. Cook and Alexander Wedderburn, Library edn (London, George Allen, 1901) vol. 15, p. 227; George Eliot 'Belles Lettres', *Westminster Review*, 67 (January 1857) 306–10, and *The George Eliot Letters*, ed. Gordon Haight (New Haven, Yale University Press, 1954) vol. 2, p. 342; Kathleen Barry, *Susan B. Anthony: A Biography of a Singular Feminist* (New York, Ballantine, 1988) pp. 121–3.

20. *Elizabeth Barrett Browning* (London, Gerald House, 1928) pp. 92–3.

21. *The Mother–Daughter Plot: Narrative, Psychoanalysis, Feminism* (Bloomington, Indiana University Press, 1989) p. 43.

22. See my article, 'Bile and the Brownings: A New Poem by RB, EBB's "My Heart and I", and New Questions About the Brownings' Marriage', *Browning Studies*, 1 (1994) 1–20.

23. See 'The Old Right', p. 206–7, 219, 221; and *Intellectual Women*, pp. 97–143 (in the Selected Bibliography).

24. Lee Holcombe, *Wives and Property: Reform of the Married Women's Property Law in Nineteenth-Century England* (Toronto, University of Toronto Press, 1983) pp. 70–1; *Elizabeth Barrett Browning's Letters to Mrs. David Ogilvie 1849–1861*, ed. Peter N. Heydon and Philip Kelley (New York, Quandrangle, The New Times Book Co., & The Browning Institute, 1973) p. 140.

232   ELIZABETH BARRETT BROWNING

Notes to Chapter 2

1. McGann, *The Romantic Ideology*, pp. 107–30.
2. *The Anxiety of Influence* (New York, Oxford University Press, 1973) p. 66; *A Map of Misreading* (Oxford, Oxford University Press, 1975).
3. *My Life A Loaded Gun: Female Creativity and Feminist Poetics* (Boston, Beacon Press, 1986) p. 10.
4. 'Old Father Nile: T. S. Eliot and Harold Bloom on the Creative Process as Spontaneous Generation', *Engendering the Word*, p. 55.
5. 'Romanticism and the Colonization of the Feminine', *Romanticism and Feminism*, ed. Anne K. Mellor (Bloomington, Indiana University Press, 1988) pp. 13–25.
6. Hallam Tennyson, *Alfred Lord Tennyson: A Memoir* (London, Macmillan, 1906), p. 475.
7. 'Romantic Quest and Conquest: Troping Masculine Power in the Crisis of Poetic Identity', *Romanticism and Feminism*, p. 26.
8. Forman, *Our Living Poets: An Essay in Criticism* (London, Tinsley Brothers, 1871) p. 182; Lubbock, *Elizabeth Barrett Browning in her Letters* (London, Smith, Elder, 1906) p. 11.
9. Linda M. Lewis, *The Promethean Politics of Milton, Blake, and Shelley* (Columbia, University of Missouri Press, 1992), pp. 157, 162.
10. *The Poetry of Life: Shelley and Literary Form* (Toronto, University of Toronto Press, 1987) p. 172.
11. *Feminist Milton* (Ithaca, Cornell University Press, 1987) pp. 42–3, 66.
12. '*Poems*. By Elizabeth Barrett Browning', *North American Review*, 94 (1862) p. 348.
13. *Shirley*, ed. Andrew and Judith Hook (Harmondsworth, Penguin Books, 1974) p. 315.
14. Truman Steffan, *Lord Byron's Cain: Twelve Essays and a Text with Variants and Annotations* (Austin, University of Texas Press, 1968) p. 33; Mervyn Nicholson, 'Female Emancipation in Romantic Narrative', *Women's Studies*, 18 (1990) 309–29; and Caroline Franklin, *Byron's Heroines* (Oxford, Oxford University Press, 1992).
15. *LEBB* 1:172; Ruskin, *Works*, vol. 36, p. 197; '*Poems*. By Elizabeth Barrett Browning', *Athenaeum* (30 November 1950) p. 1243.
16. *Dante and the English Poets from Chaucer to Tennyson* (New York, Henry Holt, 1904) pp. 236–8.
17. Muriel Rukeyser, cited by Alicia Ostriker, 'Women Poets and

Revisionist Mythmaking', *Signs*, 8 (1981), rpt. *The New Feminist Criticism*, p. 316.

18. Beth Newman, 'Narratives of Seduction and the Seductions of Narrative: The Frame Structures of *Frankenstein*', *English Literary History*, 53 (1986) 141.

19. Cited by Sparks, *Engendering the Word*, p. 58.

Notes to Chapter 3

1. *Bishop Percy's Folio Manuscript: Ballads and Romances*, vol. 2, part I (London, N. Trubner & Co., 1867) pp. xviii–xix.

2. Malcolm Laws, Jr, *The British Literary Ballad: A Study in Poetic Imitation* (Carbondale, Southern Illinois University Press, 1972) pp. 151–8, 89–93.

3. Nancy K. Miller, *Subject to Change: Reading Feminist Writing* (New York, Columbia University Press, 1988) p. 208.

4. *The Victorian Popular Ballad* (London, Macmillan, 1975) pp. 4–7.

5. Hermann Fischer, *Romantic Verse Narrative: The History of a Genre*, trans. Sue Bollans (Cambridge, Cambridge University Press, 1991) pp. 24–35, 53, 90; Albert B. Friedman, *The Ballad Revival: Studies in the Influence of Popular on Sophisticated Poetry* (Chicago, University of Chicago Press, 1961) p. 298.

6. Stephen Parrish, *The Art of the Lyrical Ballads* (Cambridge, Mass., Harvard University Press, 1973) pp. 86–90; Mary Jacobus, *Tradition and Experiment in Wordsworth's 'Lyrical Ballads' (1798)* (Oxford, Clarendon Press, 1976) pp. 209–32, 277–83.

7. Tilottama Rajan, *The Supplement of Reading: Figures of Understanding in Romantic Theory and Practice* (Ithaca & London, Cornell University Press, 1990) p. 140.

8. *Subject to Change*, p. 208.

9. *Honey-Mad Women*, p. 117.

10. Thomas Percy, *Reliques of Ancient English Poetry, Consisting of Old Heroic Ballads, Songs, and other Pieces of our Earlier Poets, Together with some few of later Date* (London, J. Dodsley, 1765) vol. 3, pp. 310–13.

11. For a more detailed analysis of revisions and textual echoes in 'The Poet's Vow' and 'The Romaunt of the Page', see the version of this chapter published in *Victorian Literature and Culture*, 21 (1993).

12. See *Reliques of Ancient English Poetry*, 1765 edn, vol. 3, p. xviii. Barrett acquired the 5th edition of Percy's *Reliques* in 1826; see Kelley and Coley, p. 156.

13. *Warrior Women and Popular Balladry 1650–1850*, Cambridge Studies in Eighteenth-Century Literature and Thought (Cambridge, Cambridge University Press, 1989) pp. 146, 172, 164.

14. *The Poetical Works of Mrs. Hemans*, ed. W. M. Rossetti (New York, Hurst & Co., n.d.) p. 235.

15. *Warrior Women and Popular Balladry*, p. 149.

16. Cited by Mary Poovey, *Uneven Developments: The Ideological Work of Gender in Mid-Victorian England* (Chicago, University of Chicago Press, 1988) p. 147.

17. Leighton notes the probable influence of Byron's *Lara* as well (1992, 81).

18. 'Last Poems and Other Works of Mrs. Browning', *North British Review*, 36 (1862) p. 527.

19. *The Proper Lady and the Woman Writer: Ideology as Style in the Works of Mary Wollstonecraft, Mary Shelley, and Jane Austen* (Chicago, Chicago University Press, 1984).

Notes to Chapter 4

1. On Marian's role in Aurora's artistic and sexual development, see Gelpi, Leighton (1986), Cooper, Stephenson, Mermin, Loeffelholz and especially Zonana.

2. See Friedman, S., p. 208; Stone, 'Genre Subversion', pp. 123–4; and Mermin, p. 184.

3. DuPlessis, p. 84; Case, p. 94. See also Stephenson, pp. 91–116, and Sutphin.

4. George P. Landow, *Elegant Jeremiahs: The Sage from Carlyle to Mailer* (Ithaca, Cornell University Press, 1986); and John Holloway, *The Victorian Sage: Studies in Argument* (1953; rpt and New York, Norton, 1965).

5. Nichol, 'Aurora Leigh', *Westminister Review*, 68 (1857) p. 412; Eliot, 'Belles Lettres', *Westminster Review*, 67 (1857) pp. 306–7.

6. Ruskin, *Works*, vol. 36, pp. 247–8; Aidé, *Letters from Owen Meredith to Robert and Elizabeth Browning*, ed. Aurelia Brooks Harlan and J. Lee Harlan Jr (Baylor University, Browning Institutes Series 10, vol. 39, December 1939) p. 132; and 'Mrs. Browning's "Aurora Leigh"', *Edinburgh Weekly Review* (28 February 1857) pp. 7–9.

7. '*Aurora Leigh*', *British Quarterly Review*, 25 (January and April, 1857) pp. 263–5.

8. Gates, *Studies and Appreciations* (New York, Macmillan, 1900)

p. 39; Texte, *Etudes de Littérature Européenne* (Paris, Armand Colin, 1898) p. 240 (my translation).

9. '*Aurora Leigh*', *The Leader* (29 November 1856) p. 1142.

10. Holloway, *The Victorian Sage*, p. 9.

11. Holloway, *The Victorian Sage*, pp. 9–10.

12. Cited by Holloway, p. 17.

13. See Kaplan, 'Introduction', *Aurora Leigh*, pp. 28–34; Blake, 'Elizabeth Barrett Browning and Wordsworth'; Freiwald on the Carlyle connection; and Taylor, ' "School–Miss Alfred' ", and Stone, 'Genre Subversion', on the debate with Tennyson.

14. *A Map of Misreading*, pp. 102–03 and 129.

15. *Spectator* review, rpt. *Little's Living Age* (2nd ser, vol. 16 (1857) p. 430.

16. 'The Laugh of the Medusa', *Signs* (Summer, 1976); rpt. *New French Feminisms: An Anthology*, p. 256.

17. Holloway, *The Victorian Sage*, p. 13; Yaeger, *Honey-Mad Women*, p. 33.

18. On the echoes of *Corinne*, see Kaplan, pp. 16–22; on the Sand connection, see Thomson and Kaplan, pp. 22–3; on *Ruth*, see Kaplan, pp. 24–5 and Cosslett; on the echoes of *Jane Eyre*, see Zonana, p. 258.

19. For biographical interpretations, see Woolf, p. 137; Taplin, p. 313; Friedman, S., p. 208; and Lootens, p. 229. On Aurora's unreliability in love, but not in art, see Case, pp. 17, 24.

20. See Tompkins, p. 10; Taplin, '*Aurora Leigh*: A Rehearing', p. 20; Leighton (1986) p. 8; and Lootens, p. 308.

21. *Barbara Leigh Smith and the Langham Place Group*, ed. Candida Ann Lacey, Women's Source Library (New York & London, Routledge & Kegan Paul, 1987).

22. *The Life of Frances Power Cobbe By Herself* (Boston, Houghton & Mifflin, Riverside Press, 1895), vol. 1, p. 344.

23. 'Last Poems and Other Works of Mrs. Browning,' pp. 514–15; *The Collected Writings of Thomas De Quincey*, ed. David Masson (London, A. & C. Black, 1897), vol. 5, p. 406.

24. 'Mrs. Browning's *Aurora Leigh*', *The Spectator*, 22 November 1856; rpt. *Littell's Living Age*, 2nd ser., 16 (1857) p. 430.

25. Typescript of *LEBB*, 42.229 f. 525, in the British Library.

26. See David, *Intellectual Women*; Loeffelholz, p. 73; and DuPlessis' comments below.

27. *Beyond Feminist Aesthetics*, p. 2.

28. Kathleen Barry, *Susan B. Anthony*, pp. 121–3.

29. Cited by Yaeger, *Honey-Mad Women*, p. 199.

30. H.D. *Tribute to the Angels*, cited by DuPlessis, p. 119.

Notes to Chapter 5

1. *The Political Unconscious: Narrative as Socially Symbolic Act* (Ithaca, Cornell University Press, 1981) p. 86.

2. Cited by Barton Levy St. Armand, *Emily Dickinson and Her Culture: The Soul's Society* (Cambridge, Cambridge University Press, 1984) p. 120.

3. Poems 593, 312 and 363 in *The Poems of Emily Dickinson*, ed. Thomas H. Johnson, 3 vols (Cambridge, Mass., Harvard University Press, 1955).

4. *The Letters of Emily Dickinson*, ed. Thomas H. Johnson and Theodora Ward (Cambridge, Mass., Harvard University Press, 1958) vol. 2, p. 404.

5. Cited by Dorothy Hewlett, *Elizabeth Barrett Browning* (London, Cassell, 1953) p. 291.

6. See Arinshtein, Gladish, and Stone ('Cursing') in the Selected Bibliography; Lootens, pp. 392, 403; and Harriet Waters Preston, below.

7. *Victorian Poetry*, ed E. K. Brown and J. O. Bailey (1942; 2nd edn, New York, Ronald Press, 1962) p. 352.

8. Cited by Dolores Rosenblum, *Christina Rossetti: The Poetry of Endurance* (Carbondale & Edwardsville, Southern Illinois Press, 1986) p. 1.

9. *Sexual Anarchy: Gender and Culture at the Fin de Siècle* (New York, Viking Penguin, 1990); *Idols of Perversity: Fantasies of Feminine Evil in Fin-de-Siècle Culture* (New York, Oxford University Press, 1986); Gaye Tuchman with Nina E. Fortin, *Edging Women Out: Victorian Novelists, Publishers, and Social Change* (New Haven, Yale University Press, 1989).

10. 'Last Poems and other Works of Mrs. Browning', pp. 514–16.

11. '*Poems*. By Elizabeth Barrett Browning', *North American Review*, 94 (1862) pp. 338, 344–6, 353.

12. 'The Works of Elizabeth Barrett Browning', *Edinburgh Review* 114 (1861) pp. 520, 525, 533; 'Mrs. Browning', rpt. *Littell's Living Age*, 3rd ser., 14 (1861) p. 492.

13. 'Poetesses', rpt. *Littell's Living Age* 9 (4th ser.) (1868) p. 822.

14. Texte, *Etudes* p. 240; for Waddington, see the Selected Bibliography.

15. Forman, *Our Living Poets: An Essay in Criticism* (London, Tinsley Brothers, 1817) pp. 11, 99–100, 182–3, 231–7, 261, 481–5.

16. Lewis E. Gates, *Studies and Appreciations* (New York, Macmillan, 1990) p. 32. For Herridge and Bradfield, see the Selected Bibliography.

17. *The Letters of Edward Fitzgerald*, ed. Alfred McKinley Terhune and Annabelle Burdick Terhune (Princeton, Princeton University Press, 1980) vol. 1, p. 407.
18. 'Poetesses', rpt. *Littell*; 'Elizabeth Barrett Browning', *Saturday Review*, 66 (1888) p. 466.
19. Cited by Lootens, pp. 413 and 408; and by Ann Thwaite, *Edmund Gosse: A Literary Landscape 1849–1928* (London, Secker & Warburg, 1984) p. 116.
20. *The Complete Works of Elizabeth Barrett Browning*. By Elizabeth Barrett Browning (Cambridge, Cambridge University Press, 1900); 'Robert and Elizabeth Browning', *Atlantic Monthly*, 83 (1899) 812–26.
21. *The Victorian Age in Literature* (New York, Tait, Sons & Co., 1892) vol. 1, pp. 227, 231.
22. John W. Cunliffe, 'Elizabeth Barrett's Influence on Browning', *PMLA*, 23 (1908) 169–83; Laurie Magnus, *English Literature of the Nineteenth Century: An Essay in Criticism* (London, Andrew Melrose, 1909).
23. (Cambridge, Cambridge University Press, 1910) pp. 287, 252, 327, 360, 328, 343, 366.
24. *The Age of Tennyson* (1897; rpt. Port Washington, New York & London, Kennikat Press, 1972) p. 235.
25. See Taplin's list in *The Life of Elizabeth Barrett Browning*, pp. 419, 453.
26. *E. B. Browning* (London, Gerald Howe, 1928), pp. 9, 13, 44, 80.
27. *The Victorian Temper: A Study in Literary Culture* (New York, Vintage Books, 1951) pp. 61–3.
28. *English Literature of the Victorian Period* (New York, Appleton-Century-Crofts, 1949) p. 149.
29. *The Book, the Ring, and the Poet* (New York, McGraw-Hill, 1974) pp. 348–9.
30. *Victorian Prose and Poetry*, ed. Lionel Trilling and Harold Bloom (New York, Oxford University Press, 1973) p. 689; *A Map of Misreading*, pp. 28, 36, 33.
31. 'Lyric Poetry and Society,' trans. Bruce Mayo, *Telos*, 20 (1974) 57–8.
32. *English Poetry of the Victorian Period*, Longman Literature in English Series (London, Longman, 1988) p. 88; *Aurora Leigh*, World's Classics Series (Oxford, Oxford University Press, 1993).
33. *Robert Browning: His Poetry and His Audiences* (Ithaca, Cornell University Press, 1984) pp. 104, 108.
34. *The Stone Angel* (1964; rpt. Toronto, McClelland & Stewart, 1968) p. 126.

Selected Bibliography

Agajanian, Shaakeh, *'Sonnets from the Portuguese' and the Love Sonnet Tradition* (New York, Philosophical Library, 1985).

Alaya, Flavia, 'The Ring, the Rescue, and the Risorgimento: Reunifying the Brownings' Italy', *Browning Institute Studies*, 6 (1978) 1–41.

Arishtein, Leonid M., ' "A Curse for a Nation": A Controversial Episode in Elizabeth Barrett Browning's Political Poetry', *Review of English Studies*, n.s. 20 (1969) 33–42.

Armstrong, Isobel, 'The Brownings; in *New History of Literature*, vol. 6, *The Victorians* (New York, Bedrick, 1987).

Auerbach, Nina, 'Robert Browning's Last Word', *Victorian Poetry*, 22 (1984) 161–73.

Barnes, Warner, *A Bibliography of Elizabeth Barrett Browning* (Austin, University of Texas Press & the Armstrong Browning Library, Baylor University, 1967).

Battersby, Christine, *Gender and Genius: Towards a Feminist Aesthetics* (Bloomington, Indiana University Press, 1989).

Bayne, Peter, *Two Great Englishwomen: Mrs. Browning & Charlotte Brontë, with an Essay on Poetry, Illustrated from Wordsworth, Burns, and Byron* (London, James Clarke, 1881).

Blake, Kathleen, 'Elizabeth Barrett Browning and Wordsworth: The Romantic Poet as a Woman', *Victorian Poetry*, 24 (1986) 387–98.

Blake, Kathleen, *Love and the Woman Question in Victorian Literature: The Art of Self-Postponement* (Totowa, NJ, Barnes & Noble, 1983).

Borg, James, 'The Fashioning of Elizabeth Barrett Browning's *Aurora Leigh*', Diss. Northwestern University, 1979.

Bradfield, Thomas, 'The Ethical Impulse of Mrs. Browning's Poetry', *Westminster Review*, 146 (1896) 174–84.

Byrd, Deborah, 'Combating an Alien Tyranny: Elizabeth Barrett Browning's Evolution as a Feminist Poet', *Browning Institute Studies*, 15 (1987) 23–41.

Case, Alison, 'Gender and Narration in *Aurora Leigh*', *Victorian Poetry*, 29 (1991) 17–32.

Chesterton, G. K., *The Victorian Age in Literature*, Home University Library Series (1913; rpt. London, Thornton Butterworth, 1933).

Cooper, Helen, *Elizabeth Barrett Browning: Woman and Artist* (Chapel Hill, University of North Carolina Press, 1988).

Cosslett, Tess, *Women to Women: Female Friendships in Victorian Fiction* (Brighton, Harvester Press, 1988).

David, Deirdre, *Intellectual Women and Victorian Patriarchy: Harriet Martineau, Elizabeth Barrett Browning, George Eliot* (Ithaca, Cornell University Press, 1987).

David, Deirdre, 'The Old Right and the New Jerusalem: Elizabeth Barrett Browning's Intellectual Practice', in *Intellectuals: Aesthetics, Politics and Academics*, ed. Bruce Robbins (Minneapolis, University of Minnesota Press, 1990).

Donaldson, Sandra, *Elizabeth Barrett Browning: An Annotated Bibliography of Commentary and Criticism, 1826–1990* (New York, G. K.Hall, 1993).

Donaldson, Sandra, 'Elizabeth Barrett's Two Sonnets to George Sand', *Studies in Browning and His Circle*, 5 (Spring 1977) 19–22.

Donaldson, Sandra, ' "Motherhood's Advent in Power": Elizabeth Barrett Browning's Poems About Motherhood', *Victorian Poetry*, 18 (1980) 51–60.

DuPlessis, Rachael Blau, *Writing Beyond the Ending: Narrative Strategies of Twentieth Century Women Writers* (Bloomington, Indiana University Press, 1985).

Edmond, Rod, *Affairs of the Hearth: Victorian Poetry and Domestic Narrative* (London, Routledge, 1988).

Erkkila, Betsy, *The Wicked Sisters: Women Poets, Literary History and Discord* (New York, Oxford University Press, 1992).

Falk, Alice, 'Elizabeth Barrett Browning and Her Prometheuses: Self-Will and a Woman Poet', *Tulsa Studies in Women's Literature*, 7 (Spring, 1988) 69–85.

Forster, Margaret, *Elizabeth Barrett Browning: A Biography* (London, Chatto & Windus, 1988).

Freiwald, Bina, 'Elizabeth Barrett Browning's *Aurora Leigh*: Transcendentalism and the Female Subject', in vol. 2, *Proceedings of the Tenth Congress of the International Comparative Literature Association*, ed. Balakian, Anne et al. (New York, Garland, 1985).

Friedman, Susan Stanford, 'Gender and Genre Anxiety: Elizabeth Barrett Browning and H.D. as Epic Poets', *Tulsa Studies in Women's Literature*, 5 (1986) 203–28.

Gelpi, Barbara Charlesworth, '*Aurora Leigh*: The Vocation of the Woman Poet', *Victorian Poetry*, 19 (1981) 35–48.

Gilbert, Sandra, M., 'From *Patria* to *Matria*: Elizabeth Barrett Browning's Risorgimento', *PMLA*, 99 (1984) 194–211.

Gilbert, Sandra M. and Susan Gubar, *The Madwoman in the Attic: The Woman Writer and the Nineteenth-Century Literary Imagination* (New Haven, Yale University Press, 1979).

Gladish, Robert W., 'Mrs. Browning's "A Curse for a Nation": Some Further Comments', *Victorian Poetry*, 7 (1969) 275–89.

Harrison, Antony H., *Victorian Poets and Romantic Poems* (Charlottesville, University Press of Virginia, 1990).

Hayter, Alethea, *Mrs. Browning: A Poet's Work and Its Setting* (New York, Barnes & Noble, 1963).

Herridge, William T. 'Elizabeth Barrett Browning', *Andover Review*, 7 (1887) 607–23.

Hickok, Kathleen, *Representations of Women: Nineteenth-Century British Women's Poetry* (London, Greenwood Press, 1984).

Hoag, Eleanor, 'Fragment of "An Essay on Woman" ', *Studies in Browning and His Circle*, 12 (Spring, 1984) 7–12.

Homans, Margaret, *Women Writers and Poetic Identity: Dorothy Wordsworth, Emily Brontë, and Emily Dickinson* (Princeton, Princeton University Press, 1980).

Kaplan, Cora, 'Introduction' to Elizabeth Barrett Browning, '*Aurora Leigh* With Other Poems' (London, Women's Press, 1978).

Karlin, Daniel, *The Courtship of Robert Browning and Elizabeth Barrett* (Oxford, Clarendon, 1985).

Kelley, Philip and Betty A. Coley, *The Browning Collections: A Reconstruction With Other Memorabilia* (Winfield, Kan., Armstrong Browning Library of Baylor University, The Browning Institute, Mansell Publishing, Wedgestone Press, 1984).

Leighton, Angela, ' "Because men made the laws": The Fallen Woman and the Woman Poet', *Victorian Poetry*, 27 (1989) 109–27.

Leighton, Angela, *Elizabeth Barrett Browning*, Key Women Writers Series (Brighton, Harvester Press, 1986).

Leighton, Angela, *Victorian Women Poets: Writing Against the Heart* (Charlottesville, University Press of Virginia, 1992).

Loeffelholz, Mary, *Dickinson and the Boundaries of Feminist Theory* (Urbana, University of Illinois Press, 1991).

Lootens, Tricia, 'Elizabeth Barrett Browning: The Poet as Heroine of Literary History', Diss. Indiana University, 1988.

Lupton, Mary Jane, *Elizabeth Barrett Browning* (Long Island, Feminist Press, 1972).

Markus, Julia, 'Introduction', *Casa Guidi Windows*, ed. Julia Markus (New York, The Browning Institute, 1977).

Marxist-Feminist Literature Collective, 'Women's Writing: "Jane

Eyre", "Shirley", "Villette", "Aurora Leigh" ' in *1848: The Sociology of Literature*, ed. Francis Barker et al. (University of Essex, 1978).

Mellor, Anne, *Romanticism and Gender* (New York, Routledge, 1993).

Mermin, Dorothy, 'The Domestic Economy of Art: Elizabeth Barrett and Robert Browning' in *Mothering the Mind: Twelve Studies of Writers and Their Silent Partners*, ed. Ruth Perry and Martine Watson Brownley (New York, Holmes & Meier, 1984).

Mermin, Dorothy, *Elizabeth Barrett Browning: The Origins of a New Poetry*, Women in Culture and Society Series (Chicago, University of Chicago Press, 1989).

Moers, Ellen, *Literary Women* (New York, Doubleday, 1976).

Morgan, Thaïs (ed.), *Victorian Sages and Cultural Discourse: Renegotiating Gender and Power* (New Brunswick, NJ, Rutgers University Press, 1990).

Morlier, Margaret M., 'The Death of Pan: Elizabeth Barrett Browning and the Romantic Ego', *Browning Institute Studies*, 18 (1990) 131–55.

Moser, Kay, 'Elizabeth Barrett's Youthful Feminism: "Fragment of an 'Essay on Woman' " ', *Studies in Browning and His Circle*, 12 (Spring, 1984) 13–26.

Munich, Adrienne Auslander, *Andromeda's Chains: Gender and Interpretation in Victorian Literature and Art* (New York, Columbia University Press, 1989).

Ostriker, Alicia, *Stealing the Language: The Emergence of Women's Poetry* (Boston, Beacon Press, 1986).

Phelps, Deborah, ' "At the roadside of humanity": Elizabeth Barrett Browning Abroad' in *Creditable Warriors 1830–1876*, ed. Michael Cotsell (London, Ashfield Press, 1990).

Porter, Katherine A., *Through a Glass Darkly: Spiritualism in the Browning Circle* (New York, Octagon Press, 1972).

Prins, Yopie, 'Elizabeth Barrett, Robert Browning, and the *Différance* of Translation', *Victorian Poetry*, 29 (1991) 435–51.

Raymond, Meredith B., 'Elizabeth Barrett Browning's Poetics, 1845–1846': "The Ascending Gyre"', *Browning Society Notes*, 11 (August 1981) 1–11.

Ridenour, George, 'Robert Browning and *Aurora Leigh*', *Victorian Newsletter*, 67 (1985) 26–31.

Rosenblum, Dolores, '*Casa Guidi Windows* and *Aurora Leigh*. The Genesis of Elizabeth Barrett Browning's Visionary Aesthetic', *Tulsa Studies in Women's Literature*, 4 (1985) 61–8.

Rosenblum, Dolores, 'Face to Face: Elizabeth Barrett Browning's *Aurora Leigh* and Nineteenth-Century Poetry', *Victorian Studies*, 26 (Spring, 1983) 321–38.

Sanders, Valerie, *The Private Lives of Victorian Women: Autobiography in Nineteenth-Century England* (New York, St. Martins, 1989).

Sharp, Phillip D., 'Poetry in Process: Elizabeth Barrett Browning and the Sonnets Notebook', Diss. Lousiana State University, 1985.

Showalter, Elaine, *A Literature of Their Own: British Novelists from Brontë to Doris Lessing* (Princeton, Princeton University Press, 1976).

Smith, Fred Manning, 'Mrs. Browning's Rhymes', *PMLA*, 54 (1939) 829–34.

Stedman, Edmund Clarence, 'Elizabeth Barrett Browning' in *Victorian Poets*, rev. edn (Boston & New York, Houghton Mifflin, 1903).

Steinmetz, Virginia, 'Images of "Mother-Want" in Elizabeth Barrett Browning's *Aurora Leigh*', *Victorian Poetry*, 21 (1983) 18–41.

Stephenson, Glennis, *Elizabeth Barrett Browning and the Poetry of Love* (Ann Arbor, UMI Press, 1989).

Stone, Marjorie, 'Bile and the Brownings: A New Poem by RB, EBB's "My Heart and I", and New Questions About the Brownings' Marriage', *Browning Studies*, 1 (1994) 1–20.

Stone, Marjorie, 'Cursing as One of the Fine Arts: Elizabeth Barrett Browning's Political Poems', *Dalhousie Review*, 66 (1986) 155–73.

Stone, Marjorie, 'Genre Subversion and Gender Inversion: *The Princess* and *Aurora Leigh*', *Victorian Poetry*, 25 (1987) 101–27.

Stone, Marjorie, 'Taste, Totems and Taboos: The Female Breast in Victorian Poetry', *Dalhousie Review*, 64 (1985) 748–70.

Sutphin, Christine, 'Revising Old Scripts: The Fusion of Independence and Intimacy in *Aurora Leigh*', *Browning Institute Studies*, 15 (1987) 43–54.

Taplin, Gardner, B., '*Aurora Leigh*: A Rehearing', *Studies in Browning and His Circle*, 7 (1979) 7–23.

Taplin, Gardner, B., *The Life of Elizabeth Barrett Browning* (New Haven, Yale University Press, 1957).

Taylor, Barbara, *Eve and the New Jerusalem: Socialism and Feminism in the Nineteenth Century* (New York, Pantheon Books, 1983).

Taylor, Beverly, ' "School-Miss Alfred" and "Materfamilias": Female Sexuality and Poetic Voice in *The Princess* and *Aurora*